SPEECH★LESS

MATT LATIMER

SPEECH ★ LESS

TALES OF A WHITE HOUSE SURVIVOR

Crown Publishers

NEW YORK

Library of Congress Cataloging-in-Publication Data is available upon request.

ISBN 978-0-307-46372-2

Printed in the United States of America

10 9 8 7 6 5 4 3 2 1

First Edition

For my blue-state parents
from their red-state son

CONTENTS

SPEECH★LESS

WHERE'S GOOFY?

It was a fall day in 2008. I'd just picked up my usual can of Diet Pepsi from the White House Mess when all I knew about the world seemed to come to an end. As a speechwriter for George W. Bush during the final years of his presidency, I'd seen any number of crises and controversies. But nothing had prepared me for what was ahead: the imminent collapse of America's free market system.

I was in my office with another speechwriter, a young man named Jonathan, when we first heard the grim news. Tall and lean with a tuft of black hair, Jonathan was such a team player that for weeks he'd worked at a desk he could barely fit his legs under. I used to watch him hunch down in his chair, Quasimodo-like, whenever he wrote a speech. But Jonathan wasn't one to complain. Far more inconvenient for him than his desk, it turned out, was his last name: Horn. This conferred on him the honor of being the only speechwriter with a presidential nickname, though not a particularly inventive one. The president called him "Horny" (which, incidentally, is not a sentence I ever expected to type).

Contrary to some people's belief, President Bush didn't behave like a deranged frat boy, walking around the White House handing out nicknames to everyone. But for whatever reason, he did take a shine to Horny—the name, if not the person. He especially liked the moniker because it made the quiet, studious Jonathan visibly uncomfortable. But then I think all of the writers felt a vague sense of unease over sitting in the Oval Office while the president of the United States said things like "Let me show you what I mean, Horny." It always seemed that we were one slip of the tongue away from a Ken Starr investigation.

Horny and I were chatting casually when Chris Michel came into the office. Chris was the president's favorite speechwriter. He was in his midtwenties with sandy blond hair. Chris was extremely talented and, like Jonathan, had started at the White House as an intern. Their short professional lives had been almost entirely in the service of George W. Bush.

Chris was usually chipper, except he wasn't today. At the moment, his face was so pale that he had to have been the whitest man in the Bush White House. And that was no small accomplishment.

Chris had just come from a secret meeting in the Oval Office. Without so much as a hello, he placed his notebook down and announced, "Well, the economy is about to completely collapse."

"You mean the stock market?" I asked.

Chris continued to cushion the blow. "No, I mean the *entire* U.S. economy," he replied. As in the American way of life. As in capitalism as we know it. As in hide your money in your mattress.

Jonathan and I looked at each other. Was this a joke? We looked back at Chris, his face shaken and somber. Nope. Not a joke. Yikes.

The scenario sketched out that day by the gravelly voiced secretary of the treasury, Hank Paulson, was dire. Every bank in America was at risk of closing down. Americans across the country might not be able to get loans. Large businesses could fail. There would be massive job losses. The stock market, which was already dropping by triple digits every day, could plummet even further. It was so terrifying that I immediately wanted to call my parents in Michigan and warn them to take their money out of everything. Then I realized that I wasn't allowed to tell anyone what I knew. Not only was the information extremely confidential, Chris said, but the slightest hint about it before the White House was ready to announce a plan could start a panic. He didn't have to convince me of that. I already was considering melting down the silver crowns in my mouth for currency.

Chris said we'd have to write a speech for the president announcing his bold plan to deal with the crisis. (The president loved the word bold.) We also had to reassure the American people that everything was going to be okay. As it turned out, Secretary Paulson—who'd been pretty much a nonperson at the White House until that very day—had a plan that would fix everything: a $700 billion bailout of the financial system (except we couldn't call it a bailout).

The plan, like the secretary himself, seemed to have come out of nowhere—as if it had been hastily scribbled on the back of a couple of sheets of paper in the secretary's car on his way to the White House. Basically, it could be summed up as: *Give me hundreds of billions of taxpayer dollars and then trust me to do the right thing, even though 99.99 percent of you have no idea who I am.* There was no denying it. This plan was certainly "bold."

Clearly, Chris, Horny, and I had a lot of work ahead of us that day. But it was nearly noon, so we decided to get a quick lunch first. Jonathan and Chris were going to order some food from the carryout window of the White House Mess. I wasn't a big fan of the mess in any event, and especially now—look what had happened when I went to get a Diet Pepsi. Instead, I walked two blocks down Pennsylvania Avenue toward the nearest Subway. (Horny hated going with me to Subway because I got refills of pop while I was there. He thought taking free refills was "stealing.")

For me, it was always comforting to get out of the White House and walk around in the real world. And that day it seemed especially important. The other Subway customers had no idea, of course, that their country's sputtering economy was being held together by fumes, Scotch tape, and Hank "Trust Me, Baby" Paulson. I was holding on to a dark, terrible secret, and I couldn't warn any of them.

I ordered the same thing so often that the workers behind the counter could make my sandwich without my saying a word. But if our economy was really in its death throes, I was going out with a bang. When I got to the counter, I threw the whole Subway system off balance and ordered an extra bag of potato chips.

Probably the most worrisome thing about the financial crisis of 2008 was how it seemed to strike without much warning, at least to the people who were supposed to be keeping an eye on the economy. Though there were a few midlevel people in the administration who had predicted a calamity, most of official Washington was caught off guard—the Democratic leadership in Congress and the Republican administration in the White House. For many months, there'd been news stories about individual financial firms failing and recurring troubles in the housing market. But each time some problem bubbled up, elected officials in Congress did what they always did: walked around rubbing their chins and looking troubled. Then someone at the White House would tell the public that it was all being taken care of. Nothing to see here.

Time after time, we speechwriters were given talking points from economic experts that were variations on the same theme: *Even though we're in a rough patch, things are bound to get better.* That, in fact, was exactly what I had heard them tell the president. Like everyone else at the White House, I scoffed at critics who insisted the economy was worse than we were saying. I figured they were just playing politics. This time, at least, it turned out they were right. I hated it when that happened.

When the Bush administration announced a plan to have the federal government directly invest in U.S. banks, a number of conservative critics expressed concern. To them, the government owning pieces of banks sounded suspiciously like socialism. So Chris and I were asked to write a speech for the president that explained why what we were doing was not nationalizing the banking system.

Neither Chris nor I had the slightest idea how to explain this, so we went to the man at the White House who was our point person on the economy. Keith Hennessey was the director of the National Economic Council and one of the president's top economic advisors. Up until that point I knew two main things about Keith. The first was that he was in charge of a "pen pal" program that paired White House staffers with athletes competing in the 2008 Summer Olympics. The second was that he owned at least one hand puppet. I'd first encountered the puppet some months earlier while sitting in the chief speechwriter's office in the West Wing. We were crashing on remarks for the president when I caught a glimpse of a large cloth bird peering in to look at us. All work stopped while one of the president's chief economists staged a mini version of The Muppet Show for our (non)amusement. So I guess you could say that my most indelible image of Keith was not that of an economic Yoda, though whether Keith in fact owned a Yoda puppet remained an open question.

Chris and I entered Keith's wood-paneled office on the top floor of the West Wing. He was sitting in a wingback chair. In front of him was a jar filled with jelly beans—the Gipper's favorite. (Keith thought of himself as a Reagan conservative.)

As usual, Keith was solicitous. He also appeared as if a mountain had just fallen on him. As we sat down across from him, he started explaining what the administration was trying to accomplish to steady the economy.

"We're supposed to write a speech that explains why what we're doing isn't nationalizing the banks," I replied.

Keith looked perplexed. "We *are* nationalizing them," he said.

"Oh," we replied. We told him we had to write a speech saying that we weren't. He gave us a look that said, *Good luck with that, buddy.*

Keith then outlined the dire economic scenario our country was facing. All the options before us, he said, were equally terrible. The banks weren't lending money to one another. Consumers were nervous about spending. Economic growth was coming to a halt. The best-case scenario, it seemed, was a long, deep recession. I was feeling sick to my stomach. My dad was retired and my mom was close to it. They'd be counting on retirement savings to get by—but investments they'd made might tank, perhaps forever.

In the middle of explaining the economic horrors that awaited us, Keith reached for something near his chair. It was a Mouseketeer cap. As in Mickey Mouse. *What on earth?* I wondered.

Without a word of explanation, he placed the cap on his head. Then he continued talking as if nothing at all strange was happening.

I looked at Chris, who looked at me. Then we stared back at Keith. One of the president's top economic advisors was describing the end of the world while wearing mouse ears. There had to be a metaphor around here somewhere.

As we sat there on the top floor of the White House, at the center of power, I couldn't help wondering how it had all come to this. And as the days passed, each more surreal than the last, another question haunted me: what the heck was I doing here?

CHAPTER ONE

SHINING CITY ON A HILL

I guess there's a point in most children's lives when they believe that their hometown is the worst place in the world. Well, those kids can choke on it, because I actually did come from the worst city in America—a fact certified by one of the largest publications in the nation. When I was growing up, Money magazine ranked the major cities in the United States from the perspective of which was the best place to live. My hometown of Flint, Michigan, ranked at the absolute bottom. I must admit, even I was surprised by that. Second to worst, maybe. But the worst of the worst? Wow. The townspeople of Flint made a big show of burning the magazine in effigy, but no one could credibly argue our case.

Flint became internationally famous in the documentary Roger and Me, directed by that self-appointed spokesman for working-class outrage and future millionaire Michael Moore. The film chronicled Flint's economic decline after the one company that had been keeping it alive, General Motors, packed up most of their automobiles and sputtered out of town. It wasn't the smoothest departure the world had ever seen. Basically, the company broke up with Flint by e-mail and then changed its phone number.

I was born in the heart of the city to two liberal teachers. My dad, Maurice, was born while the country was still reeling from the Great Depression, and he was the first boy in his family to go to college. He had thick jet-black hair and looked vaguely like Ricky Ricardo. My mom, Larcia, was the second of ten children and didn't have a single enemy in the world. During my childhood, Mom had round glasses and a brown beehive hairdo that she painstakingly wrapped up every evening with tissue paper. Sometimes I'd wake her at night when I had a scary dream. She'd shoot up in bed with white cream on her face and her hair wrapped like a mummy. (I think that's where my troubles began.)

My parents lived in Flint several years before I was born. When I was about one, they adopted a baby girl. My sister, Jennifer, was born on an Indian reservation in Canada. One of the first things I did when I was young was kick her in the eye. Otherwise, we were very close.

We grew up in a neighborhood filled with people of many different income levels and races. There were abandoned homes a few doors down and vacant lots where you could always find trouble. Everyone in our neighborhood knew where the drug houses were. There were at least two within a block of our home. It wasn't uncommon to hear police sirens at all hours of the night. Once on my way home I was stopped by the Flint police. They put me in the backseat of the squad car and started demanding proof that I lived in the neighborhood. I was young, white, with a nice car. I think they suspected I was on a drug buy.

We had a beautiful brick Tudor-style house with five bedrooms. If it had been built in any other city, it would have been worth more than a million dollars. In Flint, it was worth about $50,000. But whatever Flint's problems, my parents were stick-it-out types. Even if our house had exploded, Mom and Dad would have sat in the rubble and camped out with tents.

My parents often invited random people to come to stay, sometimes for months or years at a time. When my sister and I were very young, Mom and Dad brought foster children into our home. For most of my childhood, young men would move into our house as our temporary brothers. Most of them had been abandoned or abused by their biological parents and, understandably, had severe emotional problems. One guy who shared my bedroom used to hide under a blanket while wearing my sister's bathing suit. Another guy took apart our electronic equipment—cameras, remote controls, VCRs—to see if he could repair them. He couldn't. One day I was sitting with him at the breakfast table when our cat, Mindy, walked by. His eyes darkened, then he pointed at her. "You will pay for your actions," he vowed. (Didn't ask. Didn't want to know.)

Another day one of the older guys who lived with us disappeared. Years later, he showed up with a garbage bag. He was slurring his words and acting strangely. He put down the bag and said he'd come back to ask my dad for my sister's hand in marriage. We weren't sure if the bag was part of a trade (we never opened it). Dad, of course, had no intention of entertaining the offer. "Hey, Dad," I whispered, "let's hear the man out." No one else thought that was funny, especially my sister. Dad took the man for a ride somewhere, and we never saw the guy again. (Didn't ask. Didn't want to know.)

I always knew Mom and Dad would be there for me when I really needed them. But when they got home from work they had to prioritize. My "crisis" over getting a B on a homework assignment didn't rate quite as high as one of the foster kids threatening to burn down our house, being accused of indecent exposure, or breaking into the house next door. So I tended to fend for myself. I did household chores without being told. And I did well in school, at least academically. I even taught myself to read. Socially, well, that was another story. For most of my childhood, I was a classic nerd with thick glasses, cowlicky hair, and pale skin. I was shy and quiet, and could go for hours without saying a word. In first grade, everyone in the class made papier-mâché puppets of ourselves. Mine didn't have a mouth.

To add to those woes, I was really overweight. But I finally beat my weight problem the old-fashioned way: by becoming a subject of total humiliation. I was with my parents, my sister, and one of our foster brothers on a summer vacation in the Pocono Mountains. We all decided to go horseback riding, which was the most exercise I'd had in my entire life. My usual workout routine was trying to get as many scoops of ice cream as I could before The Dukes of Hazzard came back after commercials.

As we waited to get assigned horses, another vacationing family waited with us. They had two kids, a girl and a boy. The boy was about my age and extremely overweight. I felt bad for him. The horse people brought out horses for everyone—my parents, my sister, the other kids' parents, his sister. Finally, it was down to the fat kid and me. As we stood there, I saw them bring forward the biggest horse I'd ever seen, the T. rex of the equestrian world. I overheard the workers talking on their way over. One asked which one of us he should give Horse-zilla to.

"Give it to that fat kid," the other worker replied.

I felt so terrible for the boy standing right next to me. He could hear them too. How awful. Then they brought that giant horse right up to us and handed the reins . . . to me. They'd been talking about me! From that day forward, I never drank a glass of regular pop again. I started walking and running. I lost thirty pounds over the next two months, and I did it completely on my own. I was becoming a believer in the power of self-sufficiency.

While my family and I were facing these and other challenges, Flint was facing several as well. Our valiant civic leaders always seemed to have some new scheme certain to pull us out of our Depression-like doldrums. The most infamous of these brainstorms was AutoWorld. AutoWorld was, in the wisdom of our leading citizens, a no-lose proposition: an amusement park that would be a tribute to the auto industry and its origins. Except, as it turned out, there were hardly any rides and not a single roller coaster. Instead the "attraction" was a walk-through history of Flint. Come one, come all, to hear about the famous Sit-Down Strike and the birth of the United Auto Workers! All the family will want to listen to a mannequin of town father Jacob Smith talk about Flint's founding! Did you enjoy building dioramas in high school? Now you can actually walk through one—and come back to walk through it again and again. AutoWorld was going to cost millions to build, but everyone was sure it was going to be Flint's salvation. The city tore down homes to build large parking lots for the overflow crowds that would certainly teem in. The Hyatt Regency built a hotel downtown to host all the expected guests. City officials went to the trouble of installing signs on highways and streets to help guide the expected tourists. "What if too many show up for the opening?" the local newspaper fretted.

Predictably, every prominent politician in Michigan rushed to glom on to the AutoWorld magic—and free publicity—on opening day. Governor Jim Blanchard, who was rumored to be considering a run for president, offered his typical bromides. "This is a great day for Flint," he said, "but it is also a great day for the entire state of Michigan!"

"AutoWorld is a magnificent dream come true," Senator Don Riegle gushed. "And many of you dreamers are here tonight."

Not to be outdone, Flint's mayor compared AutoWorld's opening to America's decision to declare independence from Great Britain.

My parents took me to AutoWorld—once. I didn't really care what an assembly line looked like or how an engine was built. I attended for one reason only: to see the Cosby kids. Somehow, AutoWorld had lured Theo and Rudy Huxtable from the hit TV program The Cosby Show. What those two had to do with the world of automobiles I didn't know. They weren't even old enough to drive. But I wanted to see them. So did a whole bunch of other kids. All of us were behind a fence staring at little Rudy, who was five or six years old and probably a millionaire. Some beside me were screaming: "Hi, Rudy!" "Little Rudy!" "Come here, Rudy!" Rudy clung to her fake brother, Theo, for dear life. The crowd was so frenzied that if either kid had moved a millimeter closer to the fence, it would have been all over.

Sadly, for all their glamour, even the Cosby kids couldn't save AutoWorld. It folded within a year. Hordes of people did not want to spend money to walk through a giant diorama after all. Eventually, the entire building—the "miracle"—was torn down. The Hyatt Regency people, who knew a loser when they saw it, pulled up stakes. All the politicians who had come to AutoWorld's grand opening were noticeably absent at its grisly collapse. It was probably a wise decision. We didn't have much in Flint, but we could still get our hands on tar and feathers. The good citizens of our town would have been better off if they'd just poured all of our tax dollars into lottery tickets.

Even after AutoWorld's spinout and fiery crash, city leaders couldn't help themselves—they kept dreaming up other big comeback plans. One assignment that preoccupied them was devising a new slogan. The city was dying economically, so of course the solution was a catchphrase. One suggestion was "Flint—that's right, you made the wrong turn." They settled on "Flint: our new spark will surprise you." (If there were any sparks in Flint, it was probably due to arson.) As president, Ronald Reagan talked about "a shining city on a hill." But Flint wasn't it.

I didn't blame Flint's troubles on corporate America or the auto industry, though. I blamed Flint's sad fate on us. We allowed ourselves to become dependent on one corporation for our survival or, failing that, the tender mercies of government bureaucrats. We elected bad managers who made bad choices and didn't diversify when times were good. Then we kept the same people in office over and over again. In Flint, the Democrats, whether competent or incompetent, rule with impunity. The Republicans don't even bother. Our United States congressman had been in office since I was a child. Decades later, he's still there, promising that Flint's new dawn is just around the corner.

Every election year, Democratic candidates came to Flint to pay homage to the city's grit and make sure the citizens turned out to vote. Bill Clinton once came to extol the city and its mayor, Woodrow Stanley. "They used to call me the 'Comeback Kid,' " President Bubba said. "You ought to call Flint the 'Comeback City' under Woodrow Stanley." Actually, under Mayor Stanley's mismanagement, Flint's debt rating was lowered to the level of junk. An auditor discovered that Mayor Stanley's city budget included "phantom" revenue of $10 million. When a newspaper questioned the mayor's leadership, Stanley defended himself by calling the newspaper racist. The city's voters finally got smart and threw our version of the Comeback Kid out of office in a recall election. But a few years later, Stanley was back—elected to the county Board of Commissioners. He ran for a seat in the state house of representatives—and won. (He reportedly has his sights on higher office.)

As I witnessed the sad fate of my hometown, I came to the conclusion that government largesse, dependence on handouts, and the noble intentions of liberals had achieved nothing. I didn't know if any political party had better answers. But we'd tried it the Democrats' way and got zip. So I looked for something else.

I started getting interested in politics at a pretty young age. The boys I grew up with could tell you the latest baseball scores or recite all the statistics about the Detroit Lions (the most pathetic football team in history). I could tell you how many electoral votes Iowa had or what states Jimmy Carter won in 1980.

I was even excited when former vice president Walter Mondale came to our school assembly in 1984. Mondale was running for president against Ronald Reagan. We were supposed to be enthusiastic about him. All of our parents were, and most of our teachers. Every leader in town endorsed him. He'd recently picked the first woman vice presidential nominee in history—New York congresswoman Geraldine Ferraro—and that was especially exciting. At the school rally, I was handed a large Mondale-Ferraro sign. It was one of the coolest things I'd ever seen—a part of history. (I still have it.)

Mondale gave a pretty bland speech in a high-pitched, nasal voice.

The kids I was sitting next to were so bored that they were even thinking about going back to class. As Mondale went on and on, I remember wondering, *What's he doing here anyway?* There wasn't a single person in the auditorium, except for a handful of teachers, who could vote. A few months later, he lost forty-nine states. I remember how disappointed Mom was. Then I started thinking that maybe this Ronald Reagan guy might not be as terrible as everyone said. A huge majority of the country seemed to like him just fine.

Reagan was the first president I could remember. For a long time the only thing I knew about him was that everyone seemed to think he was going to start a nuclear war. Then I started listening to him. I found appealing his belief that government was not the solution to our problems. I was attracted to his philosophy of responsibility, accountability, and pulling yourself up by your bootstraps. Yes, government had a certain duty to help those who couldn't do it for themselves. But as a last resort. I was suspicious of sending more money to government to create bigger programs that didn't really solve anything, as had been the case over and over again in Flint. I supported welfare reform to break a cycle of dependency and encourage people to find work. (Even Bill Clinton would support that.) The Republican Party may not have been hip, but they were the responsible, competent grown-ups. At least, that's what Republicans were supposed to be.

I read the great speeches of Lincoln, Kennedy, and Reagan, and, more than anything, I dreamed that one day I could go to the White House and write eloquent words for a president that would also ring through history.

Every Sunday after church, I turned on every political news show I could find: Firing Line, The McLaughlin Group, CNN's Late Edition. I found myself rooting for the conservative panelists on the shows, people like William F. Buckley Jr., Fred Barnes, and Kate O'Beirne. I joined the Genesee County Republican Party and went to a meeting. Unfortunately, the local Republicans were a small, hapless group who didn't seem to go out of their way to recruit young blood. Most seemed to have voted in every election since the time of Warren G. Harding. No wonder we couldn't win any elections. We barely had a pulse.

At first, I think my conservatism was something my family considered cute—I was their own Alex P. Keaton. But when I continued with it, they started to get worried. My parents had sacrificed to pay my way through college and law school. Now I was going to use that training to practice the dark arts of the Republican Party? This was exactly what had happened to Anakin Skywalker.

When I first confessed to Mom that I was a Republican, she told me point blank that she considered most Republicans to be selfish and greedy. I think she would have been far happier if I'd told her I was a Communist vampire who had been diagnosed with kleptomania. Mom didn't hang out with many conservatives. She was very close to her aunt Anna, the Jane Fonda of Rock Island, Illinois. A former Peace Corps worker and part-time radical, Aunt Anna wore beads, muumuus, and flip-flops and had a subscription to Mother Jones magazine. In her worldview, Republicans were nefarious monsters who wore black capes and twirled their mustaches. She truly believed this. If she had still been alive when I went to work in the White House, she would have moved into Lafayette Park to shame me every day with a bullhorn. Aunt Anna didn't play around.

Mom's opposition was especially hard for me. When I was growing up, my mom was my best friend. There was no one in the world I was closer to. Once when I was about six I got mad about something and decided to run away. I took a pile of clothes and made a big show of storming out of the house. My parents watched me from the window. I walked down our front steps and to the end of the lawn. Then I turned around and came back into the house. "Mom," I asked, "can you come and carry my clothes for me?" She would have, gladly. And even though she wished I wasn't a Republican, I was still her son.

The 1992 election was the first time I was eligible to vote. President Bush (the first one) was in a tough fight for reelection. I was so keen on voting in the Republican primary between Bush and his challenger, Pat Buchanan, that I was stopped for speeding. "Rushing to vote" was surely a new entry on the list of driver excuses. (I got a ticket anyway.) When I asked for a Republican ballot at my precinct in Flint, the old ladies who worked at the polls tried to hold back gasps. I had a feeling that as soon as I walked off they shook their heads and said sadly, "He seemed like such a nice boy."

Since 1992 was the first year I'd be voting for a president, I went to Mom with an unorthodox request. I begged her to vote Republican in

November. "Mom, you can't cancel out the very first vote I ever cast," I argued. Mom mentioned something about democracy, but I pretty much ignored her. "I beg you, Mom," I said. Then I fell back on my most shameless plea. "I'm your child!" As she left to vote, I called after her, "Please don't cancel me out!"

Mom came back from voting that day with a frown on her face. She looked at me sternly. "Just this once," she said. She voted for Bush. (I'm still not sure I'm authorized to say that out loud.) I imagined Mom walking into the polling booth wearing a trench coat and dark sunglasses, glancing in both directions to make sure none of her teacher friends saw what she'd done.

Dad wasn't particularly happy about my Republican tendencies either, for that matter, but unlike Mom, there was no way I could ever have convinced him to vote Republican. We were at heart a union family. And union families in Flint voted one way: to the left.

The only other Republican in our family was my grandma, my mom's mother. Somehow Grandma escaped the family wrath. Everyone seemed to think she was an eccentric who'd never gotten over her family's losing all their money during the Great Depression (she blamed Franklin Roosevelt). So they figured she could be a Republican if she wanted.

Grandma lived in Chicago. She and I used to walk over to a café at the Ramada hotel across the street from her condo and sit and talk politics for hours. One day we were walking back to her apartment when we saw a political sign for a man running for the local seat in Congress. The man's name was unusual: Barack Obama. He was a professor or something who had positioned himself as a moderate, at least compared to the guy he was running against, a radical named Bobby Rush.

"What do you think of him, Grandma?" I asked her.

"Oh, he doesn't have a chance," she said. She was right. He lost badly. But he launched his first political campaign in the very café Grandma and I frequented. It was our own little brush with Democratic Party history.

Meanwhile, back home in Michigan, a silent political war was being fought between my parents and me through the U.S. Postal Service. I was on all the Republican mailing lists and my parents were on all the Democratic ones. This meant that in any given month, my parents and I would receive dueling solicitations from the ACLU and the Heritage Foundation, Planned Parenthood and the National Right to Life Committee, the Save the Whales Committee and the Committee to Let the Whales Fend for Themselves.

In 1996, I received an invitation that was of particular interest. The Republican National Committee was starting a program to rally youth volunteers at the party's nominating convention—the big one—that summer in San Diego. I was invited to be part of the first-ever GOP Youth Convention. And as a youth convention delegate, I'd also get a chance to serve as a page at the actual convention itself and meet all the famous figures I'd watched on TV. I desperately wanted to go.

I went to my mom with the idea and showed her the brochure.

"Where is this?" she asked.

I told her it was in San Diego and that I'd be gone for a week. She was surprised. I'd never wanted to do anything like this before. I'd had to be forced to go to summer camp.

Then I told her how much it would cost—more than $1,000. And I didn't have a dime.

"That's a lot of money," she said. It also was money that would be going directly to the coffers of the Republican Party.

"Let me talk to your dad about it," she said. I wasn't worried about that. Dad was a little more careful with money, but there was nothing either of them wouldn't do for me if I really wanted it.

When Mom came back and told me they'd pay for me to go, I felt a little guilty. "Are you sure it isn't too much money?" I asked.

"Well, I look at it this way," she said. "You never liked to do any after-school activities. You didn't like going to camp. You didn't like taking art or music classes. You didn't play a lot of sports." (This wasn't coming out too well.) "If this is what you enjoy," she said, "we ought to give you a chance to do it." I think she liked the idea that her shy bookworm son was actually going to go out and talk to real, live people—even if they were ghouls who kicked puppies and laughed at poor children on the streets.

Before I left for San Diego, I wrote a letter to former president George H. W. Bush. I told him that he was the first person I'd ever voted for, and I was sorry he'd lost. Then I said I was going to the convention and, if he had any free time, I'd love to meet him. I don't know why I sent it, I was just a kid from Michigan no one had ever heard of, but I'd read somewhere that Bush liked letters and answered them himself. I thought if I could write a nice letter, who knows? Weeks passed and I never heard from him, and the letter was forgotten.

Just before I was scheduled to fly to San Diego, I had a panic attack. I was about to travel halfway across the country to meet thousands of people at one of the biggest political events of the year. I didn't even like talking to our next-door neighbors. What on earth was I thinking? Still, something compelled me to do this.

When I arrived in San Diego, I was assigned a room at one of the dorms on the University of California–San Diego campus. I'd be sharing it with three other guys. When I got to my room, I was surprised to find a message waiting. It was from the office of President George H. W. Bush. He'd received my letter after all! The caller had left a number in Maine for me to phone back at my earliest convenience. The guys I was rooming with had just met me, and I was getting a personal call from the former president of the United States. That didn't exactly hurt my efforts to make friends.

I dialed the number that had been given to me, and a woman in Bush's office answered. She very kindly told me that the president had received my letter. He wanted to meet with me, but he was sorry that he didn't have the time. She said he'd be in San Diego only very briefly. But they wanted me to know he was sending me a letter to my address in Michigan. She stressed that the president had signed the letter himself. It was a nice introduction to the Bush family.

But the 1996 convention was not a time to celebrate the Bushes. This time, it was finally Bob Dole's turn. Dole had been in the Senate for thirty years. He'd run for president twice before and vice president once. Now a wiser, kinder, gentler, and older Dole was at it again. He wasn't known as a staunch conservative. He once admitted that he'd first run for office as a Republican because there were more Republicans than Democrats in his district in Kansas and he'd done the math. But in 1996, he'd seen the light.

"I'll be another Ronald Reagan," he promised, "if that's what you want." (It was.)

His reinvention aside, Dole had a habit that people mocked. He liked to refer to himself in the third person. As in "Bob Dole likes apples" or "Bob Dole is getting angry." It was funny, but not in a good way.

Bob Dole was going to arrive in San Diego by boat, and we youth volunteers were asked to go and welcome him. The convention organizers didn't need to do much to encourage us. Welcoming the nominee of our party—there was nothing more exciting to us than that. I talked my new friends into getting to Embarcadero South Park as early as possible to get a good spot. The park was adjacent to San Diego harbor. It was one of the most beautiful places I'd ever seen: inviting blue water glistening under a blue cloudless sky. Even the boats in the harbor looked pristine, ivory white and shining in the sun.

We were there so early that we snagged a spot right at the edge of the rope line where Senator Dole was going to disembark. He'd be walking right past us! I stood in the blazing sun for an hour and a half waiting for him to appear—without any suntan lotion, I might add. We grabbed American flags that campaign workers were handing out along with large blue and white placards that displayed DOLE-KEMP in block letters. I used one as a sun visor.

There was a big extravaganza preceding Dole's arrival. We watched a flyover of old planes. We saw skydivers jumping. Then Senator Dole himself arrived on a large ferry, at the front of a vast armada of ships. It was a little like Horatio Nelson arriving home in Britain. We squinted to see him.

Dole was tan and waving as he approached the dock. His wife, Elizabeth, was there with a practiced smile along with Dole's new running mate, former congressman Jack Kemp. The choice of Kemp was meant to suggest that this time Bob Dole meant business. Everyone knew that the two men didn't get along. Kemp was supposed to supply the ticket with charisma, in contrast to Dole, who was seventy-three and about as dry as Kansas corn.

Kemp had been a talented quarterback for the San Diego Chargers in the 1960s, which for all of the young Republican acolytes gathered there might as well have been in the Stone Age. No one had any memory of Kemp's football days—none of us had even been alive then. But the Dole-Kemp people went to great lengths to evoke Kemp's football glory. Dole announced Kemp as his running mate by saying, "I wanted a ten, but I got a fifteen." My friends and I looked at one another and shrugged. (Apparently 15 had been Kemp's jersey number.) The whole football thing was so pathetic. It was like parents bringing out Beatles eight-tracks just to prove they used to be groovy. Sure enough, as Kemp got off the boat in San Diego, the football cheese show was on full display. The vice presidential candidate kept making hand gestures that mimicked throwing invisible footballs into the crowd. For those who didn't know any better, it looked like he was having some sort of seizure. I couldn't care less if I shook Jack Kemp's hand. But I wanted, desperately, to touch Bob Dole—which, trust me, is far less creepy than it sounds. It's not as if I'd never seen a celebrity before. I'd once had lunch with Steve Martin in Beverly Hills. He sat two tables away and had no idea who I was, but still. Yet to me at that moment, Bob Dole was the biggest star in the world.

As he arrived, Dole seemed vaguely puzzled at seeing all these screaming young people reaching for his hand. It was as if he couldn't understand why we were bothering. I got the feeling that if he'd been in our shoes, Bob Dole wouldn't have cheered anybody. Bob Dole'd be back home doing some real work.

As it happened, Dole was about to walk right by me. I don't know the clinical term for it, but I went absolutely nuts. At that moment, there was nothing more important than for Bob Dole to shake my hand. This was not as easy a task as it might have seemed. Even on a good day, Dole was not the most outgoing guy. Also, his right hand was withered and largely unusable from injuries he'd sustained in World War II. He didn't have full feeling in his left hand either. So, understandably, handshakes were not Bob Dole's favorite thing.

I was not deterred. "Senator Dole!" I cried. "Over here! Please! Over here! Oh, Senator Dole!"

If my parents could have seen their shy son then, the first thing they would have said was "What happened to you?" The second thing would have been "Yikes."

As I worked myself up into a full froth, Dole paused and looked down at me—this crazy young fellow with a sunburned face screaming Dole's name at the top of his lungs. I could see that he was debating whether he could get away with ignoring me. There was a look of uncertainty on his face as he considered shaking my hand. It reminded me of that look Bob Barker sometimes flashed when a contestant on *The Price Is Right* seemed a little too eager for a hug. As Senator Dole stared down at me quizzically, a photographer for USA *Today* snapped a picture. The next day, on the front page, was a picture of Bob Dole with that priceless expression on his face—a combination of fear and bewilderment. And though you couldn't see the face of the certifiable lunatic he was looking it, I'd have known that thick brown uncontrollable hair anywhere. That lunatic was me. I was so proud that I cut the picture out and put it in a frame.

It's hard to explain what possessed me to act that way. For the first time in my life, I was overcome with excitement. I felt so honored to be at the convention, as if I were home. The best thing about it was that there were other young people around who felt just the way I did—freshly scrubbed Republicans from all parts of the country who wanted to be part of history. We'd been following politics since we were kids, and we fraternized like fellow groupies. We became instant best friends. More than a decade later, I remember one of my convention buddies clearly—a young man named Steve McPherson, of Idaho. We did everything together, talked politics as if we'd known each other all our lives. After the convention, I never saw him again.

Walking onto the convention floor was like a Little Leaguer's dream of walking onto the field at Yankee Stadium. I was captivated by the rows and rows of chairs, the large signs for each of the fifty states, and the media skyboxes occupied by every TV network. I watched workers put up the balloons for the traditional balloon drop. I saw news anchors set up their booths. I grabbed DOLE FOR PRESIDENT signs to save for history. Even signs for people like Christie Todd Whitman, Fred Thompson—you name it.

Even more impressive was to see all the great figures of my party walking around as if they were regular people. I felt like those scientists did when they entered Jurassic Park for the first time. That look of wonder the scientists showed as they saw the dinosaurs they'd dreamed about and studied for years actually walking the earth—that was mine. (Eventually, of course, the dinosaurs started killing innocent people and demolishing everything in sight. But I digress.)

One of the cochairs of the convention was a Texas governor named George W. Bush. I heard him speak and don't remember a single word.

There were those I met at the convention who were already talking about W. in 2000, however—in the of course extremely unlikely event that Bob Dole would lose. At the time, I was more inclined toward John McCain. I'd met Senator McCain in Michigan when he came to campaign for a Senate candidate, Ronna Romney. He was charming and funny, good on almost all of the issues—a real conservative. Plus he was a war hero who'd survived a North Vietnamese prison camp. He had guts.

At night, we were asked to stand on the convention floor and fill the aisles so the place looked crowded on TV. One night I watched Nancy Reagan come out to introduce a video tribute to her husband, who was suffering from Alzheimer's. I was deeply moved by her bravery and her fierce loyalty to her beloved Ronnie. Colin Powell spoke too. He had considered a run for the GOP nomination that year but decided against it. He was the most popular man in the country. Why muck that up by governing? That night Powell was proudly Republican—and he stayed that way every single day that it suited him.

We stood in line to get other famous Republicans to autograph our DOLE-KEMP signs. I practically chased Newt Gingrich into a CNN trailer to get him to sign something. While I was waiting, I got an autograph from his press secretary, an urbane, well-dressed English-born gentleman named Tony Blankley. Blankley was getting a lot of publicity on his own in those days, which was unusual for a press secretary. When Newt came out of the CNN trailer, I asked him for his autograph. He smiled and said, "Sure." Then he scanned the Dole sign I was holding. "You got my press secretary to sign this?" he asked.

"Yes, I did," I replied.

"Why do you need me to sign this if you got the great Tony Blankley?" he asked. I laughed. Newt didn't. I wasn't sure if he was kidding or just annoyed. But he signed anyway.

I had my picture taken with Marilyn Quayle, Senator Alan Simpson of Wyoming, and Representative Dan Lungren of California. I would have taken a picture with Dan Lungren's cousin if he'd been standing there.

At the time, I was somewhat obsessed with Texas senator Kay Bailey Hutchison. She'd been elected in 1994. I thought a tough-talking Texas woman would be an ideal Republican presidential candidate someday. She was lean and attractive with a soft voice and honey-blond hair. I told my friends that we had to find her and have our pictures taken with her. I said I was going to be her convention "stalker." As it turned out, this was a poor choice of words. She actually had a real stalker. In retrospect, maybe it wasn't the best idea to walk around using that term.

One day, during our futile KBH search, we stood at the bottom of an escalator taking all the VIPs down to the convention floor. I felt sure she would show up eventually. She never did. Instead we saw her fellow Texan, Senator Phil Gramm. Gramm had run against Dole for the presidency. On the campaign trail, he used to always talk about his "mawma," which I found charming. He was proudly politically incorrect. He once offered the thought-provoking comment "I have more guns than I need and less guns than I want." And when practically everyone else in the Senate was supporting Hillary Clinton's convoluted takeover of health care, he was the only one who went to the Senate floor and vowed that her bill would pass "over my cold, dead political body." He raised a ton of money to win the White House and got flatfooted by, of all people, Pat Buchanan in the Louisiana caucuses. Losing to Pat was like being beaten up by your sister (of which I had some personal experience). After that, Gramm was finished.

As Senator Gramm came down the escalator, I decided that it would be nice if we offered an attaboy to good ol' Phil.

"Let's give him a standing ovation," I suggested.

My friends agreed immediately. So here were four young men standing at the bottom of the escalator and applauding, while tipsy Republican delegates stopped and stared. As he descended the escalator, Phil Gramm looked all around to see whom the applause was for. He was more surprised than anyone to find out it was for him.

"Why, thank you, boys," he said, looking like he might choke up.

He tried to shake our hands, but we didn't stop applauding. He was even more touched. Finally we stopped clapping and took pictures with him. Then we watched him amble away.

My other big autograph score was from Bush campaign strategist and author Mary Matalin. Mary had led the first President Bush to a humiliating defeat against Bill Clinton. Then she married the guy who beat us, political strategist James Carville—a strange-looking, bald-headed guy with a thick Louisiana drawl who talked so fast it was hard to understand him. Still, she'd worked at the White House! She'd run a campaign! She knew a president! To us, that made her a big-time celebrity.

I caught up with her as she was making her way to an event with a very impatient aide. As I approached, the aide brushed me off. "Mary is in a hurry," she informed me with a sigh.

With Carville, Mary had written a book about the 1992 presidential campaign. "I read your book five times," I said, walking alongside them. The aide rolled her eyes. Mary didn't.

"You read it how many times?" she asked.

"Five times," I said, not even slightly embarrassed by it. I also had brought her book with me to San Diego and was clutching it in my hands as we spoke. (Okay, maybe that was a little embarrassing.)

Mary laughed. "I haven't even read it that many times." She stopped, dropped her purse, and took out a pen. "Well, I've got to sign this," she said, and I handed her the book. Her aide sighed again. I beamed in triumph.

The book was inscribed, To Matt: Go get 'em. Love, Mary M.

I felt like I'd been knighted by the queen. She was right—I was going to go get 'em. And she loved me for it! I treasured that book for years.

At this point, I'd accomplished a lot—a multitude of photos and autographs from the Republican glitterati. I admit it—I was feeling cocky. I decided that I had to go after the Moby Dick of presidential autographs: that of multiple-time presidential candidate Alan Keyes. Keyes was a prominent African American Republican. This meant he was as rare as a three-eyed goldfish.

Even better for party activists, Keyes was a staunch conservative and a crusader against abortion. Unfortunately, he also had a reputation for . . . well, in polite circles we called it being eccentric. His main line of attack in a debate was to yell indignantly at everybody else. He once jumped into a mosh pit to get an endorsement. There was a story then circulating that he'd charged his hotel bills to another campaign. Still, he was never boring, and believed passionately in whatever it was he was saying.

The reception Keyes usually received from lily-white evangelicals could be summed up in one word: rapture. Sure enough, Keyes walked around San Diego's convention center as if he were a god. Though people clamored for his autograph, he remained on his mental mountaintop. He would sign nothing, acknowledge no one. That only made us want his signature even more. We surrounded him, pleaded with him as he tried to move among the masses. As our growing mob encircled him, waving pens, he did nothing. His inaction drove us all to a near-frenzy. This guy knew how to work a crowd!

I was determined to get his signature. So in the few minutes I had to strike, I tried to get into his head. And it occurred to me: Keyes craved respect. After all, he'd once staged a hunger strike because he was excluded from a presidential debate.

I remembered how proud he was of being President Reagan's representative to some United Nations agency, which meant he received the rank of ambassador. That's how he liked to be billed.

Foolishly, the people trying to get his autograph were saying, "Please sign this, Mr. Keyes" or, worse, "Alan," as if he were a mere human being.

Instead I tried something else. "Would you please sign this, Mr. Ambassador?" I asked loudly. I had to say it a few times before he heard me.

When he did, he smiled. He turned to me, took my placard, and scribbled his name on it. The rest of the autograph seekers looked at me with awe. It was my Sixteen Candles moment. I felt like Anthony Michael Hall standing triumphantly in the bathroom surrounded by his peers. Except in my case I didn't have a pair of panties in my hands, but an autograph from Alan Keyes. Sorry, Ambassador Keyes.

After the convention, MSNBC gave him a TV show mischievously titled Alan Keyes Is Making Sense. I didn't think the producers at MSNBC really believed the ultraconservative Keyes made sense. It was as if Fox News Channel, to have some fun, decided to air a show called Hillary Clinton Is Telling the Truth.

During each half-hour show, and without any explanation, Keyes would change from a suit and tie into a loud sweater, and then change back into a suit again. Why did he do this? Was it cold in the studio? Was he doing a Mr. Rogers thing? These were the kinds of questions a shy political nerd like me would ponder on a dateless Friday night.

My most interesting brush with celebrity at the convention wasn't with a politician but with someone far more powerful: a television journalist. In the days before the convention started, I'd been assigned to greet people at the airport and direct them to the rental cars and baggage claim. As I stood in front of one terminal, who should come out but the dean of the White House press corps: Sam Donaldson of ABC News. Sam came off his plane looking like the most bored person on earth. This must have been his umpteenth convention. He'd done this all before.

I went up to him nervously. "Excuse me, Mr. Donaldson," I said. "Welcome to San Diego."

"What?" he asked, with an annoyed glance.

I swallowed hard. "Um, I'm supposed to welcome you. I'm, uh, on the welcoming committee." I think I mumbled something about the Republicans.

"Where is my car?" he said.

Huh? Uncertainly, I pointed in the direction of the rental cars.

"No, I have a driver," he retorted, as if this should be perfectly obvious. He treated me like an uppity assistant who'd spoken before having been given permission.

I mumbled something unhelpful. He gave me another annoyed glance and then walked away.

A day or so later, I ran into Sam again. He was giving a radio interview to Mary Matalin at the convention's "radio row." That's how big Sam was—he was being interviewed by other journalists. For some reason, I decided to take this opportunity to verify something I'd heard Katie Couric say on the news. Many people at the time believed Sam wore a toupee. That was because the top of his hair did not seem to have a part and it never, ever moved. But Katie assured her viewers that she'd checked, and Sam's hair was his own. So while Sam was being interviewed, I walked up behind him. I was standing a few inches over him and scrutinizing his head. Mary Matalin watched me as I did this, while she was live on the air. She clearly wasn't sure what to make of this strange young man examining her guest's hairline. I don't know if she remembered signing my book. But this surely wasn't what she'd meant by "Go get 'em." Still, Mary was a cool chick, so she said nothing.

As I drew ever closer, I was almost sure I could see a plastic lining attaching Sam's hair to his scalp. I was pretty certain. I just couldn't quite tell. I needed one more second...and then, while he was still talking on the air, Sam whirled around and looked straight up at me. He fixed me with an angry, terrifying gaze.

For a moment I froze. Then I did the only thing that made sense: I ran like Seabiscuit.

I would have one last encounter with Sam at the convention a few nights later. I was filling one of the aisles between the Texas and South Carolina delegations on the night Dole delivered his acceptance speech. After the speech ended, I saw Sam standing on the edge of the convention stage, trying to push his way toward Dole. Reporters weren't supposed to be on the stage, and the Secret Service kept pushing Sam back. This went on until at one point Sam was teetering extremely close to the edge of the platform.

On a whim, I started a chant with one of my friends as we stood among the South Carolina delegation: "Jump, Sam, jump!" Some of the delegates heard me. They laughed and started chanting too. Before long, the chant spread to the Texas delegates and then across the whole convention.

"Jump, Sam, jump! Jump, Sam, jump!"

Sam heard the chant, looked in my direction, and scowled. I then changed the chant into a message for the Secret Service. "Push Sam off!" we shouted. "Push Sam off!" (They didn't.)

Sometime later, I made the national news. They played the "Jump, Sam, jump" chant as part of a PBS Frontline special called "Why America Hates the Press."

While I was in San Diego, I called my parents and tried to tell them what was happening and how exciting it was. But Mary Matalin meant nothing to them. Neither did Alan Keyes. They would have thought I was crazy if I'd told them about my impromptu ovation for Phil Gramm. Only the name Sam Donaldson would have rung a bell at all, and they probably wouldn't have liked what I did to him. I guess it was a Republican thing. They just wouldn't ever understand.

Even though it didn't accomplish what it was supposed to—Bob Dole lost big—the 1996 convention was my first real involvement in national Republican politics, and I was hooked. People were talking about ideas I believed in, like smaller government and a strong defense. There was a sense of unity against the Democrats, whom we opposed not because they were evil but because they were wrong.

After the convention was over, I called the only person I knew who might understand it all. Grandma had watched every night to see if she could catch me on television. She swore she did one night. Supposedly a camera had flashed on my face standing in the crowd.

"How did you like it?" she asked excitedly.

"It was the best time of my life!" I gushed.

"Well, you've got to go to Washington," she said. "There's no other place for you."

I knew she was right. There was no other place I wanted to be. Though the Democrats still controlled the White House in 1996, it was the Republicans, under Newt Gingrich, who were the leaders on Capitol Hill. And I wanted to be part of the action. I even hoped one day to make it to the White House—a Republican one—and help carry our party's philosophy bravely forward into the twenty-first century.

When I was in San Diego, I ran into an aide to our new Republican senator from Michigan, Spence Abraham. The aide, a man named Tony Antone, was a very nice guy who was probably in his thirties. Tony wanted to help me, but he wasn't sure whether there were any openings in the Washington office. Still, since I was there at the convention, I asked if there was a chance to say hello to the senator.

Tony looked embarrassed. "Boy, it doesn't look like the senator is going to have time to meet with you out here," he said. Curiously, Senator Abraham was standing about ten feet away at the time and appeared to be doing absolutely nothing.

"Let's stay in touch," Tony said.

Eventually, by sending my resume, calling up people in the senator's offices in Michigan and D.C., and being a general pain in the neck, I finally got an interview with the senator's state director in suburban Detroit. I was nervous and inexperienced, and I'm sure it showed. It became one of those "we'll keep your resume on file" interviews.

Many weeks passed. I was back home in Michigan considering abandoning my dream and going to work at a law firm. Then at last I received a call from Tony. He said that there was one job open in the Washington area, but I might not be interested in it. The job was special assistant to the senator. It was described as answering letters and handling constituent concerns. It was basically the lowest-level job there, just one step up from the front office assistant who answered the phones. It paid about $25,000 a year.

Since I had a law degree, Tony thought I might be overqualified for the job. I didn't care. I said I desperately wanted to work in the Senate and would take what I could get.

My parents were wary. It wasn't so much that I was going to work for a Republican, though my parents wouldn't have voted for Spence Abraham if he'd lived next door and mowed their lawn every Saturday. Their worry was money. My dad wanted me to take a job where I could use my law degree. Most first-year lawyers made three or four times the salary I was going to get. They wanted me to stay and find "real work," and I almost did. My sister had just given birth to a son, Michael, whom my parents were raising. He was a sweet kid and I wanted to help out. But I had to do this. This was my dream. And as usual, my parents quickly got 100 percent on board.

I didn't have enough money to stay at hotels, so I was going to have to stay temporarily with my friend Kim Love in her small studio apartment. Kim was from Flint too. She was a die-hard Democrat. I was a die-hard Republican. But we were both Star Trek fans, and something like that binds two people together for life.

So with my parents' blessing and some money to tide me over, I packed up my old Dodge Dynasty and said goodbye. I was finally off to Washington, D.C. As I drove into the big city, passing under bridges and green road signs, I felt like Matthew Tyler Moore.

CHAPTER TWO

"ONE CATASTROPHIC GAFFE A WEEK"

Like most Americans, I only knew about Congress from what I'd read in my civics textbooks. I'd always thought there was something magical about the place and that it took a certain special type of person to hold elected office. It never occurred to me until I arrived there that the people in charge of trillions of our tax dollars and with nearly unchecked power were just like everyone else. Congress was not some flawless institution engineered to perfection by America's Founders. It was only as effective as those who ran it.

Senator Spence Abraham was my first introduction to the workings of the legislative branch. I was in his office for about six months. He was a bright man, the son of immigrants. He also was mysteriously elusive. I don't think I even met him until days after I'd started, and then only briefly. Our office would have staff meetings that nearly everyone attended—except him. Senator Abraham had two assistants posted just outside his office door, apparently to prevent any "incidents" from taking place, such as the senator accidentally bumping into someone who worked for him. While I was there we moved to another office suite within the same building. The new suite seemed smaller, but I think the allure was that it gave the senator a personal office that was literally separated from the rest of the staff by a wall. Abraham once came to an office birthday party. It was as if Buzz Killington had just showed up. He talked almost the entire time to his two pincer guards and stayed just long enough not to come across as rude (he didn't quite make it). I hadn't known what working for a United States senator would be like.

I'm sure he was very busy. Maybe he was shy (I could sympathize with that). Still, I *had* expected that I'd, you know, get to converse with him.

I assumed that his constituents felt they would get the same opportunity. Boy, were they in for a surprise. When folks from Michigan came to the office to see him, they'd often end up being directed to people like me. I was one of a handful of special assistants, each of us in our early twenties and recently out of school. I was asked to take notes at the meetings and make apologies for the senator. He was just too busy to come. There was one occasion when he did show up at the last minute. "I know Matt's been doing a good job explaining things to you," he said. *He did? Was he talking about me?*

As special assistants, we also answered most of the letters people sent in. Sometimes they included moving stories, with a plea to the senator for help. I don't know if he read a single letter. Nearly all of the responses were drafted by one of us, the more generic the better. It was an assembly-line operation. We'd write as many form-letter responses as we could, and our letters' responses would be ultimately approved by the senator's chief of staff. The chief was not the warm and fuzzy type. On my first day he took me to lunch at an Indian restaurant. "You strike me as a fellow who likes hot sauce," he said. Before I could say a word, he poured it all over my food and watched me try to eat it. He also liked to criticize our ties, jackets, coats, hairstyles, whatever. So if Mabel Smith of Petoskey, Michigan, looked to Spence Abraham to help with the high price of prescription drugs, her plea was in the chief of staff's kind and gentle hands.

For some time, moving around our office suite, I walked past a narrow door that I'd never opened. I assumed it was a supply closet. One day I decided to look inside and found a strange-looking machine—a long metallic arm attached to a table. Blue pens were scattered around it.

"What's that thing in the closet?" I asked our receptionist.

"Oh, that's the autopen," she replied.

"The autopen?"

"Yes. That's how we sign letters." Every senator had one. No one could possibly sign every single letter he or she received, I was told. (I didn't believe her. I was sure John McCain and Kay Bailey Hutchison would never use an autopen.)

She showed me how the machine worked. I sat on a stool and put a blue felt-tip pen into the small hole on the mechanical arm. Then I pressed my foot down on a pedal on the floor. As I did this, I watched the metal arm slowly scrawl "Spencer Abraham" on a piece of paper. It looked like he had signed it. As the receptionist showed this to me, I felt like I was ten years old and sitting under a blanket with a flashlight looking at Playboy. It seemed illicit.

One day it was decided that we letter writers should start using the autopen. So on dozens of occasions, I pressed that pedal and watched the mechanical senator write "Spencer Abraham" onto a page, every blue-inked scribble sucking away a little more of my integrity. Sometimes we were even asked to give the signature a more personal touch. That was essentially the same process, except as the arm started to sign "Spencer" we pulled the letter or photo away as quickly as possible after the second e. That way the photos looked like they had been signed "Spence." This, in effect, was adding one fraud on top of another.

Actually, it started to occur to me that my entire job in the Senate was to abet a series of deliberate frauds. We were reading letters the senator never read, writing responses he apparently didn't review, and now even signing his name. Abraham didn't even have to buy postage stamps. His signature was all that was required on the top of the envelope. And that signature was printed by some machine too.

Worse than that, most of the senator's senior staff weren't from Michigan and they seemed to have only a vague idea about the state. (The one shaped like a mitten, right?) Early on, I sat in a meeting where people joked about signing on to some bill about the Great Lakes because it would make the hometown yokels happy. I was one of those "yokels" and I wasn't happy at all. The atmosphere of the entire office—cold, lifeless, mechanical—was what I thought it must be like to work on the board of directors of an insurance company.

There was, however, one member of Senator Abraham's senior staff I did like. She was an outspoken blonde, tall and willowy. A lawyer by training, she'd stand up against other people on the staff when she thought they were wrong. They didn't seem to like her much, which made her look even better to me. She was idiosyncratic. She rarely came into the office before ten unless there was a state of emergency. But she worked hard on the graveyard shift. She left messages on other staffers' voice mails at all hours of the night while she chain-smoked cigarettes.

Since she was a serious smoker and something of an outcast, the powers that be put her in a small office carrel at the end of the senator's suite. I'd go back there to talk to her sometimes and watch as she leaned back in a chair, chatting away on the phone. Occasionally she'd take a long puff from a cigarette, and I'd watch the smoke slowly cascade to the ceiling. I guess you could say I was a major, and early, fan of Ann Coulter.

The Ann I knew was a far more complex person than her caricature. She certainly could be intense. But she was a good judge of people. And she didn't like it when others were treated badly. Of course, from what I knew of Ann, the last thing she'd want people to think of her as was nice. Ugh! But she was—and now I've probably ruined her career.

Much to my surprise, I hated my first job on Capitol Hill. But I figured my experience had to be an exception, so I tried to stay with Spence Abraham just long enough not to look rude (I'm not sure I made it).

When I finally found a new job on the Hill, Spence's scheduler arranged for me to have a goodbye photo taken with the boss I hardly knew. I went to meet him just outside the Senate chamber, since it was more likely we'd run into him there than in our own office. After some delay, Spence came out with one of his aides. He looked thoroughly unhappy to have to do this.

"Thanks for all your work," he said insincerely, shaking my hand. Our picture was taken by a Senate photographer, who'd been waiting as long as I had. Small talk lasted about fifteen seconds, then the senator looked at his aide. "I've got to run to my next meeting, is that right?" The aide nodded. And he was gone. A few weeks later, I got my signed photo, a token for my service in the office. I knew from a glance that it was autopenned, and I didn't even get a "Spence."

Clearly, I was not dazzled by Spence Abraham. Though he was a smart and capable man, he wasn't remotely cut out for elective office. My tenure with him was a lesson that politics was often a lot harder than it looked.

But if I thought working for Spence was an education, that was nothing compared to what I learned from my next boss. Congressman

Nick Smith represented the farms and small towns of south-central Michigan, just north of the Ohio and Indiana borders. Nick's congressional office was a three-room suite in the Cannon House Office Building, on the same floor as the office John F. Kennedy had had when he was a representative from Massachusetts.

I'd never interviewed for a job with a member of Congress before, and Nick's chief of staff warned me to expect anything. Like most senior staff members on the Hill, Kurt Schmautz was in his early thirties. He was a graduate of the University of Michigan Law School and one of the brightest people I'd ever met. Kurt clearly admired Nick. He also told me the congressman liked to ask candidates trick questions, such as "What's the gestation period of a cow?" I hadn't the slightest clue what that even meant. (It referred to the length of a cow's pregnancy. The answer was nine months.)

What defined Nick Smith's political philosophy and the primary reason he was a conservative was his belief in being, well, cheap. So Kurt told me it was okay for me to push back on the first salary offer Nick made. The congressman enjoyed haggling, as long as it looked like he was winning. Kurt advised that even if I ended up having to take a lower offer than I expected, Nick was quick with raises if he liked you. "There's just one more thing," Kurt told me before we went to see Nick. "Be sure to put whatever you and Nick agree to in writing."

When Kurt and I entered his office, Nick sat behind a large oak desk, signing some paperwork. He was in shirtsleeves and looked deep in thought. He was impressive, fitting my image of how a congressman should appear.

We took a seat at a conference table and waited for the congressman to finish. The office was decorated with pictures of Nick with various people, including President Clinton. There were awards all around—the Taxpayer's Hero Award, the Spirit of Enterprise Award, the Guardian of Small Business Award, the Guardian of Seniors' Rights Award. It was an impressive display. (At that point, I had no clue that these same awards were given out to most Republicans in Congress every year.)

Nick rose from his desk and walked over to greet me. He was shaped a bit like a barrel, and was neither tall nor lean. His full head of hair was graying. Sometimes he wore glasses; like many things with

Nick, that seemed to depend on his mood. In all my years in Washington, I never saw a more photogenic legislator. No matter what the circumstance, he always looked tan and youthful with a broad smile.

"Nick Smith," he said, shaking my hand.

"Pleasure to meet you, Congressman," I replied.

He sat down across from me with my resume in his hand. He asked a few questions about it. He seemed friendly, businesslike. Reasonable. I didn't think he was the madcap eccentric that Kurt seemed to make him out to be.

"Tell me some of your extracurricular activities," Nick said. I started telling him about various things I'd done in college. He listened halfheartedly. Then he leaned forward.

"How about in high school?" he asked. I didn't know it at the time, but Nick's high school years included some of his proudest moments. He graduated near the top of his class (though I think the class was about fifteen people). I'd basically done zip in high school, except for Quiz Bowl. He seemed satisfied that my high school years didn't come close to competing with his.

I was interviewing to be Nick's press secretary, though I hadn't any experience working with the press. Nick didn't care. He may even have liked that fact, since it was a useful bargaining tool for what really interested him: the great duel over how much money I'd cost him.

Whenever the congressman had a difficult question to ask, he prefaced it with a long guttural sound. "Ahhhh, how much do you want me to pay you?" he asked.

It was intimidating, talking with a congressman about how much of the taxpayers' dollars I deserved.

I had no idea what to say. I'd been making something like $25,000 working for Senator Abraham, so I thought I should try for more. I suggested $35,000. Nick countered with $27,500. His eyes were lively now. The dance had begun.

I pointed out my graduate degree and my Senate experience. He rebounded, as I expected, with my lack of press experience. We went back and forth briefly. It was all good-natured. Ultimately, the congressman came up with a uniquely Nick idea. He'd pay me $27,500 for three months, and if I did a good job, I'd get $30,000 by the end of six months and then $35,000 by the end of my first year. Kurt gave me a look that said, *Take it, and we'll figure it out later.* So I did.

"Oh, just one more thing," I said, not knowing quite how to put it. "Uh, can I, uh, have this put in writing?"

At first, Nick looked as if I was saying I couldn't trust him. Then he smiled, perhaps realizing I was smart not to.

"No problem," he said. He took a piece of paper and wrote down the number we agreed to with an asterisk. Next to the asterisk he scribbled the other terms of the deal. He handed the paper back to me, and I put it in my pocket. I figured I might need it. I never did. Nick was true to his word.

I now had a job on Capitol Hill with an impressive title: congressional press secretary. Not knowing what else to do, I called up all the reporters who regularly covered Nick and introduced myself. Most reporters liked Nick. He was generous with his time. And he'd say a host of un-congressman-like things that made him clumsily charming and almost always good copy. Sometimes reporters would call our main office number and the congressman himself would answer the phone. This was unheard of, and they marveled at it: *Nick Smith answers his own phone!*

I saw him do this on many occasions. It happened most often when one of us brought up something he found boring. Once I was talking to him about some press issue when the main line rang. He shot me a disinterested glance and picked up the phone.

"Ahhhh, Congressman Nick Smith's office," he said, and listened to whoever was on the line. "Uh, okay," he finally said, "I'll pass the congressman your message." Then he hung up.

From the start, Nick and I got along famously. He seemed to think I was pretty smart. He liked to brag about my education.

Once he was talking to someone in his office and he called me in. "Ahhhh, Matt, where did you go to school again?" he asked.

I figured he meant undergrad, so I said, "Michigan."

"No," he said impatiently. "I meant that school named after a president."

I was quiet for a moment. "Do you mean Columbia?" I finally asked.

"Yeah, that's it," Nick said, satisfied. His visitor looked bewildered.

Even though the salary wasn't great, a congressional staffer enjoyed pretty nice perks. I got a choice of free Metro cards if I took the subway into work or a free parking space if I drove. I was told that I could check out books from the local library. For us, that was the Library of Congress, just down the road. We could order any book we wanted—they had them all—and a library staffer would deliver it straight to our office.

I started in Congress before devices such as the BlackBerry were in widespread use. Even cell phones were uncommon. So congressional offices found their own innovative ways to communicate. My friend Kim, for example, worked in the office of Congresswoman Debbie Stabenow, a tenacious and ambitious Democrat from central Michigan. Someone in Debbie's office came up with the idea of giving members of the staff walkie-talkies. Kim would have to carry one of these whenever she went down to the House floor. When the red-haired congresswoman headed out of the office to meet Kim, Kim would receive a message on the walkie-talkie: "Red Bird has left the nest." Kim was mortified. Her colleagues teased her with truck driver lingo. Some would call her on the phone and say "Breaker, breaker, one-nine" whenever she answered. (To Kim's delight, the walkie-talkie experiment proved short-lived.)

Sometimes Kim would stop by Nick's office to see how I was doing. She didn't care for Spence Abraham and had rarely visited me in the senator's office, but she considered Nick a lovable iconoclast. He was friendly to her whenever she came in to visit. Kim thought it was funny that Nick preferred to start all of his speeches with "Folks, . . ." For my birthday one year, Kim bought me a life-sized cardboard cutout of my favorite *Star Trek* character, Dr. Beverly Crusher. She took it into my office and put it right next to my desk. Nick came over to ask me a question and stopped dead in his tracks when he spotted this woman in a *Star Trek* uniform pointing a phaser at him. He was about to say something, but instead slowly backed off. That was too strange, even for him.

Once people knew I worked for Nick, they'd eagerly describe some encounter with him or some strange thing he'd done. Nick once told us he had a tailor in Ohio sew designer labels into his suits so that they'd look expensive. Most people saw through this ruse, however. After all, Armani suits weren't known for being powder blue. Nick prided himself on being the fastest envelope stuffer in Congress. He'd race members of the staff to see if anyone could beat him. Once Nick was driving through Michigan and got lost, so he called the office for help. "Where are you right now, Congressman?" someone asked. Nick replied, "I'm on a road with yellow lines in the middle." On another occasion, when something funny happened in the office, a staff member said, "I guess this is another example of Murphy's law." Nick replied, "Ahhhh, I never voted for that."

He was notorious for getting facts wrong. When Nick was about to lead an important group of constituents on a tour of the House, he asked our staff assistant, Dena, for some tips. Dena told Nick to be sure to point out the bullet holes in the House chamber that came about when Puerto Rican nationalists stormed into the Capitol and started shooting. Kurt, who knew more than he needed to know about everything, went into a long digression about how the nationalists had also tried to assassinate President Truman. Alas, Kurt had given Nick too much information. While on the tour, Nick pointed out the bullet holes as instructed. Then he added, "These came from some Puerto Ricans after Eisenhower was assassinated." Dena softly muttered a Homer Simpson–like "D'oh!" and tried to change the subject.

Just when you thought critics who called Nick a kook might have a point, he'd do something to impress you. Nick voted against nearly every congressional pay raise. Most years he returned to the Treasury some of the money allotted for his office expenses. Though he represented a largely farming community, he voted against farm subsidies on the principle that they weren't necessary and cost too much. He started a scholarship fund for kids in his dad's name. And before he went down to cast a vote in Congress, he always looked at a picture of his grandchildren on his desk to remember whom he was voting for. There was no autopen in Nick Smith's office.

Nick also kept his promise not to accept any contributions from political action committees. He said he didn't want to be influenced by special interests. The decision cost him hundreds of thousands of dollars, maybe even millions, in campaign contributions. The congressman once met with a group from the banking industry who were determined to get Nick's support for an important bill coming before Congress. They told Nick that if he failed to support what they wanted, it could affect their contributions to his next election run. "Ahhhh, when you put it like that," Nick said, "it makes me want to say, 'Fuck you.' "

When I joined Team Smith, about six of us worked together in two modest-sized rooms. Nick would come up and talk to any of us at any time about anything. We were also welcome to come into Nick's office anytime we wanted. Most were reluctant to exercise that privilege because we had no idea what new scheme we might be pulled into.

As Nick's press secretary, I was mostly supposed to be involved with press issues. But Nick wouldn't hesitate to ask me for help on Social Security or answering a constituent call or fixing some problem in the district. He was like that with everybody.

As Nick's chief of staff, Kurt was in many ways an ideal boss. He didn't yell. He didn't make unreasonable demands. He had a thorough understanding of issues. He also had an engagingly dark sense of humor. He kept a sign on his desk that said, THE BEATINGS WILL CONTINUE UNTIL MORALE IMPROVES. Most important, he had a knack for soothing Nick and tamping down his, well, enthusiasms. The operative rule in the office was that we should never do anything Nick wanted until he asked for it three times. We figured that if Nick actually remembered something that many times, he must be really serious about it.

Kurt and I were once invited out to the district office in Jackson, Michigan, during one of those periodic times when half the district staff was threatening to quit for being underpaid and unappreciated. Instead of offering raises or addressing the issue head-on, Nick had persuaded some management consultant from Michigan State University to give us a training session. The consultant orchestrated weird team morale exercises, like having us figure out how to cross an imaginary river MacGyver-style, using a chair, a piece of string, and a two-by-four. Then we were told to pick a name of an animal out of a hat. The consultant informed us that someone else on the staff had picked the same animal. We had to blindfold ourselves and walk around the room making our animal's sound until we found our "match." I picked a cat. My first thought was, *There is no way I am doing this.* My second thought was, *Please, don't let Nick be a cat.*

It turned out that Nick was a rooster. I knew this because Nick, a three-term United States congressman, was walking proudly around the room cock-a-doodle-dooing at the top of his considerable lungs. I refused to say anything. I shuffled around in silence, hoping no one was videotaping this. Finally I heard someone walk by me with a very familiar voice. He mumbled, "Um, I guess, meow." Immediately I yanked off my blindfold. "Kurt!" I exulted. "Thank God it's you! We're cats! We're cats!" Kurt pulled off his blindfold and laughed. We were done with this stupid exercise. (Shortly after team morale day, one person on our staff quit, followed by another a few weeks later.)

Besides Kurt and me, our cast of eccentrics in Washington included Dena Plummer. Dena was, in her own words, "the world's worst staff assistant." When she was hired, she thought she was going to help with legislation. She didn't know until her first day on the job that she was going to work at the front desk and deal with all the people who called in. Dena hated answering the phone. Most normal people in America never called their U.S. congressman, probably because they knew they'd rarely get useful assistance. That left people who either had a lot of time on their hands, were nuts, or both. One guy called every day just to talk about the weather. Another person called up because he'd taken out student loans and spent the money on drugs. He was furious that the government was now making him pay the loans back with interest. His argument was that it was the government's fault for being stupid enough to lend him the money in the first place. "I can't argue with you there," Dena responded. Dena repeatedly asked Nick to promote her. Considering the untold number of callers she hung up on, it would have been in everyone's best interest. But Nick was reluctant. At first, he offered to promote her on one condition: she had to take a pay cut. (Dena eventually became a highly successful lobbyist.)

Not everyone in the office was as indulgent of Nick's antics. Foremost among that group was Nick's legislative director, Alec Rogers. Alec shared Nick's midwestern upbringing and had attended the same alma mater, Michigan State. But that was about all they had in common. Privately, Alec was smart and witty and became one of my best friends. But by his own admission, he could be stiff and formal in business settings. He had the demeanor of an English gentleman. He wore tweed jackets and ordered shirts from a London tailor (Brooks Brothers having become too trendy).

Every morning Alec came in determined to make Nick Smith's office run like a high-class law firm. Alec's ideal congressional office was a place where lower-level staff treated senior staff deferentially and everyone had clear, assigned duties. He envisioned an environment where sober professionals helped the boss enact a disciplined, logical, well-thought-out legislative strategy. The poor guy.

To put it mildly, Nick was not an Alec Rogers kind of congressman. Alec wanted Nick to be a cross between Clarence Darrow and Sir John Gielgud. Instead he got something closer to Bozo meets Matlock—a combination I, for one, found a lot more enjoyable.

Nick came into the office one day furious with Alec that not enough of his bills were becoming law. So Nick had an unusual solution: he ordered random people in the office to come up with legislation by the end of the day or else they were fired. As Dena put it, "This plan has success written all over it."

One staffer showed up at Alec's desk in a panic. He had no idea how to write legislation. "Tell Nick to come to me," Alec said. "I have a bill for him."

Nick went over to Alec's desk. "Ahhhh, I hear you have a bill for me."

"I sure do, Congressman," Alec said. "I was thinking that if members paid the printing costs for their own bills, they'd think twice before introducing a lot of frivolous legislation." Nick was quiet for a moment as he considered this.

"Ahhhh, good idea," Nick finally replied. "But I introduce a lot of bills myself. Hey, how's our new copier working out?" Alec smiled. Crisis averted.

It didn't help matters much for Alec that Nick's relations with other members of Congress were pretty poor. That was partly because Nick didn't practice all the niceties of kissing up and making deals, which were essential to getting ahead in Congress, the world's largest frat house. He'd ask questions out of turn at committee hearings, or he'd ask things that were off point and embarrassed the committee chairman. Nick also wasn't enthusiastic about raising money for other members of Congress running for reelection, which was the real way to make friends and advance in the House. He was a member of the Agriculture Committee, but its chairman at the time hated Nick so much that when it was Nick's turn to chair a subcommittee, the chairman eliminated the committee altogether to keep Nick from having the post. For Nick this was really embarrassing, but at the time I tried to put the best spin on it. "Look at it this way," I said. "Nick can actually claim that he single-handedly reduced the size of government."

Nick also wasn't always good with names. Once I was with him in his office when he got a call from a fellow member of Congress seeking his vote for an upcoming leadership election. Nick put her on speakerphone so we could listen in.

"Hi, Nick," she said. "As you know, I'm running for a leadership post."

"Uh-huh," Nick replied.

"Well, I could really use your vote. You know, we came to Congress together."

"Uh-huh."

"I think we share the same philosophy."

"Uh-huh."

"And I think we've really worked well together," she continued.

"Uh-huh," Nick said again.

She finished by saying, "So, Nick, I sure would appreciate your vote."

Nick was silent. So she asked: "Do you have any questions that I can help answer?"

Nick thought about it. "Ahhhh, yes," he replied. "Were you the woman in the brown jacket that I saw today?" I covered my mouth to keep from laughing. Nick had no clue who she was. The congresswoman paused slightly. "Oh, yes, I was," she replied.

Nick said he'd think it over, then hung up. Even he was pretty embarrassed about not knowing who she was. For a while after that, he suggested that Kurt, Alec, or I follow him around at all times when he was at work, so we could whisper the names of people in his ear before they came up to him. It was a *Devil Wears Prada*–type moment. (Except Nick didn't wear Prada—at least not the real kind.) Needless to say, all these things didn't make Alec's job as legislative director any easier.

It was usually Alec who received phone calls from other offices angrily complaining about the latest thing Nick had done—and holding Alec responsible. I occasionally walked by Alec's desk after he'd gotten off the phone with some angry staffer. "Get me out of here," he'd say, with a desperate look in his eye. Sometimes I was nervous that his desk was so close to the window.

In light of all he went through, Alec felt perennially unappreciated by Nick. And with good reason: Nick didn't appreciate him. Sometimes Nick would introduce Alec (note the c) as "Alex" (note the x). One thing that seemed to weigh on Alec was that every year Nick would give him a Christmas gift—a congressional Christmas tree ornament. It might have been a thoughtful gesture for the notoriously frugal Nick. The only complication was that Alec was Jewish. Nick didn't seem to be aware of this rather key detail about his own legislative director.

One year, Kurt decided to try to rectify this.

"Congressman, you keep giving Alec a Christmas ornament every year," Kurt said.

"Ahhhh, that's right," Nick said.

"Well, it's a nice thought, but the thing is . . . Alec is Jewish."

"Oh," Nick replied. He was pensive for a moment. Then he walked over to Alec's desk, where he'd placed the wrapped ornament. He picked it up, took his pen, and scribbled something on it. Then he placed it back down on Alec's desk. On the card, Nick had crossed out the words "Merry Christmas" and written "Happy Holidays."

After working for Nick for several years more, and repeatedly cursing the gods for his fate, Alec finally found another job. He vowed that he would never again speak of his years with Nick. On his resume he said he would list those years as a stint working for the Bubba Gump Shrimp Company.

During my time with Nick I first became introduced to a Capitol Hill phenomenon: the superstaffer. Secretly, all members of Congress believe their mediocre staffs hold them back. They could be introducing major bills every week and serving in the top rungs of leadership if only they had that special person on their team who knew how to get there. That was what made the superstaffer's siren song irresistible. They always came into an office with an impressive-looking resume and a surplus of smooth talk.

Naturally, superstaffers were too good to be true. They conjured up an image of the snake oil salesmen of yesteryear who rolled into town with a slew of elixirs to cure wrinkles or reverse baldness. One of the most popular superstaffers was pollster Frank Luntz. Even Newt

Gingrich swore by Frank. The Speaker brought him to speak to Republican conference meetings and congressional retreats where Frank would pass out this book filled with a whole bunch of buzzwords and gimmicks that congressional press secretaries were supposed to scrupulously follow to manipulate voters. Don't say "fix" Social Security; say "strengthen and improve" it. Don't call it "tax cuts"; use "tax relief." There was nothing voters loved more than hearing their elected officials spout canned rhetoric from some PR expert in Washington. Frank probably made millions off stuff like that. (Later we learned that our Republican message guru had tried to defect to the Clinton administration.)

Nick had his own version of the superstaffer: Harrison Fox, Ph.D. Harrison worked for all sorts of well-known people. He'd written a book, which was out of print, and was the head of some organization he'd created whose goal was to build a sound economy. Harrison also wielded "Liberty's Toolbox." This was a persuasion prop full of things like a mock airline ticket that might be "Your Ticket to the American Dream." I think there was also a key that opened the door to the "House of Your Dreams." At first, I thought these items were clever. Then I wondered, what exactly did they do? (I wasn't supposed to ask that.)

Harrison was a man of great enthusiasm, which made him fun to be around. He had grandiose notions. He once said something like "Nick Smith is Speaker of the House in 2010. Now let's work backward." Dena and I said to each other, "Well, first there's a massive chemical and biological attack that has killed every other member of Congress and most of their staffs . . ."

Harrison was believed to be the highest-paid member of our staff, and he focused exclusively on one issue: Nick's Social Security reform bill. (Nick was one of the first people to advance the concept of partial privatization, a pretty gutsy move at the time.) On my first day, Harrison told me a major Democrat was going to cosponsor our bill any day now. When I happened to mention that I went to law school with Harold Ford Jr., a Tennessee Democrat, Harrison asked if I'd call him and ask him to sign on. (That's when I started to figure out we were in trouble.) Eventually Nick grew frustrated with Harrison's lofty promises and no results. To be fair, Harrison's job wasn't exactly easy—bipartisan agreement on meaningful Social Security reform still hasn't happened. But our superstaffer picked up on Nick's growing discontent. One day he suddenly announced that he'd found another great opportunity. Then he packed up his potions and elixirs and was gone.

About a year or so after I started working for Nick, he asked me to go home to Michigan to run what was turning out to be a tough reelection campaign. Most Americans are under the impression that they actually have a choice when they vote for congressional candidates, but they usually don't. Most congressional districts have been set up so that one party almost always wins it. It takes a certain type of politician to turn one of those safe seats into a nail-biter. Nick Smith was such a politician. Nick had gotten into the habit of spending almost no money on his reelection campaigns, despite the advice of political consultants. (Nick thought they were just trying to take his money.) As a result, his name identification in the district declined and his margins of victory narrowed. That made him vulnerable to a well-funded Democrat.

I was in my twenties and had no campaign experience. But I'd had no press experience either, and that had worked out pretty well. So I figured, why not give it a try? As Nick's campaign manager, I'd be paid entirely by the Nick Smith for Congress campaign, which was, in fact, funded with Nick's own money—money he'd raised or donated to the campaign. This obviously was a recipe for trouble.

Nick didn't want to pay for me to rent a car while I worked on the campaign. So he lent me his four-door Dodge Neon. The car had more than a hundred thousand miles on it. It shook on the highway when you went past 60 miles per hour, and it was the color of a tongue. Actually, this was better than what Nick had offered his previous campaign manager—use of his old truck, which, literally, had a dead cow in the back.

Nick lent me a cell phone that came in a large box. When I say box, I don't mean you opened a box and took the cell phone out. I mean, the phone itself resembled a box. It looked like one of those phones that soldiers used in World War II. The only way it worked was to take an antenna, which came with a rubber attachment, and hang it out of the window. Most of my driving was across barren farmland with few cell towers. If I was lucky, I could have an entire conversation without being cut off.

Also to save money, Nick suggested that I stay at a motel in Jackson, Michigan. It basically seemed to serve as a halfway house for convicts recently released from the state prison. We weren't allowed visitors after certain hours, and there were no phones in the rooms—just a pay phone down the hall. I shared a bathroom on the floor with large, older men. At all hours of the night, I'd hear a creak outside my door and see the shadow of someone standing outside it. Then slowly the person would walk away. A friend who visited me there said, "So this is what skid row looks like."

On my first day of the campaign, I looked for our volunteer list. We didn't have one. I looked for our old campaign office. It didn't exist. County Republican chairs? Most hadn't seen a good political fight since Nixon ran for president. Press spokesmen? None. Full-time campaign staff? Two girls recently out of college. Support from other state Republicans? Lukewarm at best. The campaign treasury? That was the best news. It was in decent shape, since Nick never spent any money. But we'd need several hundred thousand dollars more, and fast.

Nick's campaign advisor, a real pro named Cliff Pintak, had worked for Nick on his very first campaign for Congress. From day one Cliff and I understood each other perfectly. Half facetiously, Cliff jokingly told me my job as campaign manager was simple: to limit Nick to "one catastrophic gaffe a week."

After six years in office, Nick had become involved in all sorts of mini-controversies that alienated what should have been his natural support base in the district. He antagonized Michigan Right to Life by suggesting that all the fighting over abortion would end just as soon as Congress approved RU-486. Nick was also taking heat for appearing to backtrack on his term limits pledge. When he first ran for Congress, Nick apparently had insisted he'd only serve for three terms, or six years. He now was seeking his fourth term, extending his reign to eight years. Even Nick couldn't deny that eight was bigger than six.

When Nick first realized he might want to stay in Congress longer than six years, he did his best to muck up the issue. He went around telling people that he endorsed a six-term limit in Congress, or twelve years. Eventually he amassed a pile of news clips saying he endorsed six terms, while reporters dangled their own clips saying he'd limit himself to six years. One reporter at the Jackson paper kept telling me he specifically remembered Nick pledging six years, not six terms. Why, he asked, wouldn't Nick just admit he'd changed his position?

Nick was vexed that the question wouldn't go away, but one day, when we were driving in the car, he had an epiphany. He decided that he'd start interchanging the words *years* and *terms* in conversation. He'd say something like, "Such-and-such happened six terms, I mean, six years ago." That way people would think that maybe he confused those words all the time. I knew right then that this campaign wasn't going to be easy.

There was still another controversy brewing, this one odder than any other. I was still in the Washington office when Dena received a copy of a flyer from a union in the district. The union claimed that Nick was so extreme, he'd even supported killing his mother. This was one of the ugliest charges I could imagine. I took the flyer directly into Nick's office.

"Congressman, you will not believe this," I said excitedly. "This union claims you tried to kill your mother!"

Nick gave me a blank look.

"We need to hit back on this hard," I said, getting myself worked up. "There is no way they can defend themselves!"

As I spoke, Nick was curiously silent. Then he uttered words that I'll never forget: "Ahhhh, I can explain that." My heart sank. *Oh, no.*

Nick claimed his mother had needed an operation. The family had to decide whether to spend money for the operation or use it to pay expenses on the farm and buy land. They voted, and the farm won.

I couldn't believe what I was hearing. "Congressman, are you actually telling me you chose the farm over your mother's life?" I asked.

Nick shook his head. "It's not as bad as it sounds," he said. "She got a vote too."

On another occasion during the campaign, I suffered an embarrassment of my own. Probably unwisely, I became involved with a young woman who worked for the campaign. As a matter of fact, I fell in love with her.

One night, she and I were watching TV at my motel/halfway house. It got to be very late, and we fell asleep. Then she woke up and finally went home. (She lived with her parents, about an hour away.) That night, the pay phone in the hallway was ringing and ringing, but no one picked it up. (There was no way I would ever leave my room in the middle of the night.) Finally, the ringing stopped, and I thought nothing more of it.

The next morning, I went to a breakfast with leaders from the county party. I was supposed to speak on Nick's behalf—but unexpectedly, Nick showed up. He was friendly, but he kept giving me strange looks.

When the breakfast was over, Nick walked up to me and ushered me into a small room. Then he closed the door.

Nick was usually a loud talker, and this was the first time I'd heard him lower his voice. "Ahhhh, this is sort of awkward," he said. "But, ahhhh, Nicole's mother called me at two A.M. and woke me and Bonnie up."

Nicole's mother. We fell asleep. The pay phone in the hall. Uh-oh.

"Anyway, she thought something had happened to her," Nick said. "And we tried to get hold of you. She even wanted to call the police."

I knew what was going to happen. Nick was going to fire me. This was going to be a scandal. How mortifying.

"Congressman, I-I'm so sorry," I stammered. "It was perfectly innocent and—"

Nick interrupted. His tone was soothing, almost fatherly. "If you're going to fool around with someone you work with," he said in a stage whisper, "be really careful that she doesn't turn on you. You don't need it." It may have sounded like I was listening to G. Gordon Liddy, but I got the impression that Nick had covered for me. In his own way, he was trying to help.

Nick's opponent in the campaign, Jim Berryman, was the son of an autoworker from Flint. Berryman had moved to the small college town of Adrian and become a well-regarded state senator. He was one of those guys who could dazzle people with a few buzzwords and syrupy compliments. Adorned in a double-breasted suit and sporting a pinky ring, he looked like an extra from the cast of The Sopranos.

Apparently quite taken with himself, Senator Berryman came up with the idea of painting a giant cartoon picture of his head, complete with cheesy mustache, onto the side of an RV and driving said monstrosity all over the district. It was a curious campaign expenditure. I kept imagining voters coming home and saying things like, Sorry I'm late, honey, but Jim Berryman's huge head slowed down all traffic on Route 127.

Berryman was working the district harder than any Democrat had in a long time. He was getting union endorsements and the Democratic Party was pledging a lot of money. Nick's seat was said to be targeted for defeat that fall.

Since Nick was going to have a credible opponent, we knew he'd have to hold one-on-one debates. The press would insist on it. Nick hadn't been in a real debate in some time, and it was anybody's guess how he'd do. Myself, I thought after it was over, we'd see his picture next to depictions of the sinking of the *Titanic*, the Bob Dole campaign, and other great disasters in history.

I helped Nick prepare for debates by standing in for his opponent in rehearsals and videotaping his performance. At first, Nick and our campaign consultant were uncertain that I was the right person to debate. They didn't think I'd be tough enough on Nick. I promised that I would. I really thought it would be fun.

Before our first practice session our consultant came up to me. "Savor this," he whispered. "Not many people get a chance to go after their boss and get paid for it."

Nick and I conducted three mock debates, the full ninety minutes each time. I went after Nick on every issue I could think of, portraying him as an aloof and heartless conservative. I had an advantage that Nick didn't have: I knew his voting record better than he did. Before the debate, I looked for every possible obscure vote I could find to rattle him. And I discovered a perfect one: he'd apparently voted in favor of an obscure provision that cut off money for air conditioners for welfare recipients.

"Nick Smith is so heartless, so out of touch, that he'd put lives at risk by cutting off air-conditioning for families with children," I charged.

Nick had absolutely no idea what I was talking about. He looked like I'd struck him. At first he ignored the charge. Then after I repeated it two or three times in the debate, he finally took the bait.

"Ahhhh, I have no idea what vote you're talking about!" he snapped.

At another point, I read a fake letter from one of his constituents saying that she'd tried repeatedly to get hold of Nick and he never answered her calls or letters. She'd wanted to talk with him about a matter of life and death, and Nick had ignored her. There was always some constituent who was complaining about something like that, whether true or not.

Nick was proud of his constituent service. He held office hours regularly across his sprawling district and signed and approved the letters that the office sent to constituents. I figured he wouldn't like the charge that he was blowing constituents off. He didn't.

"You're picking out someone I never heard of!" he raged. "I have no way of knowing what this is about or if this is even real!"

After our second debate, Nick wouldn't look at me. "Matt, I don't really like you right now," he said.

For the third debate, our advisor instructed me to tone down my attacks. "Go easy on him this time," Cliff said. "I had you go after him hard to teach him a lesson. Now we have to build him back up." Nick did better in the third debate, but he still wasn't great. After it was over, in true Nixonian style, the congressman ordered Kurt to destroy all copies of the tapes.

Nick debated Berryman—twice. The first debate took place in the shadow of a tragedy in Washington. Two police officers in the Capitol building had been killed by intruders. The story was national news, and for a moment we considered canceling the debate. But Nick wanted to go ahead.

While we were getting ready, I casually suggested to Nick that he might want to start the debate with a prayer for the two officers.

"Why would I do that?" Nick asked. "I didn't know them."

No, I said, but they were heroes and—

"They weren't heroes," Nick interrupted, in obstinate mode. "They weren't killed in combat like a member of the military." I pointed out that a police officer was by nature heroic. Nick grudgingly seemed to agree but wouldn't admit it. This was not an auspicious beginning.

When the debate started, Nick surprised all of us by talking about the officers and saying we should all pray for their families. I smiled with pride.

In fact, Nick was great throughout the debate. Berryman was more poised and articulate. He was a man who owned a pinky ring, after all. But Nick held to his message and kept focusing on what he believed in—lower taxes and smaller government. I thought he won.

When it was over, I was so excited I ran up to him and hugged him. He smiled sheepishly and then looked at our two female campaign aides. "I'd rather get a hug from them," he said.

Then he laughed. "You were way tougher on me than Jim Berryman was," he said.

From then on, things went pretty well for Nick and the campaign. He was well ahead in the polls. We were raising money. We even got Newt Gingrich to come down and hold a fund-raiser. The Speaker was not a big Nick Smith fan. Nick had once chewed him out over the phone when Newt's office called to instruct him how to vote on an upcoming bill. Newt was the whip at the time and the instructions were pro forma, but Nick didn't care. How dare anyone tell him how to vote! It was another episode of *Nick Smith: Winning Friends and Influencing People.* But the Speaker came out to help Nick anyway and smiled grimly as he stood next to Nick for photo after photo.

By the time of the second debate, Berryman was getting desperate to shake up the race. At the end of a rather dull candidate forum in Battle Creek, Berryman's staff passed around a sheet of paper to the audience and to the press. I struggled to see what the paper said.

Berryman announced that he was handing out a letter from a local dentist who claimed that Nick had promised he'd vote in favor of legislation the dentists wanted if they'd give him campaign contributions. Berryman was accusing Nick of bribery. The charge suddenly roused the snoozing reporters. They loved stuff like this. Watergate all over again!

I thank God every day that Nick had already given his closing statement. Thus, he had no opportunity to say a word in his defense and probably make matters worse.

Once the debate was over, I grabbed a copy of the letter and went up to Nick and his wife, Bonnie. Nick looked puzzled by the charge. But what I saw in his expression offered little comfort. His face wasn't saying, *How can someone say this about me?* It was more like, *I don't think I did that, did I?*

"We've got to get out of here, Congressman," I instructed. I felt that our staff needed to ascertain the facts before we said anything. I urged Nick to go home and not take any press calls. To my constant horror, some reporters knew that Nick was listed in the phone book, which meant the time bomb was always ticking.

As soon as I was out of there, I got on a real cell phone, not that crazy box of a cell phone Nick had given me, and contacted Cliff, our consultant, who was home in Virginia.

I described what had happened—the charge, the letter, the reporters, the questions, everything. Then I said, "The worst part about it is I have no idea if it's true!"

"Matt," Cliff said calmly, "remember, you're on a cell phone."

Oops. "Oh, ah, of course I don't believe a word of it," I said, with my usual smooth recovery. I told Cliff I'd look into the whole thing and call him back—from a landline.

The name of the dentist making the accusation was on the letter Berryman had sent around. But as I read the letter closely, I realized that it didn't actually accuse Nick of soliciting a bribe. It just said Nick had made these dentists feel uncomfortable. Heck, that was nothing. Nick made me feel uncomfortable all the time.

As it turned out, Berryman was even more clueless than we were. The dentist wasn't prepared for press calls and seemed unaware that Berryman was going to make the charge. That didn't stop the newspapers from blaring the next day: "Berryman Accuses Smith of Bribery." Nick was furious over the headlines, more so as soon as he reassured himself that he was innocent. We even considered suing the papers for libel. Eventually we just let the whole thing drop.

Instead we went after Berryman on our favorite issue: taxes. We stated running ad after ad highlighting legislation Berryman had introduced that proposed higher taxes on haircuts, on dry cleaning, on movie tickets, and a whole list of other things. Our tagline was: "Liberal Jim Berryman. He keeps taxing and taxing."

Now it was Berryman's turn to be infuriated. He was losing the election. He was being outspent. Most galling of all, Nick Smith of all people, whom all the pundits held in such low regard, was running circles around him. Even his crazy giant-head RV was not turning the tide.

On the eve of the election, I went in Nick's place to a legislative forum sponsored by the National Rifle Association in Berryman's hometown of Adrian. There was an empty chair reserved for Berryman, but no one expected him to come. What would have been the point? He'd already lost the NRA endorsement and the crowd wouldn't be welcoming.

I, however, had at least two friends in the audience. Kurt and Alec had taken vacation time to help with the final campaign swing. The most exciting thing we expected was to go out for nachos after the forum was over. In the middle of the forum, however, we received an unexpected show. The door to the room swung open and in walked Jim Berryman in full, cheesy getup. Defiantly, he took his seat on the podium.

I looked at Kurt, who looked at Alec, who looked at me. What on earth was this about?

After Berryman was welcomed by the surprised moderator, the state senator stood up to say a few words. He turned in my direction and glared. "I wanted to come here tonight because I've heard a lot of misrepresentations about my record," he fumed. "And they're coming from that man!" He turned one of his long, bony fingers toward me. The moderator looked at me. The other candidates looked at me. The audience looked at me.

Berryman insisted that I take back the charges being made against him on the radio concerning his tax record. "They're despicable!" he sputtered.

As it happened, I had a questionnaire in front of me that Berryman had submitted to some public interest group. It outlined in his own words his position on different issues, including taxes.

With the eyes of the room upon me, I took a deep breath. "Senator, I'm sorry you're so upset," I replied. "But I have your positions right here in front of me—which you submitted yourself." I started to read from the questionnaire.

Berryman tried to see what document I was referring to. His face turned red. "Don't listen to what I wrote!" he raged. "Listen to what I'm telling you now!"

Everyone's mouth hung open. What a mistake. "That's just what a politician would say," I replied calmly. "Don't pay any attention to the record."

When the forum was over, Berryman came up to me. I thought he might hit me. Instead, he patted me on the back. "Nice to see you, Matt," he said. "Good job."

I didn't know what to say. For me, it was personal. For Jim Berryman, fuming at me and calling me a liar was just part of the game.

I called up Cliff Pintak and told him what had happened. He was as baffled as I that Berryman would waste the last days of the campaign at an NRA forum defending his record.

"Those radio ads are driving him nuts," I observed.

"You know what that means?" Cliff asked.

I didn't.

"It means we double the ad order," Cliff said.

As Berryman seemed to grow more unhinged, so did my relationship with Nick. Nick didn't like being cooped up in Washington. He didn't like not knowing what was going on. And Nick was, after all, still Nick. He wanted to take ownership of the campaign.

For example, when he was in the district and I was driving him around, he'd insist that I stop at people's houses. Without asking the residents, he'd have me join him in putting Nick Smith signs on their front lawns. "Ahhhh, I know these people," he'd say. "I'm sure they'd want one." Often these weren't just little signs but big cardboard placards that had to be stabilized with heavy fence posts that we hammered deep into the grass. We did this sign planting all the time without permission. Every day I lived in fear that we were going to get arrested for trespassing.

On another occasion, Nick sent Kurt and me out to a local football game to distribute Nick Smith flyers. We certainly had more important things to do, but Nick wanted to feel in charge. So we did it. There was only one problem: Nick's tongue-colored Dodge Neon had recently been in an accident and the front bumper had fallen off. (Unfortunately for everyone, the driver had been Alec.) Nick's response to the accident was to fix the bumper to the front of the car with duct tape. I wasn't sure it was sturdy enough, but Nick was satisfied, and he was in charge. So Kurt and I were off.

Unfortunately, once we got the car past 55 miles per hour on the highway, it began its predictable shaking. Then I heard this thud, followed by a sound of clump-clump-clump.

I peered through the windshield to the car's front. "Oh my God!" I shrieked. "The bumper is coming off!"

Kurt leaned forward and eyed what was happening. "Yep," he observed. "It sure is." (Kurt was the most Zen-like person I knew.)

The sound kept getting louder. The bumper was going to fall off any minute. "I *knew* that duct tape wasn't going to work!" I yelled. Then I had a haunting thought: *Nick wasn't going to rest until he killed us all.*

I pulled the car to the side of the road. We ended up throwing the bumper in the backseat. The next time I saw Nick I told him what had happened.

"Huh. I guess the tape didn't hold," he replied.

I wanted to snap, *Do you think?* Instead I said, "Yes, that's right, Congressman. The tape failed to hold at sixty miles per hour."

Nick and I had one last falling-out on the campaign trail. It was about campaign yard signs again. Nick had just landed in Detroit and was driving back to his home south of Jackson when he called me up in a rage.

He was driving through Tecumseh, Michigan, a small town near Ann Arbor, and he suddenly noticed that he wasn't seeing any Nick Smith yard signs anywhere. "You must not be doing your job," he snapped.

I was livid. I was doing everything for the campaign—raising money, serving as Nick's spokesman, debating his opponent, fending off bribery charges, surviving at a halfway house. I'd had it.

"Do you know *why* there are no yard signs in Tecumseh?" I asked.

"Ah, no," he replied.

"It's because it is *illegal* to have political signs up in Tecumseh," I said triumphantly. At least, that's what someone on the campaign had told me. I hoped it was true.

Nick continued to fulminate, complaining about one thing after the other. I hung up on him. I hung up on a United States congressman.

"I quit!" I snapped at Kurt, and walked out of the office. Then I drove around Jackson for about an hour.

After I cooled off, I returned to the office. Nick was waiting for me. At first I expected him to yell at me, but I saw that he was holding my favorite kind of cookies—sugar with icing on them.

"Bonnie says I was too tough on you," he said. "I brought you these." I was so stressed out, so tired, so aggravated, and so surprisingly touched by Nick's gesture that I almost cried.

"I sure appreciate all you've done," Nick said sheepishly. "I hope we're still friends."

Yes, I said, we were still friends.

In the end, we won the election easily, 57 to 40 percent. Since Nick's birthday was around the same time, we brought out a cake for him. He may have been a winner that night, but Nick was still Nick. He plopped his thumb right into the middle of the cake and pulled out a chunk of it to eat. Message to everyone else: *Get your own cake.*

Despite it all, despite all the eccentricities and the mental roller-coaster ride that characterized daily life in his office, I really did like Nick. As infuriating as he was, he was authentic. He was a consistent conservative on most issues. He was a budget hawk who never strayed from his belief in lower federal spending. I would have gladly reelected him, which is something I can't say about most people in Washington, D.C.

After the election was over, I returned to Nick's office on Capitol Hill. But my stay was short. After everything I'd endured on the campaign, Nick was complaining about reimbursing me for some of my expenses. I realized he wasn't ever going to change. He was going to muddle on in Congress, not really making an impact, and getting us enmeshed in one scheme after another. Nick was often entertaining, but I just knew there had to be more to Washington than this.

CHAPTER THREE

THE PURSE BOYS

After a few years in the nation's capital, I took stock. I'd worked for a senator I hadn't much appreciated—one I wasn't even sure I'd vote to reelect. Then there was Nick, a man I personally liked but who wasn't going to set Washington on fire. (I could, however, see him setting his house on fire.) My excellent adventure in Washington was not turning out as I'd thought it would. I was no closer to my dream of working at the White House than I'd been when I arrived.

I decided to give the Senate one more try, but this time I was going to be a little more choosy. I sent my resume to the offices of only those senators I thought I'd really like to work for. Each was a solid conservative with a good reputation. But they were usually not the sort of Republicans most Americans had ever heard of.

The media tended to like two types of Republicans: right-wing eccentrics (think Pat Robertson) and principled mavericks (someone like Chuck Hagel, "principled" every time he disagreed with his party). These were the Republicans who got asked to be on all the Sunday shows so the media could look balanced. Neither type represented me. My friends and I laughed as we watched cable news anchors say things like "Now for the Republican view, here's Alan Keyes" or "Now telling us why he disagrees with his fellow Republicans, here's conservative Lindsey Graham." It was as bizarre as saying "And now representing the Democrats, here's Cher" or "For the Democratic view on the war in Iraq, here's mainstream Democrat Joe Lieberman."

After weeks of sending out resumes and receiving no replies, I finally was called in to interview with Arizona's junior senator, Jon Kyl. At the time I didn't know much about Kyl. The only Arizona Republican I'd ever heard of was John McCain. (Kyl got that a lot.)

Kyl's office was in the Hart Senate Office Building. Hart was generally considered the worst of the three Senate office complexes, so most of the junior senators were housed there. The inside was shaped like a hollowed-out Rubik's cube, with floor after floor arranged into squares with balconies that wrapped around a vast, sunlit atrium. The atrium had a strange, neomodern sculpture that was meant to represent birds and mountains. Hart was designed in the 1970s, so I guess we were lucky there weren't love beads and shag carpeting. There was one good thing about Hart, however. Down the hall from Kyl was the office of the junior senator from Michigan, Debbie Stabenow. Red Bird had defeated Spence Abraham in the 2000 election. One of her campaign ads focused on Spence's terrible support for constituents. It was the proverbial poetic justice. Debbie's election also meant that my friend Kim worked right down the hall. Awesome!

As for Spence, his demonstrated ability to lose a race he'd been leading by double digits apparently made him a shoo-in for a cabinet post in the George W. Bush administration. He was joined there by another former senator, John Ashcroft of Missouri, who may or may not have turned out to be a fine attorney general but who lost his senate re-election bid to a dead guy. That didn't bode well for my view of the acumen of the Bush White House, but Abraham and Ashcroft were examples of a familiar Washington phenomenon: recycled losers. I saw it many times. No matter how badly a person screwed up, sooner or later he'd turn up somewhere else, with everything forgiven and forgotten.

Senator Kyl had a lot more political savvy. And he was a true conservative in every way—in his positions, his demeanor, his hairstyle, his shoes, his dress. He chose his words sparingly and carefully. He voted against tax increases. And to make the case against wasteful spending, he joined with John McCain to vote against earmarks for his own state. This didn't win him a lot of points in the Arizona media. But he was respected by voters back home because he was principled and dignified. He explained his positions on issues without attacking those who disagreed with him. Senator Dianne Feinstein, a liberal Democrat, worked with Kyl frequently and was one of his closest colleagues on the Hill.

She said she'd find it hard, if not impossible, to campaign against him, which was a rare thing for a liberal to say about a conservative.

I'd interviewed for a job with the title of speechwriter. But Senator Kyl also figured that since I had experience as a press secretary, I could work with the print reporters who covered him. So by the fall of that year, I was serving as Kyl's communications director.

Kyl wasn't particularly interested in the media, which didn't make my job very easy. The most dreaded words anyone in my position can hear from their boss are "I don't care if I get any press." Of course, few senators ever said that. Kyl was different, though. After a leadership meeting in the Capitol, most senators would walk right toward the waiting bank of microphones. Kyl would go the other way; he had another meeting to attend. Many Senate offices had four or five people devoted to getting their boss attention in the press. Senator Kyl had just two—me and his press secretary, Andrew Wilder.

Andrew used to work in radio back in Arizona and had the perfect radio announcer voice. We shared a tiny cubicle—dubbed "the press shop"—not far from Kyl's own office. We were about the same age and had the same sense of humor. We loved to talk about old TV shows or washed-up celebrities. We'd go to bad movies just so we could laugh at them. We were probably the only two people in the world who celebrated Jamie Farr from M*A*S*H and could write a new TV pilot for him in our spare time.

Every day, Andrew and I struggled to get the media's attention. Senator Kyl didn't have time for long palling-around sessions with reporters. He was a speed walker who resembled a grayish blur as he zoomed past reporters hanging around the Capitol. When he was cornered by reporters he gave careful, precise answers, like the lawyer he was. He didn't care for sound bites, which he found phony. So guess how much reporters like to quote Jon Kyl? At Senate press conferences, most senators would crane their necks to get the best position in front of the cameras as their savvy press aides cheered them on. Senator Kyl stood in the back. Sometimes he'd let other senators push ahead of him. They'd move past him as if he were some sort of country rube. Other press secretaries would watch this. Then they'd look sadly at Andrew and me as if we were the uncoordinated kids in gym class.

Kyl's exact opposite was Democrat Chuck Schumer. Schumer

loved media attention so much that I was half convinced he slept every night in a suit and tie and full TV makeup. My favorite Schumer fact was that the senator decided his positions on issues by discussing them with people he invented in his head. For this purpose, he conjured the Baileys, a typical family in New York who shared with Schumer all their concerns about real-life America—except they weren't real, weren't alive, and therefore weren't Americans. "Though they're imaginary," Schumer once said, "I frequently talk to them." I didn't know which was the bigger problem for Schumer—that he carried on conversations with fictional people or that he was unable to find flesh-and-blood voters who benefited from his positions. Yet no one on Capitol Hill was the slightest bit troubled by the senator's imaginary friends. The media loved Schumer. The Republicans shrugged, and the Democrats elected him to the Senate leadership.

I admired the fact that my boss wasn't one of the Schumers of the world. Unfortunately, because Kyl wasn't a media darling, few really knew what kind of person he was. So Andrew and I were determined to utilize any means possible to augment Kyl's presence, especially around his state. Andrew was in charge of the senator's monthly cable access show, *Report to Arizona*. We both knew that only a small number of people bothered to watch—how many people in Scottsdale wanted to hear Jon Kyl and Senator Lamar Alexander talk about Republican proposals on health care reform?—but it was better than doing nothing. The senator was enthusiastic about the shows. He thought that if people listened to his explanations of the issues, they'd at least respect his position, even if they didn't always agree with him.

For someone who was relatively reserved in private, Kyl was a natural as a talk show host. He made his guests feel at ease. He asked good questions and never stumbled or looked nervous. Most impressively, he could walk onto the set and start the show in one take. (Kyl didn't like to waste time.)

One guest the senator was eager to book was his colleague from North Carolina, Elizabeth Dole. (I would have preferred Kay Bailey Hutchison, naturally, but nobody asked me.) There were few interesting Republican personalities in the Senate—for example, nobody had heard of people like Mike Enzi or Chuck Grassley. Senator Dole, however, was a legitimate Republican celebrity. She was the wife of Bob

Dole and had run for president against George W. Bush, then bowed out graciously and campaigned for him across the country. As a senator, she had a reputation as being notoriously high-maintenance, but didn't they all? We thought she'd be a great guest.

One day, Andrew called a friend in Dole's office to see how he might approach inviting her on the show.

The Dole aide responded with a tone of despair. "*Please* don't ask us to do this," he said.

Andrew assured his friend that it was going to be an easy interview. Kyl would talk about whatever Dole wanted. He was not exactly Mike Wallace.

"But you don't understand," the Dole aide replied. "If she agreed to do the show, there would be no end to the work we'd have to do to get her ready. We'd have to prepare a briefing book on every possible question." I imagined Elizabeth practicing in her apartment at the Watergate Hotel, with her husband standing in for Kyl: *Bob Dole is glad to have you on Bob Dole's cable show.* Andrew was nice enough not to push for the Dole invitation, and we let it drop.

With the Elizabeth Dole experiment a bizarre failure, the cable show still lacked a certain pizzazz. Though I had a limited role in the whole process, I did sometimes sit in the control booth of the Senate TV studio with Andrew and pretend I was a co-producer. I sometimes joked with Andrew about ideas to spice things up. For example, Senator Kyl could have an Ed McMahon–like sidekick who said things like "Senator, you've done it again." I also suggested surprise guests who could come out in the middle of the program—Arlen Specter's high school girlfriend or Bill Frist's mother-in-law. Or maybe we could have a giant gong that we would ring when the guest became unbearably boring. (According to my own unscientific calculations, the record was about four minutes.) Those ideas never made it off the cutting-room floor. It was probably for the best.

The Senate could be intensely busy. But there were slow days too, especially during the frequent congressional recesses. Many Januarys, for example, senators would come in from their Christmas break to gavel the Senate back into session. Then after a grueling two- or three-day workweek, they'd be off on a retreat. So there were many days when those stuck in the office would have a much lighter workload. With Andrew and me, that always meant trouble. During our free time, we came up with sitcom ideas centered on characters in our office, then handed them a draft script and asked for their comments. (They never responded.) We had Andrew's sister, Becky, pretend to be a constituent coming to the office from Phoenix. She made all sorts of absurd demands of our staff, such as having the office install extra electricity outlets to prepare for her arrival.

One day I was writing the senator's weekly column, which went out to some of the local newspapers, when I decided it would be amusing if I filled it with *Star Trek* references; then I gave it to Andrew for his review. He agreed it was funny. Then I turned in the real column to the senator in his overnight folder.

Later that day our chief of staff, Tim Glazewski, came into the press office. Tim had worked for Kyl pretty much from day one. Like Kyl, he was a serious sort. Not really into frivolity.

"Matt, I have this column you wrote," he said, "and I have a question about it."

"Okay," I replied.

"Who is the Vulcan ambassador?"

Uh-oh. "What?" I asked.

"You quote the Vulcan ambassador," he said. "Who is that?"

"Oh my God," I said. "That wasn't supposed to be turned in. It was a joke." I tried to laugh.

Tim looked at me quizzically. "He's not real, then?" he asked.

I was red-faced. Andrew tried to conceal his laughter.

With our Senate IDs, staffers could walk all over the Senate complex. On any given day I might see Oregon's Bob Packwood, the senator accused of not being able to keep his hands to himself, and Joe Biden, the senator who couldn't keep his *thoughts* to himself. Or I might spot Senator Ted Kennedy walking his Portuguese water dog Splash (without question the most unfortunately named animal in history). Hillary Clinton was also a familiar sight. She'd run for the New York Senate seat about thirty seconds after applying for a state driver's license and was now surrounded by a retinue of aides with nasty eyes.

Republicans would never admit this, but we envied the Clintons. Time and again, we'd watched them wriggle out of scandals that would have ruined the rest of us. And there was something about the Clintons' naked audacity that was intriguing. Senator Clinton, for example, railed repeatedly against "the vast right-wing conspiracy," but once she got into the Senate, she made every effort to sign on to Republican bills so she could get applauded in the press for being "bipartisan" and "centrist." Clinton even attended a press conference hosted by Kyl in the office of the Republican Policy Committee—command central of the "conspiracy" that supposedly had been out to destroy her.

Andrew and I watched with awe as she walked directly into the office and sidled up to an uncomfortable Jon Kyl. It was like watching the Riddler stroll into the Batcave, and we were powerless to intercede. After the press conference was over, I swear she caught my eye. I stared at her with a frown. With a knowing smile, she looked at me, then at all the other assembled Republicans, and practically danced out of the room. *See ya, suckers!*

In truth it was easy to see how Hillary could beguile her colleagues. The Senate, as is well known, is a clubby place, and the closest Americans come to eighteenth-century French aristocracy. Senators have large staffs, free parking spaces, a choice of health insurance options, private elevators and underground trains that connect the Capitol to each of the three Senate office buildings, Dirksen, Hart, and Russell—all of them a distance of about a city block. Heaven forbid senators walk that far (though the few physically fit senators, like Evan Bayh, often did).

I always felt sorry for the subway drivers. They spent all day in a glass cage below the earth. Their entire job consisted of pulling a lever to move their train forward or backward along a single track, with no one to talk to and nothing much to look at all day long. Meanwhile, on the neighboring track was a second train operated automatically by a machine. It was faster, nicer, and cleaner, and it whizzed by the human-driven version, almost as if it were mocking the drivers as it went along.

Nearly every day of the week some senator hosted a working lunch so that other senators could go, have a meeting, and eat lunch for free— courtesy of the taxpayer. When the senators weren't having free meals, they made use of an exclusive private dining room. There was even a separate dining room inside the dining room, which was strictly senators only. No staff. No guests. The dining options were important because there weren't many options outside the Senate complex. There was La Brasserie, a French restaurant still famous for having once been the place where carousing senators Chris Dodd and Ted Kennedy made a "waitress sandwich." (It was exactly what it sounds like.) There was the Monocle, one of those be-seen places, where staffers and reporters would hang out and smoke cigarettes at the bar and pretend to be unimpressed when famous people stopped by. Other than that there was a Mexican restaurant, a German restaurant, and a Subway (my favorite).

Since the Senate was so privileged and pampered, it was really the last place in the world prepared to deal with any crisis. So I felt fortunate to be working for someone like Senator Kyl when the September 11 attacks took place. Kyl came back from the Capitol, where he was having a meeting, and immediately took command. He was certain 9/11 would be the first of many attacks on the country and that America was about to be under siege like Israel. He'd been talking about the dangers of a terrorist attacks for years. Now everyone was listening.

The senator corralled the staff outside his office. He said that all those who were married could go home to their families. Except him, of course. He'd stay at his post.

A few of us who weren't married looked around uncertainly. What about us?

It turned out we were going to stay with the senator in the office, next to the Capitol, which was under threat of attack. I was fine with that. I respected Kyl so much that if he thought we should stay there, I would. Others on the staff weren't so certain. We have to stay? Uh, come again?

My married friends looked at us with sympathy—at least, I think they did. Mostly I saw the backs of their heads amid a cloud of dust as they stampeded out of the office.

I thought about my own family back in Michigan. My mom was at school during the day, so I called my dad at home. He was watching everything on the news. He'd heard reports of more planes and bombs going off in Washington.

"Everything is going to be okay," I told him. "I'm standing with Senator Kyl right now. We're safe in his office."

At that exact moment, I spotted the door to the office's reception area fly open. A Capitol police officer rushed in and came up to where we were standing. He was in uniform with black boots and a gun in his holster. His face was grim.

"Just a second, Dad," I said into the phone.

The officer looked at us, a little surprised that we were still there. "Senator, you're going to have to leave the building immediately," he said very firmly.

Kyl said we were planning to stay in his office and we'd be okay.

The officer shook his head. "I have to clear this building now," he said. He told us the building was still a target. There was still at least one plane missing, and many people believed it was en route to the Capitol. The entire Capitol complex was being evacuated for the first time in history. We needed to move. Right now.

As I contemplated this, I forgot I was still on the phone.

"Matthew, what's going on?" Dad finally asked.

"It's okay," I said into the receiver. "We're being evacuated. I've got to go." I hung up and joined the other staff as we followed Senator Kyl out of our office. Dad, meanwhile, called my mom at work, but they couldn't locate her. So over the school loudspeaker that filtered into every classroom, the school secretary said, "Mrs. Latimer, your son is safe in Washington, D.C."

When we evacuated Hart, the scene outside was chaotic. Every block around the Capitol building was closed off. So staffers were walking for miles to get home. Senators were wandering the parking lot aimlessly, mixed in with staffers and tourists. Other senators were sitting in the backseat of their chauffeured cars in total gridlock, since most of the roads were closed. BlackBerrys and cell phones weren't working, which only increased the sense of confusion. If this had been a coordinated terrorist attack on the Hill, we would have been sitting ducks. But as my friend Kurt used to say with typical dark humor: why would anyone bother to take out a congressman? We'd just end up electing more of them.

The cliché is that everything changed after 9/11, but it did for the United States Senate the most. It became an armed camp. It was harder than ever to get into the building every morning. Police officers increased in numbers. Concrete barriers were installed everywhere. We were all given training on how to use gas masks and started doing mandatory evacuation drills. Our office had a gung-ho emergency coordinator who carried around a clipboard and a detailed list of instructions for every eventuality. When an alarm sounded, everyone in our office was supposed to drop everything and meet on a grassy knoll. For some reason the drills always seemed to happen when it was freezing cold or raining. Andrew and I would walk to the knoll and then keep right on going to the nearest restaurant.

Not long after the attacks, we faced another crisis that tested the mettle of Team Kyl. A letter addressed to Senator Tom Daschle, the Senate Democratic leader, arrived in his office on the fifth floor of the Hart Building. The letter was opened by a staff assistant, and it contained a strange white powder: the potentially deadly toxin anthrax.

I was in our office two floors above Daschle's when news of the anthrax contamination reached us. We were notified about what was happening in the worst way possible. People wearing yellow hazmat suits walked in and seized our unopened mail. As I saw them, I thought, Uh, shouldn't we be wearing those things too?

When word of the anthrax attack spread, most people on seasoned, battle-hardened Team Kyl knew exactly what to do: they got in their cars and went home. Not me. Senator Kyl was in the Capitol, and I wanted to wait until he got back. I had a feeling he wasn't going to want people to leave. He didn't. He said he loved his staff and wanted them to be safe, but panicking and fleeing the building would be exactly what the person who sent the anthrax had intended. The perpetrators wanted the Senate to shut down and for everyone to panic, and he wasn't going to let them succeed.

It turned out that the senator wouldn't have that choice. The decision was made to close the Hart Office Building while the anthrax attack was investigated and traces of it were cleaned from our air system. This decision was made, in typical government fashion, days after the anthrax was discovered, during which time we'd been breathing it all in.

From that point on, the cleanup of the building was now in the worst possible hands: those of the federal government. The only thing I'd ever seen people in Washington do was spend money. I'd never seen them actually solve a problem in my life.

Teams from the Environmental Protection Agency and a whole host of other people were sent to the building. They built a large tent around the entrance with large hoses going in. People walked out of the building in hazmat suits and didn't talk to anyone. Everything looked so convoluted and secretive that I half expected to see Oompa-Loompas peering out of the windows.

The senators displaced from Hart—about fifty of them—were given periodic briefings. A person on our staff went to one and came back to update us, throwing out important-sounding phrases like "air quality controls" and "emission samples."

Andrew and I looked at each other skeptically. "They have no idea what they're doing, do they?" I asked.

"Nope," the staffer replied.

At first, Hart was supposed to reopen after four weeks, but that deadline was eventually changed to "indefinitely." Meanwhile, senators and their staffs were scattered to the winds. Some moved into the offices of their counterparts from the state. We heard, for example, that members of Dianne Feinstein's staff temporarily moved into Barbara Boxer's office. At least one of the wealthier senators rented hotel rooms for his office. Senator Stabenow's office was assigned to the loading dock in another Senate office building. I went to visit Kim there. It was right next to the building's massive Dumpsters. At three o'clock every afternoon, when the Dumpsters were emptied, the room was filled with the smell of garbage.

The core of Team Kyl moved into the senator's hideaway office in the Capitol. Nearly every senator had a hideaway office whenever they needed it to spare themselves the grueling ten-minute walk or train ride from their office buildings. Some of those hideaways were legendary for being settings for clandestine trysts.

The size of the hideaways varied by seniority. Kyl's hideaway, which he used so rarely that it wasn't clear he knew where it was, was the size of an average dining room. In fact, the room even had a modest-sized dining room table, which filled more than a quarter of the room. There was only one entrance and there were no windows. In the back, up against a wall, was a small desk for the senator. For months, Kyl was wedged into this room with our chief of staff, the scheduler, the legislative director, the office manager, Andrew, and me. That is seven people, for those counting—working eight hours a day in a single room right next to their boss.

Just to make it even more uncomfortable and inconvenient, the seven of us had two computers and three phone lines. If we needed to make a private call on our cell phones, we could wedge ourselves into a long, narrow hallway that connected to other Senate hideaways and hope no one was listening.

After our first week in this tiny, cramped dining room, someone decided that the plants back in our office in Hart needed to be watered. Supposedly the concern was first raised by Mrs. Kyl, but that might only have been because she wasn't there to defend herself. It didn't occur to anyone that with all the chemicals being sprayed into the building, the plants were either dead or had mutated into toxic monsters. The hazmat teams discouraged any of us from entering the building. But if it was absolutely necessary, they'd allow one person to go back into Hart, without a hazmat suit, for a limited amount of time.

Operation Plant Rescue was moving down the track so rapidly it could no longer be stopped. So Tim, our chief of staff, looked around the dining room table and asked if anyone wanted to volunteer for the mission. People started staring at the floor, or suddenly became fascinated with the newspaper. No one wanted to look Tim in the eye.

As for me, my lips may have said nothing, but my entire demeanor said, You must be crazy. I wasn't going to enter that toxic stew to water some Plantzilla for any reason whatsoever.

With no one on staff showing the slightest interest in volunteering, Tim volunteered himself. Our brave and trusted captain was willingly going to expose himself to any number of dangers. So the rest of us did what came naturally. We gave him a list of things to get while he was over there: an extra set of keys in a desk drawer or a letter that needed to be mailed. I asked for my Rolodex. Tim received so many requests he needed to get a paper and pen.

The increasingly unhappy members of Team Kyl lingered in that horrible hideaway much longer than even the most pessimistic of us had expected—through Thanksgiving, then Christmas, then New Year's. Capitol Hill reporters were being told by senators that their staffs were getting pretty angry about the delays. Not the senators themselves, of course. No, they could rough it as long as needed. This from a group of individuals so pampered that the easiest way to get them to stop holding up legislation was for the leadership to threaten to hold votes over the weekend.

With each passing day, talk of a full-scale rebellion took root. Rumors were afoot that many senators were plotting to storm Hart and reclaim their offices by force, if necessary. Senators or their chiefs of staff were yelling at the EPA and security briefers and the sergeant at arms and anyone else they could find. Then they'd go back to the front of the line and start yelling at them all over again. It was a rare moment of genuine bipartisanship on the Hill.

Oddly, I never heard Senator Kyl once complain about the circumstances he was in, however. And since I was no more than two feet away from him all day long for months on end, I would have heard it.

After three months in captivity, and maybe only a day or two before the ugliest riots on Capitol Hill since the 1960s would have broken out, it was finally over. We were allowed to return to Hart, even though it was never clear what exactly had been done to clean the building. We didn't care anymore. I never thought I'd be so happy to see my stapler, my pens, and my computer monitor. I finally had a phone that I didn't have to share with three people. It was a dream.

During the long, dark winter of the Hart exile, I searched for anyplace I could go that might give me a respite from sitting in that dining room and talking about what happened last night on *Frasier*. Once I even got so desperate that I went to the Senate gallery to watch senators give floor speeches. It was like walking onto the set of C-SPAN.

I recalled once reading what Alexis de Tocqueville had said about the American system of government. "The Senate," he wrote, "is composed of eloquent advocates, distinguished generals, wise magistrates, and statesmen of note, whose arguments would do honor to the most remarkable parliamentary debates of Europe." Now, sitting in the gallery, I watched and thought, *Um, not so much.*

Nothing could shake one's faith in democracy as much as watching a United States senator give a speech. Rarely was there a moment that was inspiring or spontaneous or even normal. Typically, a senator would come out with an aide and go to a lectern. The senator would carefully take out a typed speech or a few pages of bullet points. Then he'd clear his throat and start orating grandly to an audience of practically no one. Few, if any, senators were sitting in their seats. The tourists up in the gallery would whisper to one another or look at their watches. Those who suffered the most, of course, were the clerks who had to sit on the rostrum and do their administrative work while the senator droned on. The clerks had learned a technique I mastered when I was growing up with all those foster kids—how to totally tune out people. If a senator said the building was on fire, not a single one of the clerks would have heard him. Even members of the senator's own staff would start looking at the ceiling or chatting with other aides. They were bored by the speeches they'd helped write.

First there was meaningless process talk. "Mr. President, I'd like to suggest an absence of a quorum." "I drafted an amendment that was inserted at markup." "We're going to have a second-degree amendment on that." Then they paid homage to one another's greatness: "I salute the gentleman from New York for his outstanding remarks." "I am pleased to join with the distinguished senator from Oregon." "May I just say I am honored to work with such a conscientious legislator as the gentle lady from Texas."

Or they slipped into phony clichés they'd seen in *The American President* or *Mr. Smith Goes to Washington*: "I'm fighting for all those people who feel invisible out there." "This is not the time for politics as usual." "It's time to stop the partisan bickering."

One of the worst speakers of all was the future leader of the Democrats in the Senate, Harry Reid. When he was elected leader, Republicans rejoiced. Not only did he stumble over his words, he made all sorts of weird, inappropriate comments. When the Capitol Visitors Center was being built, he accidentally displayed the contempt that most senators have for the people who elect them to office. "My staff tells me not to say this," he began, which no doubt left his staff cringing, "but I'm going to say it anyway. In the summer, because of the heat and high humidity, you can literally smell the tourists coming into the Capitol. It may be descriptive, but it's true."

How, I wondered, had these people ever been elected in the first place? My theory was the senators weren't *always* that way. They became institutionalized once they entered the building. They forgot how normal people talked and started conversing in incomprehensible Senate-speak. "Great job, Senator," a bored aide would tell them with fake sincerity. The senator would beam. I was great, *wasn't* I? Then the speech nobody had listened to would be enshrined for immortality in the Congressional Record, which no one ever read. The whole exercise seemed like one expensive therapy session for a politician's ego, subsidized by U.S. taxpayers.

Of course, there were a few exceptions to the Senate's mindless tedium. Whenever Ted Kennedy appeared to speak, for example, he usually attracted attention. That's because his idea of soaring oratory was to come out and recite whatever he was saying at the top of his lungs. And many staffers, Democrat and Republican, tended to tune in whenever Senator Robert Byrd appeared at the podium. He was in his eighties by then, and he might do or say anything at any time. Sometimes he'd read poems he'd written about the change of seasons.

As he aged further, Byrd's soliloquies tended to wander to parts unknown, such as his infamous tribute to his pet shih tzu. He took to interrupting other senators' speeches on the floor with loud shouts of "Yes!" "That's right!" and "Amen, brother!" (As of this writing, he is president pro tempore of the Senate and third in line to the presidency, after Vice President Biden and the Speaker of the House.)

The Senate often had the feeling of being the set of an even older and male version of The Golden Girls. On the Republican side, we had our own Robert Byrd: Senator Strom Thurmond of South Carolina, whom I first encountered when he broke loose from one of his aides and shuffled into the wrong hearing room. He usually came to committee hearings with the assistance of an aide and read off cue cards. Some of the meaner Democrats on the panel, like Patrick Leahy, would ask follow-up questions, knowing Strom couldn't answer them. The senator just repeated what was on his card.

In the winter of 2002 Strom Thurmond, then the senior senator from yesterday, collided spectacularly with the ambitious Republican leader Trent Lott, the man of tomorrow. At Senator Thurmond's one-hundredth-birthday party Lott famously waxed nostalgic about Strom's 1948 presidential run—a campaign based on the notion of segregation forever. One would think that a senator from the Deep South such as Lott would want to avoid dwelling on that unfortunate period of history. Surely he wouldn't go there.

He went. "I want to say this about my state," he began, beaming at a barely cognizant Strom. "When Strom Thurmond ran for president, Mississippians voted for him. We're proud of it. And if the rest of the country had followed our lead, we wouldn't have all these problems over the years."

The question, of course, was what "problems" Lott was referring to. Maybe he meant the spread of Communism or the expansion of the federal government? But he didn't say so. High taxes? Hmmm... maybe. Unemployment? A bit of a stretch. "Uppity blacks"? Uh-oh.

Lott's comment was initially overlooked until a few days later, when the Congressional Black Caucus decided to be offended. Most white members of Congress are tone-deaf on race relations, and they live in terror of being yelled at by the CBC (unofficial slogan: "We get our way or there's hell to pay"). Members of the CBC, no matter who they are, receive from Congress the same deference on race relations that Al Sharpton receives from the media and business world. No matter how many ethics breaches a given member may be accused of, on matters of race his or her moral authority is unassailable. So when the CBC demanded that Democratic leaders condemn Lott and ask him to step down from his leadership post, Democratic leaders responded: "Yes, CBC. You got it, CBC."

I made common cause with the CBC regarding the Trent Lott situation for reasons having little to do with his stupid comment. Lott ticked me off for a couple of other reasons. First, he lived across the street from my apartment building, and I used to watch him blowing leaves from his front sidewalk shirtless. The vision of a half-naked sixty-year-old man who was not, shall we say, in vigorous shape spoke volumes about his judgment. Second, Lott was a member of the loathsome Singing Senators, one of those weird Washington institutions that turn normally level-headed public officials into stage performers seriously deluded about their own talent. Everyone who works with these self-deluding officials is forced to suffer through their boss's fantasies. Senator Orrin Hatch, for example, wrote gospel music. Senator Byrd had cut his own record, *Robert Byrd, Mountain Fiddler*. It contained such hits as "Turkey in the Straw" and "Forked Deer." And who could forget "Wish I Had Stayed in the Wagon Yard"?

The Singing Senators were the worst because they forced us to listen to their barbershop songs at every Republican event. It was deeply embarrassing—for them, for us, and for the Senate. That is, until the fickle hand of destiny made its appearance. Mysteriously, all of the members of the Singing Senators met an ugly fate—similar to that famous curse put on anyone associated with the Superman movies. John Ashcroft, as I mentioned, was defeated for reelection by a dead man. Larry Craig had an infamous encounter in a Minnesota airport bathroom. Jim Jeffords left the party and became a pariah. And Trent Lott woke up one day and decided to take a foot out of one of his expensive shoes and lodge it in his slick, syrupy mouth.

Once Lott's Strom Thurmond Apology Tour fizzled, the White House wrote him off and promoted as his replacement their preferred kind of Senate leader: Senator Bill Frist of Tennessee, who possessed the charm and personality of warm mayonnaise.

Years later, Lott wrote a book about the controversy that dethroned him. He called his comment about Strom "innocent but insensitive and indefensible." In other words, he called it "indefensible" and then defended it. "What do I need to do," he asked, "lie on the floor and flagellate myself?" This too was an unfortunate image, considering the treatment African Americans in his state had received not all that long ago.

I was so grateful that I had a boss I could admire. I looked forward to taking trips to Arizona with Senator Kyl, because it gave me a chance to spend time with him in a more relaxed environment. On one of my first trips, he decided that we'd drive together from Phoenix to Tucson for a media tour. Kyl wasn't a prima donna when it came to transportation. I used to laugh at people like Nancy Pelosi, who got into chauffeured SUVs to drive to the nearest gas station, then got out to complain about global warming and gas-guzzling SUVs. In Washington, Jon Kyl drove himself around in a fifteen-year-old white Crown Victoria that I think was a taxicab in another life. One of the side mirrors was held on with duct tape. Kyl drove that car everywhere.

When I arrived in Arizona, I discovered that Kyl's usual mode of transportation back home was actually worse. He proudly showed me his beat-up pickup truck. It had no air-conditioning and a steering wheel in questionable condition. Kyl had run for the Senate using a commercial that showed him driving that old, dirty truck. Nobody actually believed that, years later, he still drove the thing. But he did. I took one look at that truck and began contemplating the 120-degree heat. Was I going to have to ride in the Heatstrokemobile all the way to Tucson?

Luckily for me, the answer was no. It turned out that Mrs. Kyl had insisted that the senator buy a nicer car—one that included, for example, a reliable steering wheel. Bless her heart. Thanks to her, we drove that car, complete with air-conditioning, together to Tucson.

Senator Kyl grew more relaxed as he drove. I think the sense of forward motion comforted him. He liked to talk on long drives—to a point. I quickly learned his system. When he turned the radio volume down, that meant he wanted to converse. When he turned it up, that meant I should zip it. At one point, I was in the middle of a sentence when he reached for the volume knob. I stopped talking. It was a very logical system.

When we were in Tucson, Kyl asked the local staff to change our itinerary so he could visit the University of Arizona, his alma mater. He wanted to make a stop at the university's football stadium, which housed a laboratory that made mirrors for some of the world's largest telescopes. I later learned from a member of the Tucson staff that Kyl had visited the lab many times. She believed we went there because Kyl wanted me to see it. He thought I'd find it cool. It was.

As we drove through the campus, Kyl pointed out a large hill called "A" mountain. It was some student make-out place. I was surprised that the very proper Kyl would ever mention such a thing.

"If you ever want to upset Mrs. Kyl," he once said mischievously, "ask her about 'A' mountain."

Actually, I didn't really have a yen to antagonize the wife of a United States senator. I hardly knew Mrs. Kyl, but I got a clear vibe that that was probably for the best. My strategy with her was similar to the advice Brad Pitt gave Matt Damon in *Ocean's Eleven* when he was trying to pull off a job: "They've got to like you, then forget about you the moment you've left their sight." In short, it was my hope that Mrs. Kyl never remembered my name. I once ran into her at an event in Washington. She greeted me effusively and we chatted for several minutes. "Nice seeing you, Mrs. Kyl," I said as we parted. "You too, Scott," she replied. Mission accomplished.

On one of my trips with Senator Kyl to tour the Arizona-Mexico border we received the rare honor of being joined by the senior senator from Arizona, John McCain. Members of our staff weren't enamored of this idea. It always seemed to us that Senator Kyl would work long and hard on unglamorous Arizona issues. Then McCain would sign on to Kyl's legislation and get all the attention and most of the credit. That never seemed to bother Kyl, though. I don't think I ever heard Senator Kyl say a bad word about Senator McCain (which put Kyl in a very small minority in the United States Senate).

At one point during the trip, Senator Kyl parted company with us to attend a meeting concerning the least interesting issue imaginable to the media: state water issues. Wisely, McCain found other pressing work to attend to. We all separated and planned to meet up later at the airport to fly back to Phoenix.

When I arrived at the airport, Senator McCain was already on the plane. Kyl hadn't gotten there yet, so I milled around hoping that he'd arrive soon so I could walk onto the plane with him. No way was I going to be on the plane alone with McCain.

It should be said that my affinity for McCain had waned considerably after the 2000 presidential election. Running in the primary against George W. Bush, McCain campaigned as a Reagan conservative, supporting lower taxes and a strong national defense. But Bush won in part, McCain believed, due to dirty tricks.

He didn't take the loss well. He seemed to blame all the Republicans for "betraying" him. He'd become entranced by the media attention he'd received as the Republican "maverick." So he kept it going by siding with the Democrats in the Senate on nearly every issue. He opposed Bush's tax cuts. He became more liberal on global warming than even many liberals. He started adding Democrats to the cult of personality that was his Senate staff, and everyone believed he was going to leave the party.

McCain seemed to love sticking it to the Republicans every chance he got because such "courageous independence" won praise in the press and got him on TV. It made no difference to the media that the "straight-talking maverick" had changed positions on almost everything. But it made me wonder, as it did many other Republicans, whether Mr. Straight Talk really had any bedrock core of belief.

As I was waiting for Kyl to show up at the airport, I got a call from Elizabeth Maier. Elizabeth was the senator's legislative director, and she was with him at the water meeting.

"Hey there," she said. "Kyl's meeting is running late."

"Okay," I said.

"Is McCain there yet? He wants to know."

I said that he was.

"Well, you need to go on board and keep him company," she said.

Who, me?

"How long is Senator Kyl going to be delayed?" I asked. I tried not to sound panicked.

"Maybe forty minutes to an hour. But don't let McCain know how long it will be."

Elizabeth knew that I'd come to detest McCain. Right before she hung up she laughed and said, "Good luck."

For a moment, I considered staying in the hangar. Let McCain hurl his string of obscenities at the pilot. I didn't care. But I knew I'd never get away with it. So I swallowed hard, took a deep breath, and got on board.

We were using a U.S. Customs plane for the border trip. It was pretty nice as government planes go. It seated about six people comfortably. Every passenger had a beige leather seat. There was wood grain along the sides. We had little tables we could work at. There was an assortment of snacks and newspapers.

McCain was reading a newspaper when I entered. I settled down across from him on one of the leather seats and said hello.

"Where's Jon?" he asked impatiently. "Still at that water meeting?"

"Yes, he is, sir," I replied. "He'll be here soon."

McCain laughed like a jock scoffing at the hardworking water boy. "There's a special place for Jon in heaven for sitting through that stuff."

He went back to the newspaper. I looked out the window and prayed for a time machine or a case of sleeping sickness.

After a while, not a long while, McCain got restless. He started reading newspaper stories out loud to me and offering derisive commentary. One of the Tucson papers was the *Arizona Daily Star*, which had a very left-wing tilt. McCain, like many of us, called it "the Red Star." He was turning the pages quickly, and I knew he wasn't going to be satisfied with the papers for long. I figured it was only a matter of time before he started screaming.

Everyone in the Senate knew about his temper. During the 2008 campaign, McCain's defenders would claim the stories were exaggerated. They weren't. In Arizona, McCain was known for yelling at editors and publishers over any critical article. He hurled obscenities like a master of the craft—as in one famous incident in the Senate when he yelled "Fuck you" at John Cornyn of Texas in a room filled with people. During the immigration debate he fired a female staffer because she was working on an amendment he didn't agree with. The woman pointed out that she didn't work for McCain. McCain insisted she be fired anyway. He cursed at another female staffer (who also didn't work for him) when she tried to hand him a piece of paper at a meeting. McCain's colleagues fretted about his purple rages. "The thought of him being president sends a cold chill down my spine," Senator Thad Cochran of Mississippi once said. "He is erratic. He is hotheaded. He loses his temper and he worries me." Now I was stuck on a small plane with a known maniac.

I had to come up with something. *Think, Matt, think. What would a longtime senator want to talk about? Come on, man!*

"Senator, my dad really loved your book," I mumbled. Okay, I had no idea if my dad had read any of McCain's books. But I had seen one on his bookshelf and it was possible he might have read it. Anyway, I was desperate.

"Well, you can thank Mark Salter for that," he said bluntly, referring to his chief of staff and coauthor. I thought it was nice of him to acknowledge that. I was terrified he was going to ask me what part of the book my dad liked, so I quickly changed subjects.

"And you were so good on *Saturday Night Live*," I said. He'd appeared on the show several weeks earlier, to rave reviews.

He laughed. "Yeah, that was a lot of fun."

He told me about the after-parties that ran until early Sunday morning. He enjoyed chatting about the skits that he'd appeared in, including one when he tried to sing Barbra Streisand songs and was horrifyingly off-key.

I asked every follow-up question I could think of, sparing no praise along the way. I learned what I should have known all along: the key to most politicians is to let them focus on themselves. I had to admit, I found him enjoyable to talk to—though I wouldn't call him warm. His humor had a nasty edge, which was fun as long as you weren't the target.

I was still tap-dancing when Senator Kyl and Elizabeth finally got on the plane. They appeared shocked to see us laughing it up. McCain, in fact, was in such a good mood that he joked and chatted all the way back to Phoenix, making fun of other senators like "Borin' Orrin" Hatch.

After the flight, Kyl was visibly impressed. No doubt he'd thought he'd get on the aircraft and see McCain holding my severed head in his hand while he frothed at the mouth.

"What did you say to him?" Kyl asked.

I laughed. "Oh, I figured out how to get on his good side: shameless flattery."

I deserved a raise.

There were many other senators who were as unimpressive to me as McCain. While I was working for Kyl, my friend Alec had finally left Nick Smith's office to work for Senator Susan Collins of Maine. Like a convict out on parole, Alec was so happy to be anywhere else that he never said a bad word about his new boss. But I got to know others on the staff. They told me about Collins's nasty "hate mails"—e-mails she'd send to staff at all hours of the night, blaming them for one thing or another. She seemed to be constantly looking for a new press secretary. None ever seemed to be able to get her enough press compared to her archrival, Senator Olympia Snowe. Then there was Lindsey Graham, R-S.C. He was so shamelessly infatuated with McCain and the press attention that followed him that he really should have been dubbed "Lindsey Graham, R-John McCain." He did whatever McCain did and tended to vote however McCain voted. If I were a resident of South Carolina, I'd charge Arizona for stealing my senator. I was told of another senator, defeated for reelection, who spent many work hours shopping in Georgetown. And another who was said to be so lonely that she chatted with the OnStar device in her car.

I still had high hopes for one member of the Senate. Ever since I'd started working for Kyl, I'd occasionally wander the halls hoping I'd run into Kay Bailey Hutchison. That was Step 1 of my plan. I never could figure out a Step 2.

One day, I was walking in the Capitol with my friend Elizabeth. We headed to the elevator to take the train back to Senator Kyl's office. After pushing the button, the elevator doors opened. And there she was. Kay Bailey Hutchison. Finally. The K. The B. The H. All three initials were standing there in front of me, bathed in the glow of the elevator's illuminated lights. After all these years, I was about to enter an elevator with her. My mouth dropped open. No words could come.

The senator was standing with two young male aides. The guys were good-looking, young, and lean. They looked like they'd just stepped out of a J. Crew catalog.

I tried to think of something to say to the senator, something cool and nonchalant. This was the moment I'd been waiting for since I "stalked" her at the 1996 Republican Convention. I couldn't just let it pass by. I started to say something, and then I felt a violent yank on my arm. Elizabeth was pulling me backward. I'd totally forgotten she was there.

"Help me," she said. "I'm stuck."

I looked down. The heel of Elizabeth's shoe was wedged into the small opening between the floor and the elevator door.

Elizabeth smiled sheepishly at KBH. "I'm so sorry, Senator," she said.

I struggled to help Elizabeth pull her shoe out as the elevator doors slammed against our arms. This was neither cool nor nonchalant.

KBH stared at us impatiently. We were keeping her waiting! Oh, no! I was starting to sweat. For a moment I considered pushing Elizabeth out, but I could never pull that off gracefully.

After what seemed like many interminable minutes, Elizabeth finally yanked her shoe loose. We fell into the elevator, and the doors shut behind us. Now we were face-to-face with Senator Hutchison herself. I smiled at her. She looked at us grim-faced. There was not a hint of pleasure in her demeanor. It was almost as if she didn't want to know me at all. And I swear she had dead eyes. Black, small, not a sign of joy or life in them. They sent a cold chill through my body.

As the elevator proceeded downward, the senator turned to her J. Crew aides. They were "the purse boys." That was the nickname staffers gave them because their job seemed to consist of carrying Senator Hutchison's purse around Capitol Hill. They also were known to drive her from her house to work, a distance of approximately two blocks. They were basically taxpayer-subsidized butlers. This was an unusual day, since normally only one purse boy was with Senator Hutchison at a time. The other must have been a trainee.

As one of the boys quietly held her large purse, she started to fish through it. Then she issued a list of instructions.

"Now, I want you to take my purse back to the office," she said.

"Yes, Senator," the purse boy responded.

"Take the nail polish out and put it in the refrigerator."

"Yes, Senator."

"Take the rest of the makeup out and put that in the refrigerator too."

"Yes, Senator."

"Then put the purse by my desk." She said this as though it were her routine speech. The purse boy nodded dutifully, while the trainee looked like he wanted a pen to jot all this down. Elizabeth and I gazed at each other uncomfortably. It felt a little like entering your parents' bedroom and finding your mother putting on deodorant. You knew it happened, but you didn't really want to think about it.

Then the elevator doors opened. We moved to the side to let KBH pass. She did so regally, without a word to either us or the purse boys following close behind. In those few minutes, my enthusiasm for KBH sank to a previously unfathomable low.

In truth, everyone I knew in the Senate thought I was crazy for my KBH infatuation in the first place. Many people repeated the claim that she once slapped a staffer back in Texas. In Kyl's office, we hired a former KBH purse boy to work for us. He'd never say anything bad about her. I think he was too afraid to. But whenever her name was mentioned, he seemed to shake a little. Since I'd first come to Washington, I'd put Senator Hutchison on a pedestal. If I could be disappointed in her, I could be disappointed in anybody.

It might be easy to conclude from what I say that every senator but Jon Kyl was either a prima donna or a ding-a-ling. But that wasn't so. There were good, hardworking public servants there like Orrin Hatch and Jeff Sessions. They didn't seek out the limelight, but they were smart and capable people you could count on. I had a special fondness for John Cornyn, Jim DeMint, and Tom Coburn. They were senators who'd take unpopular positions and hold their ground because they believed it was the right thing to do. Coburn, for example, held up assistance for funding for AIDS in Africa because he thought the money was being spent without sufficient oversight. This won him nothing but widespread condemnation, particularly in the press. (Nobody cared that he was right.)

As for Jon Kyl, he was the senator I'd always hoped I'd work for—a good man who ran for office for the right reasons. He was kind enough to offer a slightly uncertain young man an example of integrity and principle in Washington. There was never a day that I worked for him that I didn't hold him in the highest esteem.

I probably could have stayed and worked for Senator Kyl for many more years. Several people on the staff had worked for him for decades. But despite the respect I had for him, the Senate had turned out not to be the elevated chamber of government I'd hoped it was. Besides, I'd come to Washington to do something else. I still wanted to make my way to the White House. Finally, I started to move a little closer.

CHAPTER FOUR

RUMMY

In early 2004, I still was working for Senator Kyl when an acquaintance, the conservative commentator Kate O'Beirne, asked if I had any interest in working at the Department of Defense. Secretary Donald Rumsfeld was looking for a new speechwriter. Did I want to meet him?

I only knew Rumsfeld from TV. To some, he was a modern-day Robert McNamara, a flinty technocrat running a failing war. To others, he was a modern-day Truman, with the same round, frameless glasses and give-'em-hell attitude. Even my dad liked him. He appreciated any man who displayed that much energy and spunk in his seventies.

Working for Rumsfeld seemed like it would put me one step closer to my goal of working in the White House. So I said, "Of course, I'll be happy to meet with him."

Sometime after I sent in my resume, I was called over to the Pentagon for an interview. The Pentagon was unlike any other office building I'd ever seen. The security procedures were so elaborate that it could easily take thirty or forty minutes just to move ten feet into the building. Once I made it through security, I came across a small town complete with several food courts, a McDonald's, a Dunkin Donuts, a CVS, a bank, a barbershop, and a jewelry store. There was even a DMV. All they needed was a 7-Eleven and I never would have left.

As anyone who's taken a geometry class might figure, the Pentagon has five floors, plus a basement and a mezzanine, and five pentagonal rings linked together by ten spoke-like corridors. The arrangement was so orderly that it was confusing—at least to people like me, who couldn't tell a parallelogram from a parasol. All I'd ever wanted to know about geometry I picked up on *Hollywood Squares*.

The Pentagon had so many suites of offices, occupying nearly four million square feet, that its designers came up with an address system that was meant to be helpful but actually was quite confusing. The speechwriting office, for example, was located in room number 2D-554. Even after three years in the building, I still didn't know what all those numbers meant. The first numeral was supposed to indicate what floor the office was on. That in itself was a mind teaser, since Floor 2 was actually on the same level as the entrance, which any normal person might assume was Floor 1. So that took me about a week to figure out. Then I had no idea what the D in 2D-554 stood for. As it turned out, that signified the ring the office was in. But that made even less sense, because sometimes I'd head down what I thought was the correct ring and the corridor would suddenly end. So I'd have to turn around and walk about a quarter-mile back to where I'd started and count the rings all over again. Since I couldn't get the 2 and the D right, I despaired of ever getting to room 554. Eventually, though, I began to figure out where places were in relation to the nearest Dunkin' Donuts.

The Pentagon itself was so vast that it would be impossible to know more than a handful of the twenty-three thousand people who worked there. Not only did its inhabitants feel isolated from the world, they were isolated from one another. People were always rushing through the halls in every direction. Many were in military uniform— white, green, blue, or khaki, representing the various services. There also were any number of young political types walking around in dark business suits and ties (usually red). It was Brooks Brothers goes to Fort Bragg.

Most offices, except those on the coveted E ring, had no windows. Which meant no sunlight. Which meant that for eight to ten hours every day people would be crammed into boxes with no sense of the outside world. I'm still surprised we didn't all go crazy.

Getting your car in and out of the Pentagon complex was such an ordeal that it usually didn't make much sense to leave the building for lunch. If you wanted to walk somewhere, it would take fifteen minutes to get to the Pentagon City mall, by foot or by Metro. I once tried to walk down the street to the mall and got yelled at by a huge, angry Pentagon police officer because I didn't use the crosswalk. (One might think the Pentagon police had better things to do.) For a long time after that, I was afraid to walk outside.

Secretary Rumsfeld's office was located in the Eisenhower corridor. In a glass cabinet were old pictures of Eisenhower at war and even a photograph of the retired general meeting a young Don Rumsfeld in the 1960s. Hanging on the opposite wall were Eisenhower's original oil paintings. They weren't particularly good. But the man liberated Europe, so I cut him some slack.

I waited in the wood-paneled lobby of the secretary's office for my turn to see the legendary Rumsfeld. He'd just finished interviewing another candidate, a rather sizable fellow who came out of there literally sweating. I wished I hadn't seen that. I imagined the guy sitting in a chair under a hot light while Rumsfeld demanded that he conjugate verbs or something. The guy gave me a sympathetic look. Then he was outta there.

Marc Thiessen followed the guy out. Marc was Rumsfeld's chief speechwriter. Nearly forty, he was a big, jovial man with black hair and a ruddy complexion. Marc tried very hard to be friendly—too hard. He was one of those people who'd nod and say "uh-huh" a lot while someone talked to him, but all the while he was looking around to see who else was in the room. He laughed loudly at even the mildest joke, always timed just a few seconds too soon to be sincere. For example:

Marc: "Hey there. How's it going?"

Me: "Oh, I guess things could be wor—"

Marc: "Ahahahahahahahaha! That's funny!"

Marc had worked for Rumsfeld practically from the beginning of the Bush administration. They'd gone through 9/11 together at the Pentagon. Most important to Rumsfeld, Marc was familiar with the secretary's habits. "I've broken him in!" Rumsfeld liked to say. I didn't know it at the time, but Marc was trying to move over to the White House. He'd been offered my dream job: presidential speechwriter. The secretary didn't like someone taking Marc away and upsetting his orderly system. So, as I learned later, it was the opinion of some on Rumsfeld's staff that the secretary was making the task of finding a suitable replacement especially difficult.

Larry Di Rita joined us for the meeting. Larry was running DoD's

Department of Public Affairs and would be my immediate boss if I was hired. Larry was almost movie-star handsome, possessed a quick wit, and had an easy charm. He was from Michigan, so he couldn't be all bad. Before he came to the Pentagon, Larry had worked in the U.S. Senate. In fact, he'd been the chief of staff to none other than Senator Kay Bailey Hutchison. Would that woman ever get out of my system?

Also working for the secretary and present at my interview was Tony Dolan. He'd been Ronald Reagan's chief speechwriter and had worked for Reagan for the entire eight years of his presidency. More recently, he'd worked for his friend Colin Powell until the two had had some sort of falling-out in 2001. A jovial Irishman with red hair and a beard, Tony had led a colorful life. As a student at Yale, he became a protégé of William F. Buckley. He also used to sing show tunes with an unknown actress named Meryl Streep. And he'd once got into a fistfight with an actor on the set of *The Merv Griffin Show*. Unmarried and in his fifties—he once told me with complete sincerity that he was saving himself for Deidre Hall of *Days of Our Lives*—Tony frequently showed up at events escorting a beautiful woman. For example, he once brought Catherine Crier, a former CNN anchor, to a Rumsfeld party. (His date caught more than a momentary glance from such guests as Alan Greenspan and Dick Cheney.) At the Pentagon, Tony worked to increase media access to Rumsfeld. A former news reporter who'd won the Pulitzer Prize at twenty-nine, Tony had a good relationship with most reporters.

Of the three men with me that day, he was by far the easiest to talk to. As we waited to go in to see Rumsfeld, I turned to him. "Should I be nervous?" I asked.

"Oh, it will be fine," Tony said good-naturedly.

Easy for you to say, I thought. *You didn't see that other guy's face.*

"Just be yourself," Tony advised. "Let him run the meeting. He'll know where he wants to go."

I'd learn later that Tony had enormous respect for Rumsfeld. One story stuck with him in particular. Several months earlier, while Rumsfeld was near the height of his popularity, Tony had received a phone call from a *Time* magazine reporter. The magazine's top editors were considering Rumsfeld for *Time's* famous "Man of the Year" issue. To a man of Rumsfeld's generation, a *Time* magazine cover was one of the biggest

tributes you could receive. People would practically kill for the prestigious honor, and Don Rumsfeld wasn't immune to positive attention.

So Tony came up excitedly to deliver the news. Rumsfeld was so
busy with a million other things that he kept putting off the meeting.
Frantically, the Time bureau chief called Tony. Didn't Rumsfeld know
what a big deal this was? There were other eager candidates in the
queue. Colin Powell, they said, wasn't showing a surplus of reluctance.

Finally, Tony convinced Rumsfeld to meet with the editors. When
they finally came in, Secretary Rumsfeld stunned them. In 1950, at the
height of the Korean War, when Rumsfeld was not yet twenty, the
"American fighting man" had been Time's "Man of the Year." Rumsfeld
said the magazine should do that again. "You don't want to give the
cover to me," he said. "Give it to the men and women of the military
instead."

At first, it may have sounded like false modesty. But Rumsfeld
worked to convince the editors that putting the military on the cover
was a better story for them. The editors were persuaded, and that was
how the "American soldier" became Time magazine's "People of the
Year" in 2003.

After waiting in the lobby for several minutes, Rumsfeld's secretary, Delonnie Henry, came out. Delonnie was the classic put-upon secretary. On good days, she was lukewarm. She inspected me briefly, then
turned her attention to Larry.

"The secretary's ready," she said.

Here we go, I thought as I followed Larry, Marc, and Tony into a
small passageway that led to Rumsfeld's office.

I walked into a huge room with a high ceiling, ivory-colored walls,
and blue carpeting. Mercifully, there were windows—for the first time
that day in the Pentagon I could see the sky again. Between the windows was a large portrait of George Washington. Below that was a long,
narrow table that contained two computer monitors, one of which was
marked as classified. There was an in-box that was empty and an out-
box that was full.

Across from that table was a large desk that had color-coded file
folders on it, all neatly arranged. I had the sense that they were put in
that exact spot for a specific purpose and that one moved them with
enormous reluctance. There was also a smaller, round table nearby with

four chairs circling it and two yellow lined notepads on top—again arranged with precision.

As we walked in, Secretary Rumsfeld was at his famous stand-up desk. He was silhouetted against an American flag, and his face glowed in the sunlight that filtered in from the nearby window. He couldn't have looked more impressive if he had staged it. He was dictating into a small tape recorder in his hand. We stayed quiet as he spoke. Then, after a minute or two, he turned off the tape recorder and directed his attention to us.

He looked exactly as I'd seen him on TV. He was wearing his Truman-like glasses. His silver hair was carefully swept back and his face was lined by fewer wrinkles than you might expect of a man in his seventies who'd worked for four presidents.

He was in shirtsleeves with a tie and a dark blue zip-up vest. He walked eagerly toward me and flashed a broad, winning smile.

"Don Rumsfeld," he said simply as we shook hands. He urged me to sit down at the small table and then sat across from me. He was handed my resume and glanced through it indifferently. I had the feeling he'd already memorized every relevant detail. Then again, it might have been the first time he'd ever looked at it. It was hard to know. He just seemed confident and prepared for anything.

He fixed his eyes on me. They were inquisitive, scrutinizing. I could see why people found him intimidating.

"So I see you work for Jon Kyl," he said. He lowered his voice. "He's a good man."

I nodded in agreement. I can't explain why, but there was something about his manner that instantly put me at ease. It was a strange reaction, and certainly uncommon. But I never felt nervous in his presence again.

He asked me what my impressions of the Senate were. I told him that while I respected Kyl and a few others, it was mostly a sad, depressing place. I talked about all the long-winded speeches the senators gave to empty chambers, while their staffs praised them for their mediocrity. He loved that observation.

He asked what my parents did. I said they were both teachers. He noted that his wife, Joyce, was involved in education. Don and Joyce

Rumsfeld had known each other since high school in Chicago. His eyes twinkled whenever he mentioned her name.

Marc watched our conversation, clearly delighted that we were getting along. Tony was sitting behind me on the couch. He'd occasionally shout out something to keep the conversation going if it drifted. Larry typed on his BlackBerry.

About fifteen minutes in, the heavy door to the office opened. The door had a latch that made a distinctive click whenever it moved. We all turned instinctively to look at it. Delonnie poked her head in and glanced at the secretary. Rumsfeld motioned Delonnie off with a wave of his hand, and she closed the door again. I figured out that she'd interrupted the interview at a designated time in case Rumsfeld wanted to get rid of me. Apparently he didn't.

With a boyish look in his eyes, he leaned toward me. "Ask me some questions," he beckoned. Rumsfeld loved having questions lobbed at him, the harder the better. I think it appealed to him from his years as a high school wrestler. He loved being able to grapple with a tough question, twist it as he pleased, and pin it to the ground until it begged for mercy. That is what made his press conferences so enjoyable to the public, if not the press corps.

At that moment, I learned an important lesson about interviewing: always have good, thoughtful questions ready. Oh, how I wish I'd considered that rule beforehand. As the great Donald Rumsfeld looked at me expectantly, I had nothing.

To stall for time, I asked a lame, generic question that fell apart in the air like a poorly packed snowball. "How do you prefer to work with speechwriters?" I could see the question disappointed him, and I didn't get a particularly interesting answer.

Then I asked another question that was more interesting. Rumsfeld had received bracing criticism for referring to our traditional allies, such as France and Germany, as "old Europe." There were a lot of people who agreed with him, however, including yours truly. The French and Germans always seemed to enjoy talking down to Americans even while they depended on us for their protection.

"Why did you decide to use the term 'old Europe'?" I asked him. "Was it intentional?"

He chuckled merrily. "Actually, it was an accident," he said. He told me that he'd been asked by some reporters why so many NATO allies were expressing opposition to the war in Iraq. A number of newer NATO members, those in Eastern Europe, did in fact support the effort in Iraq. He meant to refer to critics of the war as being part of "old NATO." But instead he slipped and said "old Europe," which created an international uproar.

He smiled. "It turns out it was the smartest thing I ever did."

At the end of the meeting, he asked for my writing samples. I gave him a few columns I'd written for Senator Kyl. He collected them in a folder. "I'm going to read these," he said, as if the words came as a surprise to him. After a few more minutes, I shook his hand and left.

As I was walking out, Tony pulled me aside. "That went really well."

A few days later, I was offered the job.

Senator Kyl was gracious about my decision to leave. "I really wish I could tell you not to take the job," he said. "I'm sure it's going to be pretty exciting." That turned out to be an understatement.

Working as Rumsfeld's chief speechwriter was like taking a final exam every day. He hated giving speeches. To him, they were basically a way to clear his throat until he could get to the Q & A. A speech seemed phony, someone else's words. He'd muddle halfheartedly through his remarks and then take questions on any issue anyone wanted to ask about. Usually it was whatever came out of the random Q & A, not the message of the speech, that won press attention.

By his own admission, Rumsfeld was the kind of editor who could ruin a perfectly good speech. He'd edit remarks all the way to the podium and even as the words came out of his mouth. A speechwriter who once worked for Rumsfeld was drawn one day into a long debate with him over a speech. Finally, the writer threw up his hands. "Mr. Secretary," he said, "you can edit this speech to death if you want, but there's one thing you can't do. You can't edit a quote from Pericles."

Rumsfeld grabbed the speech, scribbled on the section that quoted Pericles, and handed it back to the writer. On the page, Rumsfeld had written: "As Pericles should have said . . ."

As the secretary's chief speechwriter, I became one of the primary recipients of Rumsfeld's infamous snowflakes—short memos that con-

tained his thoughts or directions on an impossibly wide range of top-
ics. My assistant, Bonita Ruff, filled three massive binders full of them
during the three years I was at the Pentagon. They included things like:

"I never use the word *very*. It is a very weak word."

"I think we ought to do a State of the Pentagon op-ed or speech
(or both)."

"Develop a page or two about what the world might look like if the
extremists won."

"Please give me a copy of all upcoming speeches I have where
Libya is mentioned."

"I am concerned. My edits may not be finding their way into the
version of speeches you return to me."

"We have to get remarks going much faster and earlier than we are
doing."

"We have piled too many events where I am speaking too close to
each other."

Our battles over the length of his speeches went on forever. I always thought they should be a little longer. He always wanted them
shorter. I think it was because he was forced to sit through so many boring speeches that he wished would end more quickly.

Before I began working at the Pentagon, my image of the place
was that it was a well-run, über-professional institution that focused on
winning wars. It was nothing like that. There may (or may not) have
been a lot of intelligent people around Rumsfeld, but from my observation few possessed much emotional intelligence.

By all accounts, Deputy Secretary Paul Wolfowitz was a brilliant
man. I didn't know him very well. What I remembered most about him
was that his office looked like a briefcase full of papers had exploded.

I knew Undersecretary of Defense for Policy Doug Feith a little
better. In private he could be charming and quite interesting. He also
was a workaholic and a notorious perfectionist. He enjoyed treating
staff to one-sided monologues. He once called me to his office because
he wanted me to write some speeches for him. His own writer had
failed miserably at drafting some upcoming testimony to Congress.
Feith was so incensed by the speech's first line that he read it aloud to
me. "Mr. Chairman, thank you for inviting me to testify today." " 'Thank
you'?" Feith snapped, as if he couldn't believe it. " 'For inviting me'?" I

still don't know what was wrong with that sentence, but Feith was so spun up about it that I felt like I needed to apologize. (Rumsfeld didn't like anyone else using me as a speechwriter, so mercifully the idea of working for Feith was dropped.)

Then there was Stephen Cambone. Cambone had worked for Rumsfeld on and off for years. Early on at the Pentagon he was Rumsfeld's special assistant, which meant he was the link between the Office of the Secretary of Defense and the rest of the building. This was a terrible, perhaps unrecoverable mistake. Tall, lean, and glum-faced, Cambone had perfected mannerisms that somehow managed to make him look smart and foolish at the same time. He could be disdainful of lower-level employees and could have stood next to subordinates for days without acknowledging them. His demeanor posed unnecessary complications to some of Rumsfeld's early relationships with the military and civilian leadership. There was no choice but to promote him. In a bit of cosmic comedy, he was put into a newly created position: undersecretary of intelligence.

Cambone had an unusual way of speaking. He'd fill a sentence with so many oddly timed pauses that people stopped listening before he arrived at the end. They figured that anyone so long-winded simply had to be saying something smart. For example, he'd say, as he did at one senior staff meeting, "Today ... is ... the start ... of ... baseball ... season," and people would nod sagely. He had another technique he'd mastered that involved repeating whatever Rumsfeld had said back to him as if it were Cambone's idea. Rumsfeld would say, for example, "I'm going to get questions about Al Qaida on the Afghanistan-Pakistan border." A few minutes later, Cambone would tell him, "Mr. Secretary, there's something you need to be aware of. There's been news coverage of Al Qaida on the border ... between ... Pakistan ... and ... Afghanistan. So ... that's ... out there." For a moment, you could see people around the room thinking, *Didn't Rumsfeld just say that? There must be some high-minded nuance we're missing.* There wasn't.

One of the other senior officials in the secretary's immediate orbit was the White House liaison at the Pentagon, Jim O'Beirne, whose wife was Kate O'Beirne, the journalist who'd tipped me about the Pentagon job opening. Jim's job was to vet all political appointees who were hired at the department. The odd thing about the Pentagon was that

Rumsfeld didn't control most of the hiring in his own department—the White House, led by O'Beirne, did.

Jim was a brick wall of a man in his late fifties. He was very tall, with silver hair and glasses. In September 2006 his management style was portrayed in a popular book on Iraq by *Washington Post* reporter Rajiv Chandrasekaran. The book, *Imperial Life in the Emerald City*, claimed that Jim's office based hiring for key positions in Iraq on loyalty to the Republican Party regardless of any other qualifications. This included putting a twenty-four-year-old party loyalist who'd never worked in finance in charge of reestablishing Iraq's stock exchange, and a contractor with no previous experience in charge of guarding a closed airport, for which he was paid millions. In sum, the book alleged a string of "absurdities, incompetence, and bureaucratic failings" that undermined America's efforts to stand up postwar Iraq.

I was in Rumsfeld's office when O'Beirne, in a rage over the book, entered and demanded that the department come to his defense. "Mr. Secretary," he began with utmost gravity, his jowls shaking in fury, "my integrity is being questioned. Let me assure you that everything alleged in this book is untrue." But nearly everybody could cite examples of O'Beirne's office pushing unqualified candidates, or blocking the hiring of candidates they didn't like. I tried to hire an editor in the speechwriting office whom O'Beirne and his deputy, Margaret "Ducky" Hemenway, spent years—literally years—blocking. They came up with all sorts of shifting excuses. Each time I countered one, they came up with another. They even refused to bring this impeccably well-qualified woman and staunch conservative on board when Rumsfeld personally insisted on it (which meant the hard-charging secretary of defense had little power in picking people for his own department). Finally, I was told she had a "dark secret" that disqualified her. I had strong reasons to suspect what they were referring to—her sexual orientation. And they seemed to be blocking other candidates with sterling credentials across the department, with seemingly little justification.

I understood the need to want to hire Bush supporters for political jobs. Democratic administrations did the same thing. But the White House liaison office's ideal candidates for Pentagon jobs seemed extraordinary. They tended to possess one or more of the following characteristics: they were just out of college (usually an evangelical one), they had no relevant work experience, or they had been home-schooled. It made no sense. The speechwriting department was one of the few areas of the department actually trying to help Rumsfeld communicate and the White House personnel system was working constantly to deny us what we needed.

Rumsfeld grew so fed up with O'Beirne and Ducky that he threatened to fire them both. (Ducky ended up being moved to another office in the department.) But it's doubtful the secretary really could have banished O'Beirne, who seemed to have powerful backing from the White House. In fact, it was well known that the White House liaisons were minions of Karl Rove and that he ultimately was responsible for their activities, such as refusing to hire a candidate, as I was convinced, because of her sexual orientation. Rumsfeld personally brought her case and others to Rove—and lost.

Since it was so hard to bring in people to work for me in the speechwriting office, I generally had to make the most of the people we had. When I started, my office included four writers and two fact checkers. Almost all were political appointees. We had one military officer, an army lieutenant colonel named Randy Lee, and a program assistant—basically an office manager—who was a career civil service employee named Bonita Ruff. Whenever I had a problem with the bureaucracy, Bonita, a skilled bureaucrat of long standing, usually could solve it. But sometimes you just had to shake your head at the way things worked. Career employees stayed from administration to administration, and because of civil service protections, they were almost impossible to demote, punish, or fire. This gave them a lot of power and also had the potential to make them less responsive to whatever administration happened to be in charge.

As manager of an office, I was introduced to the Pentagon's rating system for career employees that determined raises and promotions. There were three main ratings a manager could use for an employee; "exceeds expectations," "meets expectations," and "does not meet expectations." The Pentagon was such an everyone-is-doing-fantastic sort of place that none of the ratings was used the way they were intended. If I thought someone was doing a good job, I had to rate them as "exceeds expectations" whether I thought they were exceeding my expectations or not. If, by contrast, I thought someone wasn't doing a good job, I had to say that they met my expectations. This was considered a terrible insult.

"Under what circumstances do I rate someone as not meeting expectations?" I asked.

"Oh, we never use that one," I was told.

Early on I realized why the Pentagon had become notorious over the years for conspicuous waste. One day, I was sitting in my office when a Pentagon employee came in and placed several boxes on my black leather couch.

"Here are your lampshades," she said.

"Lampshades?" I asked, looking up from my desk. "I didn't order any lampshades."

"Well, here they are," she replied sweetly.

I looked at her. Then I got up and walked over to look at the boxes. "The office doesn't even have that many lamps," I observed.

She had a ready response. "Oh, I can order some more."

"Wait. We don't need any more lamps," I said. "Why don't we just send the lampshades back?"

She smiled at my naïveté. "Oh, we never send things back," she said.

Our office once ordered a shipment of Hi-Liters. The Pentagon supply store sent us five thousand, and not a single one was yellow. We received boxes and boxes of printer cartridges that didn't fit any of our printers. And, of course, we never gave anything back. Instead, we lined up the superfluous items along one of the office walls until we could find a way to barter with another office for them.

Adjusting to this sort of system obviously demanded flexibility. But nothing, I mean nothing, ever prepared me for dealing with our office researcher, a woman I will call Sandy.

Officially, Sandy worked for me. In her mind, though, I worked for her and so did everyone else. She had dark hair that was almost always worn tightly with a bow and a gloomy disposition.

Sandy appointed herself the protector of Secretary Rumsfeld and the undisputed guardian of his remarks. She appeared to dedicate her life to the job. She was there early in the morning and late into the night. In fact-checking documents she was so exacting that she once required a writer to provide documentary support to prove that the 9/11 attacks had happened. If anyone bridled, she took offense: "Are you saying we shouldn't make sure the secretary's speeches are accurate?"

Rumsfeld liked her; he had no reason not to. She would show up at nearly every Rumsfeld speaking event in the building and station herself in the front row with a broad smile. I hadn't even known that she had teeth. Rumsfeld sent her a snowflake praising her once. It only seemed to embolden her.

She informed me that Rumsfeld had ordered that no one change any of his edits to speeches, even if his edits made sentences ungrammatical. She attended meetings with the secretary without my permission and even showed up on an overseas trip without my knowing a thing about it. She had a locked safe in her office that she didn't give me the combination to. She'd constantly come into my office with some complaint about my job performance and everyone else's. Eventually, I learned she was spending significant amounts of time in other parts of the building complaining about me and others in the office. She was a manufacturer of drama. Every day, it seemed, there was a major crisis that seemed likely to bring the Pentagon to its knees. I once had to literally order a lieutenant colonel on our staff not to spend more than fifteen minutes per day dealing with her complaints and concerns, because she had almost broken him with her constant complaints.

It got to the point that every other person in the speechwriting office signed a document that they then presented to me. It said that though Sandy was skilled in the technical aspects of her job, she was impossible to work with because of her "malicious," "insubordinate," and "unprofessional" behavior.

But as yet another example of the Pentagon's dysfunctional management system, when I suggested that she be moved to another office—few at the Pentagon ever actually got fired—Larry Di Rita demurred. Even after I presented the signed memo from everyone else on the staff, Larry said she could leave only if she found something else she liked. I had no idea what magical powers this woman possessed, except that Larry liked her. When she finally did leave, the office celebrated as if it were V-E Day. All we needed to do was to grab people in our arms and kiss them in Times Square.

In the spring of 2004, I attended one of my first meetings with the Pentagon public affairs team. The meeting was led by Larry in his spacious office on the second floor, which was only a few yards from where Flight 77 had crashed into the building. Usually about eight people sat around the table at these meetings: Larry; his deputy; me; Allison Barber, who as head of Internal Communications was in charge of several Defense Department websites and newspapers; Tony Dolan, special advisor to the secretary; Bryan Whitman, a deputy assistant secretary for press operations; Charley Cooper, from the deputy's office; and a representative of the chairman of the Joint Chiefs of Staff. Normally these meetings were uninteresting. Everyone went around the room and said what they were doing and then we each went off to do it. But in one of the early meetings something unusual came up.

A guy who worked for Joint Chiefs chairman Richard Myers mentioned that his office had asked the television show 60 Minutes to delay broadcasting some damaging photos from the field in Iraq. Everyone seemed to know what he was talking about, so I tried to look like I understood too. No one around the table seemed that worked up about it. It sounded important but not urgent. From the conversation, I pieced together some snippets of information. The photos were of Iraqis who were being held at a military prison in Iraq. I remember hearing the name Abu Ghraib.

Of course, the pictures of Iraqi detainees being positioned in naked pyramids or being threatened by dogs soon became an international sensation. People were equating the Abu Ghraib scandal with the My Lai massacre in Vietnam. They believed both were symbols of a failed American war. Many were calling for Rumsfeld to take responsibility for what had happened and resign.

The secretary was called to testify before the House and the Senate on the abuses. The hearings were going to be make-or-break for Rumsfeld and maybe the whole war effort. At the time Marc was still on the Pentagon's payroll, but he was taking a brief vacation before he went over to the White House. The job of writing Rumsfeld's testimony therefore fell to me. My first major writing assignment would determine whether my boss—a man I barely knew—kept his job. And, incidentally, whether I kept mine. But no pressure.

Over the next several days and weeks, I met with Rumsfeld in his office to go over what he might say. At one point, a few of us were sitting at his small round table when Rumsfeld was handed a note to take a phone call from the president. The secretary got up without a word to go into his private study, which connected to his office. The study was his sanctuary. In it Rumsfeld had hung framed cartoons of himself that appeared in the newspapers, including those that made fun of him. He got a kick out of showing them to people. He also had a framed letter from the first secretary of defense, James Forrestal, to Rumsfeld's dad when the senior Rumsfeld ended his service during World War II. Rumsfeld idolized his father, and the letter was one of his prized possessions.

I couldn't hear exactly what Rumsfeld was saying on the phone, but occasionally his voice rose a little for emphasis. Tony Dolan had lingered by the door. He heard Rumsfeld say after a long pause, "I just don't want to put more rocks in your knapsack."

After a while, the secretary came back to the table and we continued our discussion. He didn't say a word about the conversation. I didn't know it at the time, but the president had just called to tell him he wouldn't be accepting Rumsfeld's resignation. Rumsfeld had offered to resign twice over the Abu Ghraib scandal. But it would be many, many months before he'd tell this to me or to the press (and even then it was off the record). It might have made him look better—at the time all the stories were about why Rumsfeld wasn't taking responsibility and stepping down. "Look," he could have said, "I tried to resign but the president asked me to stay." For whatever reason, he never did.

Rumsfeld quickly put together a group to sort out all the detainee issues that came up from Abu Ghraib. He also ordered a probe of activities at every U.S. military prison around the world. Two men were put in charge of the investigatory group—one a civilian, the other from the military. The civilian was Preston Geren III, also known as "Pete." He was a former Democratic congressman from Texas. Everybody liked Pete, who was so soft-spoken and noncontroversial that it almost seemed that his purpose was to hang around the Pentagon to fill whatever vacancy popped up. Over four years, he'd be given at least four different jobs, including special assistant to the secretary of defense, interim secretary of the air force, undersecretary of the army, and then secretary of the army.

The other person put in charge of the detainee group was General Mike Maples. General Maples was also a friendly guy. Neither he nor

Geren struck me as hard chargers likely to drill down to the core of an issue, though. To me, General Maples bore an unfortunate resemblance to the guy who'd played Mr. Carson on WKRP in Cincinnati. I could never shake the image of General Maples as a well-meaning radio station manager who was in over his head. (Maples went on to be the director of the Defense Intelligence Agency.)

The Geren-Maples group kept holding meetings and hiring staff, but they never seemed to come up with many useful products. And Rumsfeld wanted a thorough, detailed report about what happened and what we were doing about it—what we came to call the "detainee book." It didn't appear to me that Pete Geren had the first clue what to do. But could anyone blame him? He was from Congress. So he did what any former congressman would do: look busy and wait for someone else to do the hard stuff. It was brilliant. Because of course that's exactly what happened. As Rumsfeld became more impatient, Larry Di Rita directed that the task of writing the detainee book should fall to my office. Unfortunately, because we had so much of our own work to do, the task of drafting the book kept moving from one person's hands to another. Eventually, the speechwriters turned out an eighty- or ninety-page treatise. We also were asked to put in an appendix that absolved three people being criticized in the press as architects of the detainee issue: DoD general counsel Jim Haynes, Steve Cambone, and Doug Feith. I think the exoneration idea came from Haynes, Cambone, and Feith. It was a long, convoluted digression that basically said that no one was responsible for any of the abuses that took place. And even if someone was responsible, it wasn't them.

Whenever we asked the Geren-Maples group for help in fact-checking the book, they took forever to get back to us. They seemed to have no idea how to verify the assertions we were making. At one point, in response to some of our questions, they sent us down some documents to help us. I was impressed by their unusual responsiveness. It turned out that the documents came from one of the earlier versions of the book we'd sent them. They were using our old book as their only source to verify the accuracy of our new book. This was not a good sign of the project's intellectual rigor. I guess it goes without saying that the detainee book that Secretary Rumsfeld had such high hopes for was never released to the public. It does, however, make a nice paperweight.

As Rumsfeld prepared for his testimony, the Geren-Maples group met with him every day, including weekends, to figure out what had happened and what Rumsfeld should say. I attended nearly every meeting, as did Larry and Tony.

Usually I said nothing. I just listened and took notes. Occasionally, Rumsfeld would direct instructions to me. "Steve had a good point. Make sure that's in my testimony." Or "We ought to think about putting that in, Matt." I'd nod and scribble it down. Other than that, I'm sure I didn't make an impression on anyone at all.

Everyone was giving Rumsfeld input on what he should say in his testimony. Torie Clarke, his former press aide, offered edits that made sure Rumsfeld was showing genuine regret. Karen Hughes from the White House suggested that we make reference to its being a member of the military, not the media, who first alerted authorities to the abuses. Larry also called me into his office with an idea from the White House.

"They want a Richard Clarke moment in the testimony," he told me.

Richard Clarke was the antiterrorism expert who worked for Presidents Clinton and Bush. During the hearings to investigate the U.S. intelligence failure relating to the 9/11 attacks, Clarke offered a dramatic opening statement. "Your government failed you," he said somberly. "Those entrusted with protecting you failed you." Then he added theatrically, "And I failed you." Everyone in the committee room was aghast. Members of Congress were the last people to take responsibility for anything, so to hear someone else do it was either the bravest or craziest thing they ever heard. I couldn't remember one senator or congressman who said, for example, "I voted for the war in Iraq. I was supposed to oversee its progress. I failed you in doing my job." And you could be sure no member of Congress intended to take the slightest responsibility for Abu Ghraib, even though they were supposed to oversee operations of military prisons as well. People were so impressed by Richard Clarke's profuse, dramatic apology that it didn't matter that he basically admitted he was to blame for 9/11 or that he was later found to have questions raised about his credibility. Instead he was a hero, a sensation. That is what folks in the White House hoped Rumsfeld would become.

Rumsfeld wasn't one for theatrics, though. Apologizing also meant that Abu Ghraib would be forever attached to him. He'd basically be saying it was all his fault, when many people in the Pentagon were telling him it wasn't. Still, we were told by Senate staff that if Rumsfeld didn't personally apologize for the scandal, several Republicans on the committee would call for him to step down. (This included the usual suspects: John McCain and his robotron, Lindsey Graham.) Rumsfeld wasn't the type to succumb to congressional pressure, so I had no idea whether he would apologize even if he wanted to. .

So with the guidance flowing in, I sat in my office and began to write. I stayed in there for hours every day, only coming out for brief bathroom breaks or lunch at the Pentagon Subway.

Secretary Rumsfeld was patient with me, but he'd keep sending ideas down and once in a while would ask, "How's it coming?" When I finally finished my first draft, I asked Tony to come into the office to look it over. He had no idea what to expect. Tony flipped through my pages quickly. He didn't need to read every line. He wanted to see the structure, especially the beginning and the end.

"This is good," he said, looking surprised. "This is very good." He said he'd been petrified about what I'd come up with, since I'd only been on the job a few weeks.

Rumsfeld seemed to like it too. He would, as usual, make edit after edit, sometimes just "changing happy to glad," as he put it. But it was his way of making himself comfortable with the speech. We had a cycle that we followed for the next three years. I'd draft something. He'd edit it. I'd turn around a new draft. He'd edit it again. Sometimes this would happen for five or six rounds until he wrote the magic words: "Go final." The Abu Ghraib testimony, as you might imagine, went through several rounds.

The day before the testimony, our entire Geren-Maples detainee group met with General Antonio Taguba, who was investigating the scandal. I thought General Taguba was nice enough, and he was becoming a well-known face around the country amid what was shaping up to be one of the biggest scandals in recent history.

"The famous General Taguba!" Rumsfeld greeted him. The secretary was being warm in his way. Taguba seemed shy and tentative. People asked him questions about his investigation. Rumsfeld was his usual inquisitive self. The whole meeting was cordial and respectful. It seemed useful.

Years later, I was surprised to read a completely different account of that meeting from General Taguba himself. Taguba said that everyone in the room was in denial. Were we all bewildered by what had happened? Yes. Confused about events? Certainly. But nobody in that room failed to recognize how serious the situation was.

General Taguba also characterized Rumsfeld's greeting of him as "mocking." I didn't see Rumsfeld that way. Oh, I'd certainly seen him use tones that some might consider mocking, don't get me wrong. But not this time. He had to testify before Congress and looked to the general to help him get the facts right. It wasn't in his interest to try to belittle the lead investigator or to sound out of touch on the issue. Everyone was looking at Rumsfeld in the most sinister terms. The darkest explanation had to be the right one.

At the Pentagon, I was surprised by the tendency of so many senior military officials to be such fragile flowers. There were any number of top military brass who complained that Rumsfeld was rude to them, or criticized them, or didn't go to their retirement party. These were supposed to be gruff, battle-hardened men, right? Yet the secretary always seemed to be accused of hurting their feelings. But how do you tell a man who worked his way through Princeton on a scholarship, who twice served as secretary of defense, who had been considered multiple times for the vice presidency, and who ran two corporations to please try to be a little less scary?

Finally, the morning of the testimony arrived. Rumsfeld was going to appear first before the Senate Armed Services Committee and take all their questions, then go over to the House. Nobody had told me that I could go with him in the motorcade, and it never occurred to me to ask. So I watched it on television in my office.

It looked like every senator on the committee was there for the start of the hearing, which was rare. Witnesses had to sit through entire hearings, but senators almost never did. But this hearing was the big time. All of the senators had hard-hitting questions at the ready. They had probably practiced looking outraged in the mirror. Donald Rumsfeld, the tough, hard-charging secretary of defense whom they'd all fawned over a year earlier, was now squarely in their sights.

I watched the secretary pull out the pages that I'd given him and he'd edited and place them carefully on the table in front of him. He squinted into the nearly blinding lights of almost every camera in the world. His face was serious and grave. In the next few minutes, his future in his job might very well be decided.

He delivered the remarks slowly and, I thought, forcefully. Right out of the box, we tried for our White House–ordered "Richard Clarke moment." Looking directly at the senators, the secretary said, "In recent weeks, there has been a good deal of discussion about the events that took place at Abu Ghraib prison. These events took place on my watch. As secretary of defense, I am accountable for them. And I take full responsibility."

Hours before the climactic hearing was to begin, someone had leaked to the press that Rumsfeld was going to appear but refuse to apologize. It was one of the only smart press things we ever did, because when Rumsfeld did apologize, it caught everyone by surprise. "I feel terrible about what happened to these Iraqi detainees. They are human beings. They were in U.S. custody. Our country had an obligation to treat them right. We didn't do that. That was wrong." Then Rumsfeld apologized directly to the detainees, using the short, crisp sentences he favored. "To those Iraqis who were mistreated by members of U.S. armed forces, I offer my deepest apology. It was un-American. And it was inconsistent with the values of our nation." He even said that he was looking at some way to provide financial compensation to them. The compensation idea seemed to have come from Rumsfeld personally.

In his statement, Rumsfeld also apologized to Congress and to the president for his failure to "convey the gravity of this" when the department first learned about the abuses and reported it. In total, Rumsfeld apologized about six times. At Tony's prodding, the remarks also warned the country that more photos were going to come out.

Rumors of a Rumsfeld resignation continued. At the hearing, Senator Evan Bayh asked the question everyone was thinking. "Even though you weren't personally involved in the underlying acts here," he said, "would it serve to demonstrate how serious we take the situation ... if you were to resign?"

Rumsfeld paused. He didn't mention that he'd already tried to do just that. Instead he said bluntly, and maybe a little sadly, "That's possible."

The coverage of the testimony was so widespread that every major network carried it live. They even interrupted *One Life to Live*. Large excerpts of the statement appeared in the *New York Times* and the *Washington Post*. It was the most important speech I'd ever written, or probably ever would write, and it happened in my first weeks on the job.

Unfortunately, Rumsfeld's apology and acceptance of responsibility didn't get him the Richard Clarke star treatment. But at least the Republicans refrained from calling for him to step down.

Rumsfeld soon had another surprise in store for the press. Within a few days of the testimony, I was called and told that I needed to be at Andrews Air Force Base the next day for a top-secret trip. We'd be going to Abu Ghraib prison to see the conditions of the prison firsthand. My first flight to Iraq would take place under the most stressful of circumstances: fifteen hours in the air, fifteen hours on the ground in Baghdad, and fifteen hours back. I didn't even have a government passport yet, so I had to use my own.

I met up with the secretary and maybe two dozen other people (which was actually a streamlined entourage) at Andrews Air Force Base. We took off on an E4-B, a vast military plane the same size as Air Force One. The jet had a movie theater, a sleeping area, a conference room, and a large staff office where everyone could sit at a desk. There were very few windows. What was it with the military and windows?

Rumsfeld had his own private office, complete with a shower, closet, and bunk bed. He also had a leather captain's chair and a sizable desk where he could work. Donald Rumsfeld was a working fiend. He always needed something to do. He worked all day, into the night, and on Saturdays and Sundays. The whole staff fell in love with Joyce Rumsfeld when she bought a house in Maryland and persuaded her husband to go out there on the weekends. That meant staff wouldn't have to come in to the Pentagon those days.

While on our way to Iraq, I had one of my first private conversations with my new boss. Maybe I wasn't bold enough, but in my first months with the secretary, I never felt comfortable just coming in to talk to him. And the military environment was such that informality wasn't encouraged. When Rumsfeld first started at the Pentagon, in fact, a military guard used to stand outside his office door. Talk about intimidating. Rumsfeld thought having a guy standing sentry all day was "nutty." "That guy must have had a million better things to do," he said. So Rumsfeld reassigned him.

In any event, in those early days the only way I usually talked to Rumsfeld directly was when he initiated it. I had brought on the plane a draft of a speech he was going to deliver to the troops stationed at Abu prison. He was reading something else when I entered and didn't look at me. So I placed the remarks carefully on his desk and started to walk out.

"Hey, Matt," he said without looking up. "What have you got for me?"

I told him I had a draft speech. "Good," he said. "I have some thoughts." We started talking, and I sat down in the chair across from his desk. Rumsfeld was determined to overcome the scandal. I think he was delighted to have someone new around whom he could tutor on how to weather a storm.

"I guess that testimony was your baptism by fire," he said.

I laughed. "It can't get much worse."

His eyes twinkled. "Let's hope not."

We talked about what he wanted to say to the troops in Baghdad. "It's awful what happened," he said. "They need to know that we take it seriously. They also need to be reassured."

He told me that he'd stopped reading the newspapers. He'd read press summaries, but that was it. Instead he was reading biographies, like one of Ulysses S. Grant. A lot of people were thinking about history in those days. People in the Pentagon kept giving Rumsfeld historical parallels to use. Think of the hedgerows on D-Day, for example. Eisenhower had failed to account for them and they slowed the Allied advance onto the beaches of Normandy, costing hundreds if not thousands of American lives. Horrible things like that were just ugly facts of war.

"We'll get through this," Rumsfeld said. I wasn't sure if he was talking about himself, the military, or both. "I'm a survivor," he added.

Once in Baghdad, we headed directly to Abu Ghraib prison. It was a scary visit. Iraq was still a very violent place. People were being killed by roadside bombs all the time. We rode to the prison in broken-down buses that traveled far too slowly for my comfort down bumpy dirt roads.

As we drove through the prison grounds, Iraqi prisoners slouched behind chain-link fences. The fences looked like they could topple over in a decent gust of wind.

Our bus was moving very slowly. As we passed, some of the Iraqi prisoners started to congregate. The mob started moving closer and closer to the fences. "Uh, shouldn't we be moving a little faster?" I said to someone next to me.

Most people on the bus were chatting away as if nothing out of the ordinary was going on. We were in Abu Ghraib prison, in Iraq, the site of one of the world's biggest scandals. But to them it was just another day in the office.

The detainees started raising their middle fingers at us. I could see some mouthing words. Good thing I didn't speak Arabic.

Seeing the detainees waving their fingers at us, Larry Di Rita turned to General Dick Myers, a genial Kansan. "Look, general," Larry said to the chairman of the Joint Chiefs of Staff. "The Iraqis are saying, 'You're number one.' "

As we got out of the bus, Rumsfeld walked straight past the pens holding the detainees. He was wearing a dark gray business suit and steel-toed work boots, and his face was all business. I followed just behind him in a blazer and khakis. I was carrying an extremely heavy case that contained my laptop, printer, and copies of speeches. As we were walking, photographers snapped pictures. The images of Rumsfeld at Abu Ghraib became iconic, and I inadvertently happened to be standing just behind him. One shot turned up the next day on the front page of every newspaper across the country. My mom cut it out of *Time* magazine.

The secretary next joined General Myers to give impromptu remarks to a group of troops who'd crammed themselves into a small dining hall. I was behind the crowd, struggling to hear Rumsfeld. He called the scandal a "body blow" to the department. Then he added: "Don't let anyone tell you that America is what's wrong with the world, because it's not true." The soldiers cheered. At another point in his remarks the secretary repeated what he'd told me on the plane, that he didn't read the newspapers—an admission the soldiers cheered. Then he said, "I'm a survivor," which won him more cheers and became the headline in the next day's news. After that, I knew we were going to survive the scandal but there would be many more controversies to come. And I wasn't sure we were well equippped to handle them.

One of the great untold stories of the Rumsfeld era was the near-absolute power Larry Di Rita wielded in the critical years of the Iraq war. Widely perceived as the second most important person in the building, Larry was good at solving Rumsfeld's problems. As he did, his power grew. People who needed something knew to schmooze Larry, who seemed to involve himself in nearly every aspect of Pentagon operations, his obvious closeness to Rumsfeld allowing him extraordinary authority. Larry, practically alone, had the privilege of walking into Rumsfeld's office unannounced. He could get scheduled any meeting he wanted, and cancel those he didn't. At meetings with the secretary, Larry would interrupt generals or service secretaries. Although Rumsfeld had a separate relationship with senior military officials, when it came to his civilian staff, Larry built a bubble around Rumsfeld that was not easily pierced.

Larry was aided in his efforts by a person he helped bring in as Rumsfeld's senior military assistant, Vice Admiral James Stavridis. The position of senior military assistant is probably one of the most powerful but least well known in the entire United States military. The SMA was in charge of Rumsfeld's schedule, travel, and logistics, and vetted pretty much all the information Rumsfeld received. When Rumsfeld wanted anything done, no matter how small, he usually went to the SMA first, Larry second. Shortly after I met Stavridis, he told me that he commanded a ship involved in an unsuccessful military strike on Osama bin Laden in 1998. Years later, Stavridis was in the Pentagon during the September 11 attack. "I tried to kill bin Laden and barely missed," Stav said. "And a few years later, he tried to do the same thing to me." He seemed haunted by the notion. I couldn't say for sure, but it seemed unlikely that the same thought was keeping bin Laden up at night.

Stavridis had been a one-star admiral on the verge of promotion to two stars when the job of senior military assistant presented itself. When he became the SMA, Stav was "frocked," or bumped up past the two-star rank to a rank of three stars. The leap from one star to three stars almost overnight was virtually unprecedented in the modern era. In fact, Stav was promoted faster than the architect of the Iraq surge, General David Petraeus.

One might think that a man who'd skipped ahead in line so quickly would proceed with a little care in his new position. Not Admiral Stavridis. He was so proud of his job's perks that he added more. He

made sure to have a special car on SecDef motorcades reserved specifically for the senior military assistant. He tried to get one of Rumsfeld's
personal assistants to go shopping for him while in foreign countries.
Like some other top officers, he had a young assistant carry his bags. On
trips he'd offer fawning toasts to Rumsfeld during late-night dinners.
He wrote over-the-top mash notes that praised the secretary's performances. (Years later, when the notes were discovered, they were the subject of a lot of snickering in the Pentagon's corridors.) I once saw him
trying to fix the squeak in one of the boss's chairs.

Stavridis was surprisingly political for a military man. He'd help
us craft statements to defend the secretary from partisan attacks. He
also took charge of a project to promote all of Rumsfeld's accomplishments at the Department of Defense when he was under attack from
the Democrats.

With a Ph.D. from Tufts University, Stav was undoubtedly bright.
He seemed to fancy himself a warrior-scholar, sort of a blending of
Napoleon and Aristotle. He loved fine wines, wrote books, and spent a
lot of time casually sharing this information with the Pentagon press
corps. He was one of those people who thought himself a great writer
but really wasn't. His edits to the secretary's speeches were usually unhelpful. His favorite word was *fabulous*—not exactly a word you'd like to
attach to a tough-talking secretary of defense. Still, I usually found that
he was more likely to help me if I appealed to him as a fellow scribe.

In 2005, Stav wrote an article called "Deconstructing War," a collec-
tion of clichés and buzzwords that nonetheless won wide acclaim. I
don't think many people actually read it. It began, "War is changing, and
not for the better." What exactly did that mean? Wars used to be great,
but now they are getting worse? The next sentence was a trip through
incomprehensibility. "Like much else in our world, [war] is essentially
deconstructing and re-emerging as a changed enterprise." Then Stav
made a bold prediction. "Clearly, we will continue to engage in some
form of armed conflict in the years and decades ahead." "We swim in a
strange sea," he added. And all this was only on page 1. Stav also wrote a
book on Navy life (which Larry Di Rita reviewed on the conservative
website National Review Online).

Together Stav and Larry were a devastatingly powerful combo, the
Pentagon equivalent of Bill O'Reilly teaming up with Oprah (a possibility

almost too frightening to contemplate). Whatever they wanted to happen at the department tended to happen. They even let it be known that they were drafting some of Rumsfeld's snowflakes—the most sacred of all things in the Rumsfeld pantheon. Whomever they liked and wanted to bring to the secretary's notice was usually promoted. Whomever they disliked and didn't want around Rumsfeld faced mounting obstacles. One of those who ended up facing such obstacles, as it turned out, was me.

Having gone through the Abu Ghraib experience together, Rumsfeld and I bonded—or at least, I thought we did. He seemed to like me, and I really liked him. He even told me we should meet regularly. Anytime I wanted to see him, he said, just let Delonnie or Larry know.

So time and again, I did just that. And time and again, I was told it wasn't possible. Every once in a while a meeting got on the secretary's schedule, but it was soon canceled. I'd ask Larry about it. "Unavoidable," he'd say. Or "Yeah, we better reschedule that." He didn't. Rumsfeld stopped calling me. I stopped seeing him. This went on for months. I kept writing speeches and guessing what Rumsfeld wanted to say. He'd send down edits or Larry would convey them to me, but we'd rarely speak.

Eventually, I realized that Larry wasn't trying to help me see him. He was trying to stop me. He and Stav controlled all the meetings. What other explanation could there be?

I went to Tony's newspaper-cluttered office for advice. Tony had stacks and stacks of paper around him all the time. Sometimes they were old editions of the New York Post he hadn't read, or a pile of clippings he thought were worth rereading or turning into some memo. Tony could find great meaning in a gossip item about Britney Spears.

Tony confirmed what I thought. "You can't do your job well if you can't talk to him." Tony tried to alert Rumsfeld to the problem, but even his memos to Rumsfeld were not reaching him. "You owe it to Rumsfeld to make every effort to see him," he said.

The secretary was in the middle of conducting two difficult wars and had a million other things on his plate. I didn't want to bother him about something as small as scheduling a meeting, but I'd tried everything else.

At one point, I was invited to a meeting where Rumsfeld was present. Larry and Stav would allow me to attend large gatherings where I could take notes but not have much personal interaction with the boss.

After the meeting was over, I maneuvered my way into the secretary's path. "Mr. Secretary, can I borrow you for a second?" I asked.

"Sure," he replied. It was the first time we'd spoken in ages.

"You once told me you wanted us to have regular meetings to talk about speeches," I reminded. I noticed Stav watching our conversation out of the corner of his eye.

He nodded. "Yes," he said. "We've got to do that."

"I agree. But every time I try to schedule one, it gets canceled."

"Well, push back," he instructed me, chuckling. "Don't let these guys manhandle you!"

"Okay," I said. "I'll do that."

"Good!" he replied. He glanced at his schedule, which was printed on a pocket card, and walked off to his next appointment.

After that, another speechwriting meeting got placed on his calendar. This time I had the secretary's personal backing, or so I thought. Then Delonnie sent me a note saying she was sorry, but this meeting was canceled too.

I was getting exasperated. I called Delonnie directly.

"Hi, Delonnie," I said. "Listen, I saw that my meeting with the secretary was canceled."

"Yes," she said crisply.

"Well, did you know this is the tenth meeting in a row that has been canceled?"

At first she said nothing. "The secretary was the one who asked me to cancel the meeting," she replied. She gave me the impression that he was the one who was canceling all of them.

"Oh," I said. Maybe Rumsfeld had just been being nice when he told me to push for a meeting. Maybe he didn't like me as much as I thought.

More time passed. Then I received a snowflake from Rumsfeld. (At least I assumed it was from Rumsfeld, but who knew?) It said he wanted to see me to talk about an upcoming speech. He'd even set a date and time. This was my chance, maybe my last chance. I told Tony I was determined to make my case to Rumsfeld, no matter who else was in the room. If I couldn't spend time talking with him about his speeches, I couldn't serve him well. And if I couldn't serve him well, I shouldn't be there.

Tony smiled as I left for the meeting. "Good luck!" he called after me. I wondered if he thought he'd ever see me again.

I stood in the lobby waiting for Rumsfeld, just as I had the first time I met him. Larry soon joined me, as usual acting like the BMOC. He chatted with this person and that, then joked a bit with Stavridis and laughed loudly. It was clear they wanted this meeting to be over as quickly as possible. I clung to my notebook and stood awkwardly to the side. Nobody was lining up to talk to me. If there'd been a locker around, I was sure, Larry would have stuffed me in it.

Rumsfeld, as usual, was at his stand-up desk when we came into the office. He was very businesslike. Not a lot of pleasantries. He had a folder filled with notes or memos that he wanted to share with me. I took notes furiously as he spoke. I asked him a few questions. This was how the process was supposed to work.

"This was helpful," Rumsfeld observed with satisfaction as the meeting ended. The secretary was about to dismiss us. He looked busy. But this was my chance, and I had to take it.

"Mr. Secretary, can I say something?" I said as everyone else in the room were gathering their things. Rumsfeld nodded and leaned against the desk to look at me. Everyone else froze.

"You're right. This meeting was very helpful," I said. "But Mr. Secretary, do you realize this is the first meeting we've had to discuss your speeches in months?"

"Well, you need to push for a meeting!" he said.

"I have pushed, sir," I responded. "And I've had ten meetings with you canceled in a row."

The secretary looked genuinely surprised. "Ten?"

"Yes," I replied. I pulled out a pile of e-mails I had received canceling all of my meetings. I'd brought them just in case I needed them. "I was told you asked to cancel them."

Rumsfeld's mood darkened. "I never told anyone to cancel one of them," he said. "Not one." I didn't expect him to say that.

"Well, that's not what I was told," I informed him. "In fact, I've sent you memos about this."

He looked like he didn't have the slightest idea what I was talking about.

"I just think that it's important for me to see you from time to time, not too often. It's just that it helps to hear you and—"

"Well, of course," he replied, as if that was perfectly obvious.

Rumsfeld seemed genuinely baffled. "Larry, this is your guy," Rumsfeld said, pointing at me. "You could schedule a meeting for him."

Larry nodded. "Yes. I can also cancel them too," he said, laughing. Larry always had a quip at the ready. That was his MO. What usually happened after Larry cracked a joke was that everyone laughed, including the secretary, and whatever Rumsfeld was annoyed with Larry about would blow over. Except not this time.

Larry was still laughing when I turned to him. I looked him directly in the eye. His smile started to fade.

"Excuse me, Larry, but that is *exactly* what you do," I charged. "I have asked you to help me schedule these meetings, and mysteriously they keep getting canceled. I know you like to build this cocoon around the secretary, but I don't think it's very helpful."

Oh my God. What was I doing? Was I going to get fired? I'd never before seen anyone call Larry on anything. No one had been crazy enough to do it, except for me. But it was the truth. The truth was being uttered at last. And Rumsfeld heard it.

A silence dropped on Rumsfeld's office for a moment that seemed to drag on for hours. I'm not sure anyone knew how to react.

Rumsfeld looked at both Larry and me, turning from one to the other and then back again. I imagined the penultimate scene in *Return of the Jedi* when Darth Vader is forced to choose between the evil Emperor and Luke Skywalker. Vader looks at the emperor, then he looks at Luke, then he looks back at the emperor, then he looks back at Luke again. Until, finally, he makes his choice.

"Larry," Rumsfeld began, "I need to see Matt. He needs to hear how I say things and how I think."

"Yes, sir," Larry said. "I'll make sure it happens."

Rumsfeld started to get charged up. I think he realized that the person being shortchanged the most as a result of these cancelations was not me but him. He took his recorder and dictated a memo to himself (this was where snowflakes were born). "I want to schedule a weekly meeting with Matt to discuss my speeches," he said. "It's important that we do that." He did not want them canceled, he told us. If for some reason they had to be canceled, they would be rescheduled as soon as possible.

"Yes, sir," Larry replied. I didn't look at him, but I could feel his glare on me. My heart was racing. But now I realized I wasn't going to be shown the door. I was going to win. Rumsfeld was choosing to save Luke Skywalker!

I hurried out of there as fast as I could and was in Tony's office within ten minutes. He was on a call and about to wave me away. But after one look at my face, he got off the phone immediately. I recounted the whole drama in Rumsfeld's office. Tony took it all in, completely absorbed. "That was incredibly brave," Tony said. He'd had his own tangles with Larry, which was why Larry tried to keep Rumsfeld and Tony apart.

I wasn't sure how I'd managed to survive that confrontation with Larry. But whatever the reason, no more meetings were canceled. I'd broken through. I had the feeling, though, that a lot of other people never did overcome the Larry factor. They resented Larry, but they saw the obvious affection Rumsfeld had for him. So they gave up. It's impossible to know how much damage that caused the secretary or how much information he was never allowed to hear.

It may have been my imagination, but Larry never seemed to be quite the same after our confrontation. Things got more difficult for him when Stavridis left. Stav was promoted to commander of the U.S. Southern Command, which included Latin America and the prison at Guantánamo Bay, Cuba. I wouldn't claim that Stav thought he had a lock on the job, but a few months before his nomination, he conspicuously started listening to Spanish-language tapes. This prompted some of us to wonder: how long does it take to learn *fabuloso?* President Obama recently named him to the prestigious post of Supreme Allied Commander of Europe, the job once held by General Eisenhower.

Once Larry's iron grip on Rumsfeld was loosened, my relations with the secretary warmed up considerably. The best times to get to know him were during our treks across the world. In three years I traveled with him to forty countries on nearly every continent. We took flights that circled the globe. I'd call my parents from places like Bangladesh, Morocco, Istanbul, and Ecuador. My young nephews, Michael and Eric, would track my journeys on a globe.

With Rumsfeld, almost all the trips were good-natured marches of misery. Older than his staff, in some cases by decades, he still ran circles around us: up early, to bed late, and ready to get a move on at the crack of dawn the next day. We'd pass so quickly through so many time zones that many of us were prescribed Ambien so we could sleep. On my first trip, I made the big mistake of going to the back of the plane while we were refueling in midair. When I got back to my assigned seat, I was never so grateful for the invention of air sickness bags. I was terrified that the macho members of Team Rumsfeld would notice my pathetic state—but they were all asleep. However, for the rest of the trips I took, I wore a motion-sickness patch on the back of my neck. Rumsfeld could never resist asking about it.

He took every trip in stride, no matter what the circumstances. We were once in Baghdad when it was 120 degrees. I was with Rumsfeld and two of his top aides, Bill Luti and Peter Rodman. We were all wearing business suits. We boarded helicopters for a forty-five-minute flight to Kurdistan, in Iraq's north. It was so hot that the military guys on the chopper gave us each a two-liter bottle of water and told us to drink it on the flight, because that was about how much fluid we'd probably lose from sweating. I'd never been so uncomfortable. Dust flew into my hair, my eyes, my teeth. Water dripped down my face. My suit stuck to me. When the helicopter landed, Luti, Rodman, and I disembarked. We looked like we'd just emerged, fully clothed, from a swimming pool. Just a total disaster.

Rumsfeld got out of his chopper, which was the same as ours, and looked like a million dollars. Not a hair out of place. His clothes looked untouched by dust. Not a drop of perspiration could be seen. He strolled by us as if he didn't have a care in the world. I don't know how he did it. I thought his Black Hawk must have been air-conditioned, but everyone assured me it wasn't.

One of the most memorable trips I took with Rumsfeld was to Mongolia. On the flight there, Rumsfeld was informed that he'd be given a traditional gift: a brown Mongolian gelding. The secretary was expected to name it.

This led to a furious brainstorming session where we were all asked to offer Rumsfeld suggested names. They ranged from the boring (Max) to the patriotic (America) to the thematic (Liberty). Rumsfeld listened, but never indicated which if any of our suggestions he liked. As it turned out, he had a name in mind all along but didn't bother to tell us. He called the horse Montana because the terrain of Mongolia looked a lot like that state and because Montana was where his trea-sured Joyce was from.

The horse the Mongolians presented to Rumsfeld was not exactly the crème de la crème of the equine world. But Rumsfeld loved it. Normally in Mongolia, once the horse was offered to a visiting VIP, the VIP would ask a Mongolian herder to care for it and put it out to pasture. Rumsfeld did that as well. But that wasn't what he wanted to do. For some time on that trip, he mused about getting that horse and taking it to his ranch in New Mexico. Hey, it was his, wasn't it? Why should he leave it behind?

The gift of the horse—come to think of it, the Greeks had started that tradition, hadn't they?—led to one of the only times Rumsfeld really got mad at me. When we were back on the plane, he beamed at me. "Did you see that horse?" he asked. "Wasn't it great?"

"It was very nice," I replied.

"I sure wish I could find a way to bring it back. Joyce would love it."

At that moment some bad impulse caused me to put my foot in my mouth. "Now, Mr. Secretary," I said with a tone of skepticism, "don't you think that the whole thing is a scam?"

"Scam?" he asked. "What do you mean?"

"Well, don't you think they bring that same horse out to every VIP who comes to visit? Then as soon as the person leaves, they take his name off it and get it ready for the next guy." It seemed logical to me.

"That's not true!" he said. "They wouldn't do that!" He seemed shocked by the very thought that someone would behave so dishonorably. Besides, that was his horse! At that moment, he reminded me of the dad in the movie A Christmas Story, who won some gaudy leg lamp in a contest and believed it was the greatest treasure in the world.

Eventually, Rumsfeld got over that mangy horse. He never brought it back to the States. But I still think he sometimes wonders about what might have been. . . .

Rumsfeld was a man I quickly grew to like and admire. But he was on a downward path after the Abu Ghraib scandal. And things weren't going to get any better for him.

CHAPTER FIVE

"I'M GOING TO DIE WITH THESE DUMMIES"

When Secretary Rumsfeld once was asked if the Department of Defense ever had a communications plan for the war in Iraq, he replied bluntly, "If we had one, we obviously didn't do a very good job." Rumsfeld was preoccupied with the department's ability to communicate with the country. He was particularly concerned about the ease with which Arab media outlets publicized enemy propaganda, while our own media operations were often many news cycles behind.

He worried that in a 24/7 world the department too often showed a nine-to-five mentality. He wanted military officials to have a greater awareness of blogs, YouTube, and the Internet. He was trying to adapt himself.

Once while we were overseas, I was sitting at my desk on our airplane when the secretary asked to see me in his cabin.

When I came in, he pulled out a note that he'd scribbled to himself. One of the European defense ministers had told him that there was some place on the Internet that contained all of Rumsfeld's life history, including places he'd lived and all sorts of personal information. Since I was one of the youngest people on the trip, he probably figured I'd be the best person to know where he could find it.

"I wrote down the name of the website," he said, glancing at his note. "It's something called . . ." As sometimes happened, he'd scribbled so fast that he was now having trouble deciphering what he'd written. "Wika-wakka?" He gave me a look, as if to say, *That can't be right.*

I smiled. "Do you mean Wikipedia?" I asked.

"Yes!" he said. "Yes, that's it."

Most people would assume that a man in his seventies who had a million other things to do was probably completely computer-illiterate. Rumsfeld wasn't. He had a computer on his desk in his office. He made fun of Larry and me for our BlackBerry addiction, but I could tell he was curious about what made the BlackBerry so popular. He sometimes watched YouTube videos, including those making fun of his performances at press conferences. He read the Drudge Report and Google news. But he hadn't yet heard of Wikipedia.

I printed out his Wikipedia entry on the plane's computer. (We usually had spotty Internet access while we were in the air.) Then I brought the pages to the secretary so he could see them for himself.

Rumsfeld's Wikipedia profile concerned him, but not for the reason I thought. It wasn't that he was concerned about how he was depicted. Rather, he wanted to make sure that information about his kids—their names and where they lived—wasn't available to the general public.

Still, Rumsfeld being Rumsfeld, he couldn't help editing the pages I gave him. "This isn't right," he said, looking at some factoid. "Neither is this."

He wanted to know how the site got its information in the first place. I told him that anyone could edit a profile on Wikipedia. So he told me to go and correct his. I suggested that might not be a good idea because Wikipedia could track the IP address of anyone who edited an entry. If we edited his, I said, there'd no doubt be some press story saying Rumsfeld was so vain that he was updating his Wikipedia profile.

"But some of this isn't true!" he said, genuinely puzzled that someone would post information on the Internet that wasn't accurate. Then he shook his head and laughed. "But you're probably right."

Rumsfeld was determined to fix our public affairs operation, however. And that needed a lot of work. The Pentagon's press operation was run by a very large staff of civil servants and military personnel. Maybe twenty or thirty public affairs specialists sat among a maze of carrels while the director of the room sat in a glass cage and watched over them. It was reminiscent of a secretarial pool from the 1950s or '60s, without the Smith-Corona typewriters. I sometimes expected to see Lucille Ball walk in with a steno pad looking for Mr. Mooney.

Most of the press officers were probably Democrats, but the

problem was not that they were partisan. The problem was that those who wanted to help were given no direction and the rest were mostly inert. Many would come in around 8:30 or 9:00 and breeze out by 4:59 P.M. Nothing would prevent their on-time departure—not some major crisis abroad, not even a war. At night, that giant room was so deserted that tumbleweeds blew by desks. A sizable number of them lacked any sense of urgency or interest in what the administration was doing. One Pentagon reporter compared prying information from them to going on an Easter egg hunt. Sometimes you'd want to put a mirror under their noses to see if they were breathing.

Forget about their being proactive. They rarely, if ever, came up with an interesting story to pitch to a reporter. Their job was to wait for the phone to ring and hold morale-building events. There was almost always a party going on with cakes and cookies and people telling jokes and giving one another awards. There was an annual chili cook-off. If ever you needed a sugar fix, you could find something almost any day in the press room.

Our speechwriting office was connected to the press room by a corridor, so we were all part of one massive office suite. My deputy in the speechwriting office, Thayer Scott, thought that we speechwriters had a PR problem. Compared to the rest of the press room, we looked like a bunch of young, preppy Ivy League guys who thought we knew everything. I had a degree from Columbia. Thayer had gone to Princeton. Two others on staff had gone to Dartmouth. Even our intern was from Yale.

I could see how we could sometimes come off as arrogant and aloof. One day, one of the longest-serving women in the press room came up to me when I was standing in the hallway. She always seemed overly interested in everyone's comings and goings, and was very touchy-feely. She reminded me of the woman in the movie *Office Space* who approaches people and says in the most annoying tone, "Looks like someone has a case of the Mondays." So that's what I called her: "Case of the Mondays."

"I just don't know why you don't come by more often and say hello," she said to me, grabbing my arm.

"Thanks," I said.

"You just need to come down and introduce yourself to everyone," she said. "People don't know who you are."

"I will," I said politely. Then I asked, "Who are you again?" Her face fell.

In addition to Case of the Mondays, the press room included a guy who wore headphones all day. His job appeared to be to go to a small room, take out VHS tapes that were recording news programs, label them, and then put in a new tape. What was being taped? What happened to the tapes that were taken out? I had no idea.

Other members of the press room would come to us for the most basic information. Considering that they were supposed to be the press professionals, it was sort of disquieting. I was struck by how much the people who were supposed to be in charge of press relations didn't know what the secretary was saying or doing. Members of the press room staff would regularly come into our office and ask things like, "Has the secretary said anything about Iraq lately?" One person on the staff asked Thayer to edit a letter she'd written to a reporter who'd complained about the lack of transparency at the terrorist holding facility at Guantánamo Bay. In her first line, she wrote, "We have used extreme measures to ensure access at Guantánamo Bay." Considering the outcry over interrogations at the prison, Thayer pointed out that she might want to find a different way to say that.

One of the senior press people, a naval officer with more than twenty years of experience, came in to tell us she'd just been put in charge of outreach to "our blog guys." Naturally, she had absolutely no idea what bloggers were or how to find them. She was amazed to learn that you could put colors and graphics into an e-mail. Our intern, a brilliant young man named Keith Urbahn, put together a list of some of the top military bloggers and handed it to her. It was a shudder-inducing thought. At the Department of Defense, representing the most fearsome military on earth, our Internet communications strategy was in the hands of a twenty-one-year-old kid who hadn't yet graduated from college. Considering the alternatives, we were lucky. By 2008, the head of our outreach to "blog guys" had been put in charge of all new media for the Department of the Defense and encouraged to talk about the subject at conferences across the country. It would be like Donald Trump teaching Jazzercise.

One of the worst things anyone in the public affairs office of the Pentagon could do was have an original idea that required work or innovation. Like a fool, I had one. During my first weeks at the Pentagon, the woman who tipped me to the Rumsfeld job opening, reporter Kate O'Beirne, called the public affairs office to write a story about some of the troops who'd received medals in battle in Afghanistan and Iraq. Her aim was to help support the war effort by putting a human face on the thousands of Americans who were proudly fighting overseas. Whether one supported the war effort or not, our men and women who performed acts of heroism deserved recognition that was as broad as possible.

Kate called several people in the public affairs office for help. And the press room did what they always did—sent her from one person to another without ever answering her request. Their lack of assistance was all the more notable since Kate's husband was the head of personnel at the Pentagon. The press room people didn't care. Getting the list of soldiers who won medals took work, and they didn't want to do it. And since they were civil service, no one could do anything about it as long as they looked like they were trying to help.

Members of Congress experienced the same frustrations that Kate did. Senator Rick Santorum of Pennsylvania actually introduced legislation to require the Pentagon to inform members of Congress when troops from their districts received medals. The Pentagon, through its do-nothing bureaucracy and public affairs ineptitude, was frustrating its own efforts to try to put out positive information about the troops!

So to me it seemed like a good idea for our office to start putting together a one-pager on medal recipients under the title of "Heroes." Our plan was to pick three people per week who'd received awards for heroism and send their names and a brief summary of their heroics to anyone who might be interested—members of the media, other offices in the Pentagon, the White House, Capitol Hill, et cetera. I also proposed that our staff create a product called "Fifty Heroes from Fifty States" to highlight a service member from every state in the Union. This would be followed up on a DoD website that showed a map of the United States. Anyone who clicked on a state would find profiles of medal recipients with their photos.

The idea was simple. The objections within Public Affairs, and the broader Pentagon, were immediate. First, people in our press room told us we were violating privacy rights of military personnel by highlighting them without permission. We responded that all of our material came from press releases that these soldiers had already approved (the problem with the press releases was that no one outside the military ever saw them). Next, the naysayers said that others in Public Affairs should be responsible for highlighting these people, not the speechwriters. But no one ever volunteered. Then our critics said we were exposing troops to danger and terrorist attacks by listing their names and where they were located. We responded that we wouldn't be listing specific locations. At one point, representatives from the Air Force flatly refused to cooperate. We informed the Air Force that this would mean we'd be focusing solely on medal recipients with the Army, Navy, and Marines.

Nothing motivates the services more than their rivalry with the other branches. The Air Force decided that they wanted to be involved after all. Still, this was becoming a total pain in the neck for our office. I decided to show Secretary Rumsfeld an example of what we wanted to do. If he liked it, maybe it would help.

He liked it. So did General Peter Pace, the new chairman of the Joint Chiefs of Staff. And so, apparently, did President Bush. This changed things considerably, at least for a while. Suddenly the military services were calling us to provide their assistance.

This was terrible news for our friends in the public affairs world, though. Now that the secretary wanted this project to go forward, the press room staffers were being assigned to help us. In fact, the guy who sat in the glass cage and ran the room was told to be a key part of the project. He was supposed to corral all of the people under his command—radio and TV bookers, the woman in charge of "our blog guys," maybe even Case of the Mondays—to make this effort a success.

If a great artist ever wanted to construct a sculpture of bureaucracy in its essence, he ought to first meet the man who was sent over to my office to help make the Heroes program work. His every movement and facial expression gave the appearance of complete exhaustion. He wore one of those too-short ties that lay on top of his noticeable paunch. Words seemed to come with great effort. He was as quick as a tub of molasses, as flexible as a rusted fork. And keep in mind: this man had ascended to the top rungs of power in the Pentagon's press room. He was their best. I called him Mr. You Can't Do That. I'd say, "We want to pitch our heroes to the *Today* show." He'd respond wearily, "You can't do that." I'd say, "We might want to highlight them for a CNN segment." Again, he'd reply, "You can't do that."

As you might expect, the press room's idea of promoting DoD heroes was to do as little as possible. The person who ran the radio outreach effort at the Pentagon had a staff of two other people. Their entire workload for the week appeared to be booking one or two low-level Pentagon officials on a few local stations. That was it for the week. And that was all they wanted to do for the Pentagon's heroes.

I don't think the press room folks *wanted* to undermine us. They were just unmotivated and had grown comfortable with doing nothing. A larger than expected number of them had advanced to a civil service level that allowed them to earn more than $100,000 a year for work that in most offices would be done by interns. They would outlast the Bush administration. They couldn't be fired. They were philosopher-kings without the regal bearing or any hint of a philosophy. These also were the people who were managing our communications during a time of war on behalf of the American taxpayer. Most, of course, are still there. If you want to find them, make sure you get to the Pentagon before five o'clock.

Though Larry Di Rita was head of public affairs, his role as taskmaster in the Pentagon meant he was often away from his public affairs office. This meant that he needed able public affairs assistance. Larry sought that assistance from his longtime FOL (friend of Larry's) Eric Ruff. Ruff—no relation to my assistant, Bonita—was a veteran Republican communications operative who'd worked in the Senate for— guess who?—Kay Bailey Hutchison. A shortish, friendly man with glasses and a hyperactive personality, Eric seemed to treasure three things in life: golf, Larry, and Rumsfeld—probably in that order. (Eric's e-mail address was RuffOnGolf.) Eric and I had at least one thing in common: a passion for Diet Coke. In fact, one of my first conversations with Eric concerned where to get the best fountain soda. He was not a fan of 7-Eleven, for example, because they never got the carbonation right. He also didn't like many of the fast-food restaurants because the mix was too syrupy. But McDonald's—they knew how to make a Diet Coke sing.

One of Eric's early challenges was that the McDonald's in the

Pentagon charged for refills. So Eric shrewdly negotiated a deal with the manager that allowed him to get refills for free. He must have drunk four or five Diet Cokes a day (even more than I did), which was disturbing, because Eric was a high-voltage personality to begin with. He was always rushing down some hallway somewhere, flying into a meeting at the last minute. The last thing he needed was caffeine. Nearly every memory I have of Eric in the Pentagon includes an image of him walking down the corridor with a paper cup from McDonald's. Unfortunately, the enterprise Eric showed in fulfilling his caffeine needs turned out to be lacking in other areas.

As a master of the public affairs game, Eric's solution to nearly every problem was an op-ed. Instability in Iraq? Let's write an op-ed on that. Rumsfeld under fire? An op-ed will do the trick. And guess who ended up writing all these op-eds. Eric Ruff? No sirree. He was usually off somewhere with Larry, laughing at his jokes. No, it was my office that was assigned the task of writing dozens of Eric Ruff specials. The routine was usually the same. We'd spend hours writing and editing an op-ed. We'd send it to Eric. Days later, he'd come back asking where it was. We'd give him another copy. He'd go off, and we'd never hear about the op-ed again. In a bizarre way, Eric's strategy worked. By the time we were done writing op-eds, losing them on his desk, and resending them to him, the crisis was usually over. However, with that strategy, we never effectively rebutted an attack on Rumsfeld or the Pentagon.

At one point, Larry assigned Eric the task of overseeing the speechwriting operation and, undoubtedly, keeping me in line. It was a flawed strategy, to say the least. He often appeared not to have read speeches in their entirety, and rarely commented in a timely manner. Eric also had a short attention span and was easily distracted.

Time and again, he'd come to my office with some idea that didn't seem all that well thought-out. As he talked, I'd listen respectfully from my desk. Then as soon as I got a chance, I'd look at him and say something like, "Eric, where did you get that tie?"

Eric would stare down at his tie and smile. He was very proud of his fashion sense. "This?" he'd ask. "I got it at Nordstrom's."

"I love it!" I'd say. (They usually were pretty nice.)

"Oh, you do?" he'd ask, flattered. For the next fifteen minutes, we would discuss how he'd bought the tie and which associate he'd worked with at Nordstroms to get it. Sometimes he'd give me the associate's card and urge me to go see him. We talked about his technique for matching a striped shirt with a patterned tie. Then he'd leave.

"Oh, I'll get right on that other thing you wanted," I might say. Of course, Eric had forgotten it by then anyway.

I met reporters who had the same impression of Eric that I did. He was a wonderfully nice guy. But he didn't seem like the ideal choice to serve as the department's spokesman at a critical time for the nation. Reporters would tell us that Eric didn't know the answers to questions they asked. And too often he'd have wrong information.

Eric had a cameo role in two of the biggest public relations fiascos of the Bush administration. Eric went in Larry's place on a Rumsfeld visit to the troops in Kuwait. Thayer and I went on the trip as well. We were standing in a large military facility on the U.S. base while Secretary Rumsfeld held one of his famous town hall meetings with the troops.

During the question-and-answer session, Rumsfeld took a question from a National Guardsman (given to him by a reporter, as it later turned out) about the lack of sufficient armor for the military in Iraq. It was a tough, critical inquiry—the kind Rumsfeld loved. Thayer and I knew there was going to be trouble when other soldiers applauded the question. Reporters started scribbling in their notebooks. Rumsfeld gave an answer that would come to haunt him. It was actually a long, thoughtful response, but somewhere within it—the third or fourth sentence, actually—was the line "You go to war with the army you have, not as you would wish it to be." That line quickly spread onto the newswires to show that Rumsfeld was "disrespectful" to the troops. Conservative columnist Bill Kristol called for Rumsfeld to step down. The worst thing in the world for Rumsfeld's public image was the sense that he didn't care about the troops—and that's what his comment was being made to look like. It fell to Eric to try to quell this disaster in the making, which unfortunately was like expecting Charlie Brown to finally kick a football. Eric could have had Rumsfeld issue a clarifying statement or release the whole transcript of what he'd said. He could have personally lobbied reporters to get them to put the remarks in context. But instead, from what I observed, we just left the base and he didn't seem to do anything. I wasn't even sure Eric knew how bad the press reaction was going to be.

Eric even was fingered in one of the president's biggest PR blunders. When Hurricane Katrina struck New Orleans, Bush was in California at an event Rumsfeld was also attending. Scott McClellan was in charge of the president's press contingent. Eric was in charge of Rumsfeld's and was supposed to keep the reporters in a designated press area and certainly away from Bush. One of the reporters on the trip was the tenacious Martha Raddatz of ABC. According to McClellan, Martha slipped past Eric with a camera and came upon the president relaxing in a holding room. The president liked to goof around on occasion with people he met backstage. He met someone with a guitar, took it, and pretended to be playing it. Martha snapped a photo of the president hamming it up and sent it out on the wires. The photo of a grinning Bush made its way all over the country as the residents of New Orleans were drowning under hurricane waters.

Of course, the greatest crisis during my time at the Pentagon concerned the rationale for invading Iraq. Ever since the administration acknowledged that weapons of mass destruction wouldn't be found in the country, war opponents were hammering the president and Rumsfeld for lying us into war. No one was quite sure why no WMD were found. Before the war, Rumsfeld clearly believed they were there. And from time to time, weapons inspectors in Iraq would find traces of chemical weapons that most believed Saddam had used and abandoned long before the war began. The lack of WMD was a terrible embarrassment for the administration, and it almost led to yet another press fiasco starring Eric—a fiasco that was inadvertently started by me.

I had a very eager and well-meaning Navy speechwriter in my office who was fed up with the press attacking the administration for not finding WMD in Iraq. He was always offering public relations ideas, and I usually found them unworkable, at least for Rumsfeld. Every time I rejected something he wanted me to do, he seemed deflated. Now he had another idea.

At Rumsfeld's next press conference, he wanted us to write a few lines into the secretary's opening statement. It didn't matter what the topic of the statement was, as long as at some point we wrote in the following: "As you know, we found the weapons of mass destruction in Iraq." Then he wanted Rumsfeld to continue on with his statement.

The brilliance of this was so obvious to him that I struggled to see what I was missing. "You want Rumsfeld to say we found WMD in Iraq and then just keep on talking?" I asked.

"Yes," he said. Why was I not getting this?

"And then what?"

"A reporter will probably ask him about it as soon as he finishes his statement."

"Oh, I think we can guarantee that," I replied.

"Then he can point out that we found traces of chemical weapons in Iraq."

"But those weapons were old and from the first Gulf War," I pointed out.

He looked at me suspiciously. "We don't know that for sure," he said.

As I often did in situations like this, I went in to the office of one of the other writers on the staff, Justin Walker, to see if maybe I wasn't computing something right. Justin had already heard this idea. He thought it was as bad as I did.

"What are you going to do?" Justin asked.

"Well, I don't want to reject yet another idea," I said. At the same time, this one was a doozy. But it was so obviously a bad idea that no one could possibly miss it. So I came up with a brilliant solution. This time I wouldn't be the bad guy. I'd let Eric do it.

I went back to the writer and told him to put his idea in a memo and send it to Eric Ruff. "This is really a public affairs decision for our press secretary," I said. "Let's see if Eric signs off on it."

The writer sent the memo to Eric and cc'd me. Within a few hours, Eric came bursting into my office—wearing another nice tie and with a Diet Coke in hand. "Did you see this memo?" he said excitedly.

I smiled and asked Eric to close my office door. "Yes, I did." I was about to apologize for wasting his time.

"It's brilliant!" Eric said.

Uh, come again?

"I'm sending it over to the White House right now," he said.

Oh. My. God. At that moment, I debated with myself. Do I try to explain to Eric how crazy this idea is—that the last thing the White House wants is advice on how to bring up the whole WMD issue again? Or do I let him get what's coming to him?

In the end I did the only thing my conscience would allow. "Eric, can I have that memo back?" I asked.

"Well, no," he said. "It's my only copy."

"I know," I replied. "I just want to make one correction."

After Eric left, I called the writer back in with the "good news" that Eric loved his memo and was sending it on to the White House. I said I just wanted one change made: take my name off it altogether.

The reaction from the White House was, shall we say, not positive. Many months later, I was told that Eric wasn't welcome at any more White House communications meetings. Apparently he'd sent them some memo . . .

The list of public relations catastrophes, and would-be catastrophes, grew ever longer—and I haven't even mentioned Allison Barber, the deputy assistant secretary of defense for internal communications. Allison was another FOL and an unguided missile of enthusiasm. Allison had so many projects at the Pentagon, costing millions of taxpayer dollars, that nobody could keep track of them all. That was fine by Allison. But she always had a smooth, prepared answer should anyone ask about them. I never trust people like that.

As part of her many unsupervised duties, Allison organized a video town hall between President Bush and some troops in Iraq. The format was simple. The president would talk to the troops—whom Allison helped select—via video link from the White House about their concerns or suggestions. What the president apparently didn't know was that Allison had nudged the troops along regarding what questions to ask. Once the press found out, the headlines were ugly. (One was "Pentagon Coaches Soldiers for 'Candid' Conversation with Bush.") The president looked foolish, and the town hall looked like nothing more than a cynical PR stunt, which apparently it was. In the face of yet another PR catastrophe, Allison and Larry did what they always did: they laughed it off. White House officials apparently wanted to fire Allison for this inexcusable blunder, but Larry didn't do it. And Allison rolled merrily on. At one point, she was handed as much as 80 or 90 percent of the public affairs staff and budget—again with almost zero oversight. But that didn't seem to bother anyone. For example, with much fanfare, she launched the Pentagon channel for cable television—a multimillion-dollar expenditure charged to the taxpayers for a TV channel that it appeared practically no one even watched. ("Oh, well," everyone shrugged.) The channel recently interviewed hip-hop artist Flo Rida and launched a cooking show, "The Grill Sergeants." In 2008, a report by the Pentagon's inspector general found that another Allison brainchild, America Supports You, a program meant to give publicity to nonprofit groups supporting the troops, was run in a "questionable and unregulated manner." Some $9.2 million was spent between 2004 and 2007, the bulk of it with "inadequate oversight." Large sums of taxpayer dollars were directed to a public relations firm run by a friend of Allison's.

After a year or more of working in public affairs, I'd more than had my fill. It was impossible to do anything productive. I thought most of the people running things were performing a great disservice to the secretary, to the president, to the country, and to the world. Oh, and to the taxpayers too. (Funny how we always seemed to forget about them.) Still, I liked Secretary Rumsfeld. I supported the war in Iraq. And I felt an obligation to stay, out of affection and loyalty. I was the Pentagon's Michael Corleone. Every time I wanted to leave, something kept pulling me back in—but always with a deep sense of foreboding.

That foreboding intensified in late 2005 on a Christmas Eve trip to Iraq. Secretary Rumsfeld had gone off to meet with some generals, and I was left to travel with other members of the public affairs staff in a van to our VIP accommodations in one of Saddam Hussein's palaces. It was late at night in Baghdad. As our convoy made its way down one of the desert roads, our van suddenly stopped and pulled to the side of the road. The driver turned off the van's lights and everything became pitch-black. As I heard people running past my window, I naturally grew a little nervous. The rest of the staff kept chatting away obliviously until our driver told us all to be silent.

After several minutes, I finally whispered, "What's happening?"

One of the soldiers riding with us said there were snipers ahead who were firing on our convoy. So we were stopped while they "took them out." He said it all matter-of-factly, as if this were just another day at the office.

Left unanswered was the obvious question: what if there were more of them?

At this point, I probably should have said a prayer or wished for the best. I could have thought of my parents or my young nephews. Instead I looked around at the other PR flacks I worked with who were now sitting nervously next to me in our doomed motorcade. And a single thought ran through my head: *I can't believe I'm going to die with these dummies.*

In the beginning of 2006, Larry Di Rita announced he was leaving the Pentagon. Larry's departure was a shock wave. It was like Prince Charles saying he was leaving the royal family.

The president nominated a new candidate to head Public Affairs: Dorrance Smith. Dorrance had gone to school with President Bush's younger brother, Marvin, which led to suspicions that he was just another Bush Texas buddy. Those suspicions were amplified when it became known that Karl Rove had pushed for Dorrance to get the nod. Still, he seemed in some ways well qualified for the job. He'd been an ABC News producer for the legendary David Brinkley and had worked in the administration of the first George Bush.

Initially, Senate Democrats blocked Dorrance's appointment because Dorrance had written an article that seemed to accuse the media of aiding and abetting terrorists by its relationship with the Arab media network Al Jazeera. Why Democrats in the Senate were offended over an attack on the media explained all you needed to know about the cozy relationship between the two. The Bush team was determined to get Dorrance in place and Larry out. (They refused to give Larry their full backing for two different jobs at the Pentagon, which accelerated Larry's departure.) So the president finally gave Dorrance a recess appointment to get him in place.

At last, I thought, the White House recognized the communications problem at the Pentagon and was getting serious about fixing it. Dorrance wasted no time coming down and taking over the office. He proudly displayed his multiple Emmy awards, and I found him likable, funny, and impressive—a pro who actually knew something about the press. How refreshing.

But for a man who had made a career in the media, Dorrance turned out to be the most curious of department spokesmen. He was the first assistant secretary of public affairs in recent memory who never held a press briefing. In fact, he seemed to prefer to never speak to the press at all. Reporters complained that Dorrance avoided them in the hall and refused to return e-mails. When one of CNN's top Pentagon reporters, Barbara Starr, sent him a routine press inquiry, he forwarded her to someone else in his office. "I don't do daily menu orders," noted Tony, who tried to get Dorrance to speak to reporters, speculating that Dorrance still saw himself as a producer. His job was to keep the principal happy and let someone below him handle all the other stuff. So now we had Eric, who was incapable of engaging the press, and Dorrance, who actually loathed the press. If it weren't such a serious time, with two wars going on and an embattled secretary of defense, the situation would have been grist for a sitcom. A bad one.

The first real test of Dorrance's pretend-they-don't-exist press strategy came quickly. The latest of three books on the Bush administration and Iraq by veteran Washington Post investigative journalist Bob Woodward was about to come out. Since the first two Woodward books had largely depicted the administration and Rumsfeld in a positive way, the law of averages created the distinct possibility that Woodward's third book would be negative.

The open secret in Washington was that, in general, the more time someone spent with Woodward and the more information they gave him, the more favorably they'd be depicted in whatever book he was writing. We knew, for example, that Colin Powell and his top aides spent a lot of time with Woodward. Ergo, Powell usually looked good—he was typically the somber voice of reason giving eloquent sermons about how everyone else was wrong. The Bush White House encouraged everyone to spend time with Woodward. Rumsfeld resisted, though.

"Bob Woodward's books are not the Bible," he kept saying. He didn't like being part of the cattle call. Also, he had a feeling he was going to be the bad guy in Woodward version 3.0.

Woodward tried every angle to get in to see Rumsfeld, including reaching out to Tony, a friend of many years. He told Tony he hadn't reached any conclusions about Rumsfeld and wanted to give the secretary a fair shake. Few believed this, however, since the book was nearing its deadline and was likely already 99 percent written. Eventually, though, Rumsfeld agreed. Everyone kept telling him he had to do the interview. The White House wanted him to do it. So, fine, he'd do it.

As Rumsfeld went over a few notes in preparation for the interview, Tony told him that Woodward had a source at the Pentagon—naturally, some anonymous source—telling Woodward that the secretary was a terror to work for. Tony said he'd told Woodward that Rumsfeld wasn't a terror but instead said, rather mischievously, that Rumsfeld just exhibited "an amiable contentiousness." There was a brief, nervous silence. Finally, General Pace spoke up. "I understand the 'contentiousness' part," he said. Then he asked, "Where do you get the amiable?" Rumsfeld roared with laughter.

For the Woodward interview, Rumsfeld did something smart: he insisted on having his own tape recording and transcript of any interview sessions. He didn't trust Bob Woodward—which turned out to be prescient.

Woodward started his long-sought interview by quoting Rumsfeld's own words: "Bob Woodward's books are not the Bible." Woodward seemed defensive about it. "No one knows that better than me," the reporter said.

Rumsfeld alluded to what he had to do to show up well in a Woodward "history"—and made it clear he wasn't going to play along. "I'm not the kind of guy who is going to say bad things about my colleagues," he said bluntly. Woodward assured him that wasn't what he wanted.

The reporter then offered fawning praise of Rumsfeld. Woodward said that his wife believed that the intelligence about Iraq never would have been botched if Rumsfeld had been CIA director instead of secretary of defense. "You would have picked the hole and discovered that maybe WMD was not there," he speculated.

"I don't know," Rumsfeld said. "I'm not sure I'm as smart as that."

They continued talking for some time. The transcript was filled with banter. Then, months later, the Woodward book came out and Rumsfeld, as he predicted, was portrayed as a monster. The book, State of Denial, claimed Rumsfeld would tell subordinates to "shut up" and was loathed by those who worked with him. Woodward even got many of the little things wrong. He wrote incorrectly, for example, that Rumsfeld's "petty" and "annoying" snowflakes were unsigned. Even I, on occasion, received a snowflake that one might consider "annoying," but they were always signed.

It was soon clear why Woodward had been so desperate for a Rumsfeld interview. The interview constituted the book's dramatic climax. In Woodward's depiction, he'd asked Rumsfeld a question about his role as a military commander and if he felt any responsibility for errors in the war. Rumsfeld, according to Woodward, indicated he thought he bore no responsibility whatsoever—an answer so shocking that Woodward was stunned. "I could think of nothing more to say," he wrote. Cue tragic music as scene fades to black.

Here's what actually happened. Woodward asked Rumsfeld that question, all right, and Rumsfeld, as he did with everyone, parsed the question and recast it in the way that he wanted. I could ask Rumsfeld, "How did you like the speech?" And he'd reply, "You asked how I liked the speech. Actually, what you really want to know is if I learned anything from it. Did I learn something? Yes, I suppose I did." Then he could go off in any direction with his answer. Jamie McIntyre, a reporter with CNN who'd observed Rumsfeld employing this technique on several occasions, developed a riff imagining how Rumsfeld might respond if asked by his wife if he'd taken out the trash: "You ask if I took out the trash. Did I try to avoid taking out the trash? No. Have I done my share to help out around the house? Sure. Should the trash have gone out? You bet." (The trick, of course, was that Rumsfeld never answered the original question.)

So Woodward wanted Rumsfeld to say he felt responsibility for military deaths in Iraq? Well, Rumsfeld wasn't going to sob for some reporter's benefit. So he decided to answer the question a different way. It was typical Rumsfeld, and Woodward, who'd known Rumsfeld for years, understood that as well.

Had Woodward actually been so shocked by Rumsfeld's response that he was unable to speak, as his book claimed? Heck no! He joked with Rumsfeld for several more minutes. He even asked the secretary to draft a snowflake personally for him. (Rumsfeld declined.) There wasn't the slightest indication that Woodward took offense at—or even particular notice of—Rumsfeld's supposed dramatic abdication of authority.

When Rumsfeld was popular, Woodward's earlier books called him "dashing," "intellectual," possessed of "an infectious smile." When Rumsfeld wasn't popular, he was suddenly the villain. As a writer in the liberal-leaning Slate magazine noted, "Woodward does have a consistent worldview—the conventional wisdom of any given moment . . . he has changed his mind about Rumsfeld without Rumsfeld changing one iota." Woodward has made millions writing books that basically parrot what everyone in the know already knows. Nice work if you can get it. The whole episode was my only up-close observation of the legendary Bob Woodward in action. What a massive letdown. He was a bigger disappointment than the *Star Wars* prequels (which I still haven't gotten over).

Secretary Rumsfeld was correct: the chattering classes did treat the book as if it were the Bible, because it had been written by their Watergate hero. And as usual, our public affairs people didn't do much to limit the fallout. Dorrance's press instinct was to avoid talking about it at all. "Let's not give it any oxygen," he said. That strategy might have made sense if no one was talking about the book. But everyone was. It was on the front page of the *Washington Post* and on every cable news show. Rumsfeld was being raked over the coals and was virtually without defenders in his own Pentagon. We were like Cliff Barneses in a world of JR Ewings, Frank Burnses in a galaxy of Hawkeye Pierces.

Of all my colleagues in the speechwriting office, my friend Thayer was the most sympathetic to the press and the Democratic opposition. Thayer was always calming my outrages over the media's coverage of Rumsfeld. He even argued that the media's coverage of the war could have been worse. For example, broadcast journalists weren't showing grisly images every night of dead or wounded troops, much less the thousands of Iraqi civilians killed in the war. Thayer was constantly trying to get our speeches to reflect what he saw as the reality of the war: that it wasn't going as well as we wanted, and that critics were making some fair points. I jokingly called him a "sellout."

It was ironic, then, that it was Thayer who wrote the most controversial speech of Rumsfeld's entire tenure—remarks to the American Legion convention in Salt Lake City in August 2006.

Thayer thought it would be interesting to start the speech by talking about the origins of the Legion after World War I. It was a time when Europeans and many Americans were exhausted from the fighting and, as a result, were reluctant to confront the growing danger of Nazism. The speech talked about a time of "cynicism and moral confusion" among the great democracies of the West—a strange innocence that led one senator, William Borah, to comment, "If only I had talked to Hitler, all this could have been avoided." This history was being raised in the speech, as Thayer wrote it, because of the dangers we faced in the war on terror. The speech had Rumsfeld ask rhetorically, "Can we truly believe that somehow vicious extremists can be appeased?"

I didn't think there was anything particularly controversial about any of that. No one did. I actually thought the most controversial part of the speech was something I inserted in defense of the Boy Scouts. (Many liberals deplored the Boy Scouts' discrimination against gays.) The appeasement line, at least intentionally, did not refer to anyone in particular or even to the war in Iraq. We weren't trying to be cute about it. But that's how it was interpreted by the media and by the Democrats. In retrospect, we should have known better. We violated one of the first rules of speechwriting: avoid any references to Nazis or appeasement.

After the speech, an AP reporter came up to me. "Great remarks," he said. "My editor in New York really likes it. They're going to run with it."

"Really?" I said. That seemed strange. Most of the time the press ignored Rumsfeld's speeches unless they could turn it into some controversy.

Shortly after that encounter, Eric came up to me bursting with excitement. He showed me a headline on the *Drudge Report*. It said something about Rumsfeld's accusing war critics of appeasement. Eric was beaming. This was great! He looked at my horrified expression. Wasn't it great?

As I stood there, Eric showed the headline to Secretary Rumsfeld. Rumsfeld gauged Eric's reaction and then mine and knew at once whom he needed to talk to. "Matt, show me where we said that in the speech," he ordered.

I pulled the speech out of a folder and put it on the table in Rumsfeld's holding area. Then we both looked through it.

"I never called anyone appeasers," the secretary said. He was correct.

"They're reading into the speech," I observed. "No one even asked us what we meant." At least as far as we knew. I had no idea what, if anything, Eric had already said to the reporters. Back at the Pentagon, Thayer, Mr. Let's Tone Down the Rhetoric, was nauseated when he saw the coverage. His speech was being characterized as the most partisan, over-the-top hit piece ever devised. It was my fault too. I'd toughened it up before I sent it to Rumsfeld, who'd toughened it some more. None of us had intended this, however.

The AP story was deadly. It went to every newsroom in the country. Rumsfeld's "attack" on the Democrats led every news channel. The Democrats, led by Senator Chuck Schumer (surprise, surprise), were already issuing statements denouncing us.

Eric, who'd finally figured out that he'd been singing the wrong tune, was downcast. "To be honest, I didn't really understand the speech," Eric said.

Rumsfeld wanted this fixed with the press corps traveling with us, and pronto. Eric said he'd talk to them right away.

"Matt, you go with him," Rumsfeld instructed.

"Yes, sir," I said.

I walked with Eric to the press bus. As soon as Rumsfeld was out of earshot, Eric told me I didn't need to come. He could handle this. So I left.

As the hours went by, the story took on even more life. It dominated coverage on the news channels. Rumsfeld asked me if I'd talked to the press. I told him no—Eric had done it.

Furious, Rumsfeld instructed me to go talk to the AP reporter, Bob Burns. We also tried to craft some statement that explained what the speech actually said and compared it to how it had been interpreted.

Finally, I sat with Burns in a private cabin on board our airplane on the flight back to Washington. After my entreaties, he modified the story slightly. But it was too late to have much effect. Rumsfeld was more furious than I'd ever seen him. It wasn't as if he'd tried to hit the Democrats and then changed his mind after he saw the reaction. This focus on appeasement simply hadn't been planned at all, and Rumsfeld seemed to think that the negative spin was a deliberate effort to defame him. Certainly few in the media cared what Rumsfeld had intended. To its credit, the New York Times actually pointed out that Rumsfeld had not explicitly compared Democrats to Nazis appeasers, but their reporter seemed to be the only one interested in the actual text of the speech.

Democrats on Capitol Hill were soon demanding Rumsfeld's resignation. Some even wanted to impeach him. Most congressional Republicans, who didn't have a lot of backbone on good days, were looking for an exit strategy. Worse, and perhaps not coincidentally, this was all happening two months before the 2006 congressional elections.

Years later, most Americans have forgotten about Rumsfeld's speech, but it still earned a little footnote in history. Because the speech created such a stir, a relatively unknown cable news anchor decided it merited special attention on his fledgling cable news show. He wrote a "special comment" for his MSNBC show, Countdown, that assailed Rumsfeld and his speech with a "Sir, have you no sense of decency?" tone. After that, Keith Olbermann's ratings increased dramatically and he became a liberal folk hero. In effect, the Pentagon's speechwriting team helped make Keith Olbermann a media superstar. Olbermann, we made you. (Maybe if Olbermann reads this one day, I might finally fulfill another of my lifelong dreams: to be listed as one of his "Worst Persons in the World.")

While Rumsfeld was under siege for the zillionth time, Andrew Wilder and a few of my other friends from the Senate dropped by the Pentagon to have lunch with me in the Navy Mess. They all wanted to meet Rumsfeld, of course, but I didn't dare bother him. Instead, I invited them to sit in the press studio and watch the secretary give one of his press briefings.

Earlier that day, I'd mentioned to Rumsfeld that my friends might be in the studio. I wondered if there was something I might give them as a memento.

"I can do better than that," Rumsfeld said. "Bring them by."

"Oh, are you sure you have time?" I asked.

"Sure!" he said, smiling. "I'll make you look good."

Delonnie said Rumsfeld only had about ten minutes for them. But the secretary ended up spending more than a half hour showing them around his office and asking them questions. He took pictures with each of them, then reached into his desk-drawer stash of Department of Defense cuff links and gave each a pair. He also handed them a reproduction of the famous Uncle Sam poster from World War II. It contained the question "Are you doing all you can for your country?"

My friends left Rumsfeld's presence beaming. Andrew said it was one of the coolest things he'd ever gotten to do in Washington. Another friend took the Uncle Sam poster and put it next to his son's bed. By then, Rumsfeld had been vilified. But to a small band of young conservatives, he was still a man who deserved respect. Few ever got to see him as my friends had that day—off the cuff, funny, friendly, and gracious. It was sad that things had gone so wrong for him.

On election night 2006, Republicans were tossed out of the House and Senate with surprising force. It was hard for the average American not to look at it as anything but a stunning repudiation of the Bush administration. That night I had a dream: the president would call up Rumsfeld and tell him it was time to go. Even that morning, I couldn't shake the feeling that this was the end.

I went to see Tony and told him about my premonition. He didn't believe that the president would do that. That would be handing yet another big victory to the Democrats, he said.

He almost convinced me, and I wanted to believe him, but the secretary's being pushed out just made sense to me. This would be the dramatic shake-up of the cabinet that everyone had been calling for. It would take the media by surprise—and the Democrats too. It might be a chance to salvage the Iraq war, even. That, at least, was what they were telling the president—whoever "they" were. (I learned later that the group likely included Dan Bartlett, counselor to the president; the new chief of staff, Josh Bolten; and the First Lady.)

The decision to remove Rumsfeld went against my emotional instincts—and probably the president's too. Bush had held out for a long time, even vowing only a week or so earlier that Rumsfeld would stay until the end of the administration. It was a sign of weakness to remove him, a concession the media would not praise and the Democrats would not reward. It would be open season on the administration. From then on, the Iraq war wouldn't be Rumsfeld's fault but George Bush's.

Still, I couldn't shake the feeling that this was exactly what was going to happen. I went back to my office. And it wasn't long before I received a message that Rumsfeld wanted to see me up in his office—immediately. I went with foreboding, and once I arrived, the unusual quiet of the office suite told me everything I needed to know.

I was one of the few people Rumsfeld had chosen to tell ahead of time about his decision to resign. Leaving Rumsfeld's office as I made my way to it was Steve Cambone. As usual, he didn't acknowledge my existence. He left Rumsfeld's office, oddly, with a wide smile on his face—as if he'd been let in on some great joke. I could never figure that guy out. I walked past Delonnie, noticing that her usual expression was slightly softer. She, of course, knew what was up. Then I walked into Rumsfeld's office, where I'd been many times now, and saw him as I always did: at his stand-up desk going through his papers. He looked at me and smiled. "Well, this is it," he said. "In a little while, I'm going to the White House. The president is going to announce my resignation."

I nodded. "I had a feeling about that," I said.

He seemed surprised, but looked down at his papers. "I wrote this up last night," he said. "Want me to read it to you?" Without waiting for a response, he read aloud his resignation statement, which he'd be reading to the world from the Oval Office that day. I listened in stunned amazement. Six years of ups and downs, great heights and terrible lows, and it was over. "What do you think?" he asked when he was finished. I knew that he didn't really want a critique, and I didn't know what I thought about it anyway. "It's perfect," I said, trying to be reassuring.

"Do you think I should do the Churchill quote?" he asked. He'd put in a quote that said, "I have benefited greatly from criticism and at no time have I suffered from a lack thereof." I didn't think he should use it—why dredge up all that now? It had the potential to sound bitter. "Well, there's some risk," I said, feeling protective of him. "It could be taken the wrong way." He thought for a moment, then flashed his familiar broad grin. "Oh, what the hell!" he said merrily. I laughed.

He looked at his remarks again admiringly. "Can you believe I wrote this myself?" he asked.

"Well, I figure you must have learned a thing or two from me after all these years."

He laughed. "And Joyce typed it up!" he said. "That's what I told the president when he called."

"Well, she was always the smarter Rumsfeld," I quipped.

He roared again. "You bet," he said.

Finally, I said something that I thought he needed to hear. "Mr. Secretary, the American people didn't want this," I said. "They didn't vote to fire you."

"Well," he said, "I don't want the president to have to go through this. The Democrats would be gunning for me all the time—the hearings and subpoenas. I'd be a distraction. Who needs it?"

"You've done a great job," I said. He nodded in appreciation. Then he walked to his other desk and was quiet for a moment. He started to go through his colored folders, carefully arranged just as he liked them. "When Marc Thiessen left," he said, "I didn't think we'd ever replace him." His voice had just the slightest emotion. "Then you came along. And you were a star." He paused. "You were my star," he said as he looked down at his desk. "And, uh, I probably never told you that."

Right there in his office, I started to cry. I couldn't stop it and I didn't care.

The secretary did not cry. He did not seem to be fazed at all. He was cool, controlled, just fine. "Now, you can't tell anyone!" he said. "It's a secret for a few more hours."

"Well, I can't go to any more meetings," I blurted out, wiping the tears from my eyes. "Everyone will take one look at me and they'll know."

"Then let's sneak you out the side door," he said in a consoling tone. "No one will see you." I nodded, took one last look at the office and at him, and left the room.

I called Thayer and asked him to meet me in the corridor. Then we drove away from the Pentagon and went to a restaurant across the street. It was there that I watched Rumsfeld with the president on TV. He used the Churchill quote, as I knew he would. I was dazed and sad.

When I came back to the office, some of the young men who loved and idolized Rumsfeld were in tears. Even tough-looking uniformed officers cried openly in the corridors. Those in the press operations room, some of whom despised Rumsfeld, were shell-shocked. An era was over. The years of fighting. The calls for resignation. The no-confidence votes. The contentious press briefings, the committee hearings—over. All over.

As it happened, Rumsfeld and I were already planning to travel to Kansas to give a speech at Kansas State University. Rumsfeld was also scheduled to go to a building dedication in honor of the school's most famous alumnus, the retired chairman of the Joint Chiefs, Dick Myers. There was some buzz that Rumsfeld might back out of going. He didn't, of course. I knew he wouldn't.

At Kansas State, General Myers gave a rousing introduction of Rumsfeld and a vigorous defense of his tenure. The audience applauded wildly as Rumsfeld rose to speak. We'd worked hard on what he wanted to talk about—not his tenure, not the controversies, but his hope for the future. The speech was widely considered a home run.

On the way out of the university, I grabbed a sign advertising Rumsfeld's appearance. I asked him to sign it as a memento of our last trip together. He took it back to his desk and brought it back to me some time later. "To Matt," the inscription read, "who made me sound better than I had any right to sound."

I understood that the secretary of defense gets the blame when wars seem to go bad. Rumsfeld knew that too. And I'm sure there were decisions he regretted and mistakes he made that merited criticism. But he was the only one who took the fall. Others with involvement in the big decisions, such as Colin Powell or Condoleezza Rice, were spared. Even the generals who managed the war—John Abizaid, George Casey, and others—have faded into obscurity. Rumsfeld took it all on his shoulders. After he resigned, he had numerous opportunities to leak, to point fingers, to make himself look better at the expense of others. But he didn't do it. And in the end the irony was that the man who was supposedly this fearsome D.C. operator didn't play the ruthless game that everyone played on him.

CHAPTER SIX

THE CLEANERS

On that somber November morning when Rumsfeld told me the end had come, he didn't mention the name of his successor. He didn't want to get ahead of the president, even with me. So when Robert Gates was announced as the next secretary of defense, standing with Rumsfeld in the Oval Office, I was as surprised as anyone. Gates had been CIA director under the president's dad, and he ran Texas A & M University, home to the George H. W. Bush Presidential Library. He was a solid, establishment choice. As I watched him accept the nomination, everything about him seemed enthusiastically bland: his comments, his demeanor, even his name. How could anyone ever go into a fury over someone named Bob?

I knew, of course, why Bob Gates had been chosen. He was our Winston Wolf, the character Harvey Keitel played in the movie *Pulp Fiction.* In the film, after a man is accidentally killed, Wolf is called to quietly dispose of the body and clean up the bloody mess. Less than ten minutes later, Wolf shows up at the door, dressed in an elegant tuxedo. "I'm Winston Wolf," he says. "I solve problems." Wolf was a case study of robotic efficiency, overseeing an elaborate cleanup while calmly drinking a cup of coffee. That's what President Bush wanted—a cold-blooded, competent cleaner.

Every presidential administration that gets in trouble always turns to the cleaners. They are the David Gergens and Dick Morrises of the world—guys without strong ideologies who could just as easily be moderate Democrats as moderate Republicans. They see themselves as problem solvers and pragmatists. They cultivate warm relations with reporters. And they're always lying in wait, serving on corporate boards or on the faculty of universities, until some administration needs them to come in and make everything right.

Gates was the kind of Republican that people like my aunt Darlene liked. Darlene was a proud liberal—years later, she'd drive from Chicago to Washington just to get a glimpse of Obama's swearing-in. I think the world of her, but when Aunt Darlene likes someone in my party, it makes me uncomfortable. Aunt Darlene liked Gates. (She also liked Powell and Rice.)

I understood why the president needed a cleaner to come in. Rumsfeld himself knew he'd reached a point where everything he said and did was likely to be turned into some controversy by members of Congress or the press. Bob Gates wasn't a controversial man. In fact, he may have been the most uncontroversial secretary of defense in history. It isn't easy to get worked up over a guy named "Bob."

All of us in the speechwriting office watched Gates's Senate confirmation hearing, during which Gates proved his cleaner credentials over and over. He worked hard to demonstrate that he didn't owe a thing to President Bush and would be happy, even eager, to disagree with him. Asked by senators if he shared the president's view that we were winning in Iraq, Gates provided the perfect cleaner response: we weren't winning and we weren't losing. His answer was widely considered candid and profound, since it seemed to differ from the president's view. Of course, what he said meant absolutely nothing; was the war in Iraq a tie? Gates was very deferential to the senators and wisely pretended that he cared what they thought. He listened politely to their long-winded homilies. He seemed to know roughly where Afghanistan and Iraq were located. And his name was not Donald Rumsfeld. That's all they were looking for.

After Gates was confirmed, an awkward period followed at the Pentagon. Gates wasn't immediately sworn in, so Rumsfeld was still the secretary of defense. Rumsfeld wasn't the kind of guy to sit quietly and wait for his time to run out. He wanted to visit the troops and thank them. He wanted to hold a town hall at the Pentagon. And he had a farewell speech to craft. Meanwhile, the new guy lingered in an office a floor above him with needs of his own. People were running back and forth, trying to satisfy two masters. It felt a little like a guy waiting for his divorce to be final while dating the woman upstairs.

I wished Bob Gates well, but I never felt comfortable with the idea of staying with someone whose very purpose seemed to be to repudiate the man he replaced. I'd long ago tired of the Pentagon's bureaucracy and incompetence. Still, some people in the secretary's office who were staying on with Gates wanted me to stay on too, including Dorrance. So I was asked to meet the incoming defense secretary for some contrived purpose. The real motive was so that Gates and I could size each other up and see if we'd be a good match.

Before I went up to see Gates, I sought Tony's take. Tony had worked with Gates in the Reagan administration, when Gates was an underling at the CIA and Tony was close friends with CIA director Bill Casey. In those days, Gates was considered a conservative. He had sought Tony's help in getting Casey's attention, and Tony had been happy to oblige. So Tony considered Gates a friend.

I shared with Tony my view that Gates was a cleaner. I wasn't trying to insult Gates, just pointing out that he was going to be a very different type of defense secretary. Tony waved away the idea. "Matt, unless he's changed completely, he isn't like that," Tony assured me.

Dorrance and I walked together from our offices in Public Affairs up two flights of stairs to Gates's temporary office along the E Ring. Gates was accorded a small suite of nondescript rooms and one or two assistants to help him. This temporary office was nothing close to the size of the office he'd soon inherit from Rumsfeld. It had a desk and a conference table and a few coveted windows. That was about it. I found it curious that this was the best accommodation that the folks in Rumsfeld's office could find for Gates. The Pentagon wasn't exactly at a loss for space.

The incoming secretary was relatively short, with snow-white hair that was neatly combed, an average build, and average looks. When I walked into the room, Gates shook my hand. He didn't smile. He was neither cold nor warm. Perfunctory is probably the best word to describe his greeting. I was used to the larger-than-life Rumsfeld—the broad smile, the energetic and sometimes intense demeanor, the laundry list of probing questions. Gates exhibited none of those traits.

He sat at the end of the small conference table. I seated myself to his left, and Dorrance sat across from me, to Gates's right.

Dorrance spoke first. On our way up, he'd showed me a smorgasbord of potential press opportunities for Gates based on the many things Rumsfeld had done—op-eds, press conferences, town halls, et cetera. He wanted to give Gates a full range of options. I could tell Dorrance was nervous about dealing with the new secretary. But he'd made a happy break from Rumsfeld, whom Dorrance now felt free to openly mock.

"Sir," Dorrance began, "I thought we'd go through a list of some of the activities that you might consider doing with the media. And you can tell us what you might like to do and what you'd prefer not to do."

That was fine, Gates replied. His voice was high-pitched and not particularly pleasing to the ear, like metal pipes being pulled over Texas gravel.

Dorrance said Gates could do a series of interviews with reporters if he wanted to. Dorrance had a list of reporters he recommended. Gates said he'd look at it, but he didn't seem to have any particular interest in that. Dorrance said the secretary could appear on talk radio with people like Rush Limbaugh or anyone else he liked. Rumsfeld had loved doing talk radio and had used a studio that was located downstairs near the press room. Gates seemed to have little interest in talk radio as well and even less in Rush Limbaugh. Dorrance said Rumsfeld had liked to do town halls with the troops and take their questions. Gates didn't seem to want to do that either. Dorrance said Rumsfeld would hold weekly press conferences. Gates said that press conferences really weren't his thing. He didn't think he performed well at them and he didn't like standing and taking questions for a long period of time.

On at least one occasion, Dorrance made a reference to me and my office to try to engage me and Gates. When Dorrance said something about the troop town halls, I said, "These could really be valuable opportunities to hear what the troops think. They like to ask lots of questions." Gates turned his head slightly toward me, then went back to looking at Dorrance.

At one point, Dorrance brought up the White House. "There are a lot of things that I'm going to say that the folks across the river aren't going to like," Gates said bluntly. That was an answer I might have admired, except that he said it with the tone of a boast, as if he hoped it would get back to them. I had the feeling that the folks at the White

House might soon start feeling like the kids in an episode of *The Brady Bunch* did when they told Alice to go away and quickly regretted it when her replacement was hired. Those around Bush may have wanted Rumsfeld gone, but this new housekeeper wasn't going to be any fun at all.

Dorrance started to talk about potential ways for the secretary to reach out to the country regarding the war in Iraq. Unsurprisingly by this point, Gates had little interest in that either. "Let me tell you how I look at this," he said in his most extensive comment of the whole meeting. "I feel like I've taken over a plane with one of the engines on fire. My only interest is to land it and get out in one piece." Maybe his predecessor hadn't minded being the president's flak jacket, but Bob Gates wasn't going to be a flak jacket for anybody.

Shortly thereafter, Gates turned to look at me. The move was so unexpected that I was startled. I thought maybe he wanted to talk about upcoming speeches. Or maybe he wanted to finish with Dorrance's items before he turned to mine. Then he said, "Would you mind stepping out now while I talk to Dorrance?"

I didn't expect that. "Sure," I responded, rising almost immediately. I went out and began loitering in the corridor, in case I was called back at some point. After about ten minutes, I realized I wasn't going to be summoned, so I left. I can't say I'd fallen in love with Bob Gates, but to be fair, I wasn't expecting to.

After the meeting, I went down to Tony's office. I told him everything that had happened and that I clearly hadn't made a positive impression on Gates, if I'd made any impression at all. I guess I felt a little discouraged. I wanted Gates to like me, even if I didn't want to work there anymore.

"He's probably used to an arrangement where he deals with one person in the line of authority," Tony suggested. "That's why he spent his time talking to Dorrance, who is above you. Listen, I'm going to be talking to him anytime now. And I'll tell him how valuable speechwriting is and the importance of getting you guys in there to meet with him."

Not long after my joyless encounter with the incoming secretary, something completely unexpected happened. I was sent a note from his transition office. Gates wanted to see draft remarks for his arrival ceremony. Huh. Maybe I'd made a better impression than I thought. Maybe Gates had admired the way I sat helplessly in a chair while he ignored me. Who knew?

I had no idea what to write. During our meeting Gates hadn't exactly been brimming over with thoughts he wanted to share. So with no guidance, Thayer and I sat in my office to brainstorm what we might write. We decided to craft a short statement, maybe two to three minutes in length, and pulled some general concepts from Gates's confirmation testimony. None of what we wrote was revolutionary—we needed to fight to win in Iraq, keep our eye on Afghanistan, promise to be candid and up front with the president, seek out a wide range of advice and opinions, and so on. There wasn't anything there much different from what we would have written for Rumsfeld.

We sent the draft to Gates through one of his aides and waited for his edits. This would be his first official speech as secretary of defense, his first real introduction to the country as the leader of our military, and at a time when two wars were going on. Obviously, this was a big deal for him. We were ready for round after round of edits, just like Rumsfeld would give.

Then we heard . . . nothing. Hours passed, then days. Finally, I was told by an aide that Gates was "fine" with the speech. He sent down his edits—I think there were two of them, and both were minor. He wanted to add in something about his wife. That was about it. Then a few days later Gates delivered the remarks verbatim.

Another curious thing happened. The media were so eager to make Gates the un-Rumsfeld that they discovered all sorts of hidden meanings in his opening statement. The Associated Press, for example, wrote that on Iraq "Gates said he wants to hear the views of U.S. commanders on how to improve the situation, 'unvarnished and straight from the shoulder.' The remarks seemed to contrast with critics' complaints that the man he replaced, Donald H. Rumsfeld, did not listen enough to the advice of the military's top officers." The Washington Post wrote: "Gates vowed yesterday to provide 'candor' and 'honest counsel' to the president and to listen to the professionals at the Pentagon 'who ultimately must carry out the decisions' his department makes—alluding to the perception of Rumsfeld as a Pentagon chief who didn't heed war advice from his top military commanders." Others commented on Gates's allusion to Afghanistan being at risk as proof that the new secretary was going to put renewed focus on the country after Rumsfeld had "dropped the ball." At first, the other speechwriters and I laughed about the coverage. It was just unreal. But then I found it sad because it was so cynical. It didn't really matter what Bob Gates said, just that he was the one who said it.

Time and again, Gates received credit for things he didn't do, such as successfully managing the surge in Iraq, which turned the country's prospects around. Before he was nominated as secretary, Gates in fact had been on a commission that suggested a major retreat from Iraq. (The commission was chaired by former secretary of state James A. Baker, aka "King of the Cleaners.") It wasn't Gates but rather the president who'd made the courageous decision to launch the surge, overruling nearly everyone in the administration. And it wasn't Gates but rather General David Petraeus who'd planned and carried out the surge. If Gates had any opinion about the surge when it was being contemplated, it was unknown to many at the White House. Gates wasn't stupid enough to wade too obviously into anything controversial unless he absolutely had to, especially when columnists like Ralph Peters were calling him the greatest defense secretary in history for doing two things: jack and squat. He avoided personal pleas from senior officials in the White House to go on the Sunday news shows to explain our positions or defend us on, well, anything. One excuse making the rounds was that his brother was in town. That was maybe one step up from "I have to wash my hair that day."

The real sign the cleaners were in town was when Gates persuaded President Bush to torpedo the nomination of Pete Pace for a second term as chairman of the Joint Chiefs of Staff. I didn't know General Pace very well, but the president loved Pace and thought he had done a good job as chairman. He was also popular in the military as the first Marine to lead the Joint Chiefs. Originally, Gates recommended Pace to the president for a second term as chairman—that was what Bush wanted—but members of Congress didn't like Pace. Correction: some Democratic members of Congress didn't like Pace. But the Democrats generally shied away from attacking a military officer too strongly in a confirmation hearing, so Gates helped them out, reversing himself and trying to persuade Pace to voluntarily step down. Pace wouldn't, so

Gates somehow convinced Bush to give up the fight. The Pace nomination, Gates declared publicly, in justifying his decision not to support it, would be "contentious" and "backward-looking." Senator Carl Levin, a powerful Democrat on the Hill, applauded Gates's decision. He said a Pace nomination would have been contentious—oh, and "backward-looking." Then, Levin and other Senate Democrats promptly announced a plan to hold hearings on the Bush administration's detention policies—which, as luck would have it, also were going to be contentious and backward-looking. Oh well.

There was, of course, nothing wrong with Gates's trying to work with Congress, but there was something uncomfortable, at least to me, in caring more about pleasing a few senators than doing what you thought was right. General Pace wore the uniform of our country and had risked his life in battle. Gates had wanted him to stay as long as it didn't cause Gates any problems. But maybe, just maybe, someone in the administration should have been willing to fight for him. Around Pace's office, Gates was known as the guy who'd done the unthinkable— left a man on the battlefield.

Within Gates's first year on the job, a curious number of stories started circulating suggesting that Bob Gates was looking to stick around with a Democratic administration. Whether the stories were true or not, it sure made Gates look good to opponents of the president. It was, we were all assured, a ridiculous notion. (Where do those crazy rumors get started?) As one magazine reported in 2007, "Gates scoffed at a recent article in the *Washington Times*, a conservative publication, speculating that he was maneuvering to stay on as Defense Secretary in a Democratic administration." (I guess he sure showed us.)

If I had wanted to, I probably could have stayed with Gates. He was starting to use our speeches and the office was running smoothly. I could have rewritten many of the same speeches Rumsfeld gave, only to watch them suddenly win wide acclaim. Most of the other writers stayed and prospered under Gates. Thayer, for one, really liked him. But I couldn't work for a cleaner. Gates had been a Reagan conservative when that was what he needed to be. Now he let it be known he wasn't even officially a Republican. Conveniently he hadn't registered with either party. I needed to work for someone who believed in things out of conviction, not convenience. That was why I'd come to Washington in the first place.

The question for me was where to go next. Rumsfeld wanted me to go with him, which flattered me enormously. I think I might have been one of the only people in the entire Pentagon that he asked. But in the short term I felt as though I needed to have some distance from my Pentagon experience. Also, if I went to work for Rumsfeld, I most likely would never return to government service, and I still had lingering hopes that I might get to the White House, even if only briefly. I'd met the president's chief speechwriter, Bill McGurn, and he liked me. Marc Thiessen had told me that Rummy would have prevented them from hiring me while he was still at the department, but now that wasn't a problem anymore. The only thing that had to be worked out was getting approval from White House personnel.

Big problem.

I knew Jim O'Beirne would do whatever he could to stop me from getting hired at the White House because I had opposed his absurd hiring litmus tests at the Pentagon. So as long as the same crowd ran personnel, I figured I didn't have much hope.

There was one other job possibility that sounded intriguing, though. One of the best Senate press secretaries I knew, Don Stewart, told me about a new communications center that his boss, Republican leader Mitch McConnell, wanted to create. The Democrats had formed a similar organization within their Senate leadership office—a "war room" that enabled rapid response, quick hits on Republican senators, and the capability to rally members of their caucus to speak on any particular issue at a moment's notice. It had proved really successful, and McConnell and Stew wanted to replicate that formula on the GOP side. They were looking for a staff director, and Stew suggested me for the job.

I thought it would be an interesting challenge, to say the least. As I knew from my previous tours in Congress, Republicans were always at a disadvantage when it came to communicating in Washington. Most thought, not without justification, that the mainstream media were either frivolous or biased and therefore a waste of their time. Moreover, whenever an issue demanded the attention of Congress, the Democrats

enjoyed a built-in advantage with the media because they could outhus-
tle, outwit, outspend, outtax, and outregulate even the most agile of the
GOP. Democrats were by definition the party of more—more government, more money, more spending, more regulations, and more taxes.
Conservatives, when they stuck to their principles, were the party of
less. Given a choice between covering the side calling for more action
in Washington and the side calling for Washington to, basically, do
nothing, the media acted as you'd expect.

Ever since I'd come to Washington I'd complained about how terrible Senate Republicans were at working with the press. If I wasn't
going to the White House anytime soon, how could I not try to help out
this GOP communications center? To get the job, though, I had to persuade Mitch McConnell that I was up to the task. McConnell was generally considered one of the smartest members of the Senate. He'd
helped build the Republican Party in Kentucky. He also clearly had a lot
of patience. His wife, Elaine Chao, President Bush's labor secretary, was
notorious in Washington for being—what's the word?—difficult. At various points, I was told, she had taken nearly every object on her desk—
notebooks, binders, pens, pencils, even a stapler—and thrown it at
someone on her staff. An exposé focused on her had once appeared on
the D.C. gossip website Wonkette.com—it was a savage portrait of a
temperamental maniac. Some of her employees apparently were
thrilled to see Wonkette go after her—they were like Soviet dissidents
who applauded any criticism of the Soviet government. Someone had
finally broken the silence. But nothing happened to her. She was the
only member of the cabinet who survived all eight of the Bush years in
the same job. Maybe people at the White House were too afraid of what
she might say if they let her go.

I met with Senator McConnell in his ornate office in the U.S.
Capitol. If some Washington bigwig is ever looking for an extra player
to join his poker game, I'd advise him not to call Mitch McConnell. I
met with him for forty minutes and I don't think I once saw a revealing
expression or emotion cross his face.

A person of uncommon discipline, he was bedridden as a child for
a year with polio but forced himself to recover and walk again. By the
time I met him, his every movement had become methodical, as if it
had been plotted out for weeks. Moving his hand to adjust his glasses

could be a ninety-second slow-motion act. It was almost as if his brain were having a staff meeting during which the pros and cons of a movement were debated and brought up for a vote.

Senator McConnell sat smack in the middle of a sofa—not a tad to the left or a tad to the right, but precisely at dead center. I think he smiled slightly when we were introduced. But mostly I just remember his stillness.

"So Stew tells me you're a good candidate for this job," he said quietly and calmly.

"I hope so," I replied.

"Tell me what you think the job is," he asked.

I babbled on for probably ten or fifteen minutes. I don't remember a word I said.

This was no pro forma interview. McConnell asked hard, penetrating questions. He offered scenarios and asked what I'd do in this or that press situation. He had no visible reaction to any of my long-winded responses.

At one point, while I was talking, McConnell turned his head to his left. His eyes shifted down to the BlackBerry that was carefully positioned at his side. He looked at it calmly and deliberately. Then he picked it up with his left hand and slowly moved it directly over his lap. All this while I was still talking. Finally, I stopped. McConnell continued looking at his BlackBerry, transfixed.

Many seconds of silence passed. What was I supposed to do? McConnell hadn't said a word. Then his head lifted unhurriedly and he looked directly at me.

"Excuse me for a moment," he said. Slowly his head went back down to his BlackBerry.

He typed some response. Then, little by little, he moved his Black-Berry back to its original position, placing it exactly where it had been before he picked it up. Then his hand moved slightly and his gaze returned to mine.

"Go on," he said. The interview continued.

When it was over, I had no idea how I'd done. I could have handed McConnell a million dollars in unmarked bills or I could have pulled a gun on him—in either scenario I was sure I'd get the same reaction, disciplined silence.

"I think I did terribly," I confessed to Stew.

Stew smiled. "No, you did great. He liked you." What gave that away, I'll never know. Was it a slight twitch of an eye, a brief flare of a nostril, a gentle groan? Anyway, I was hired.

At this point, I'd been out of the Senate fray for three years, during which they received repudiation from the voters and lost their majority to the dreaded liberals. Upon my return, I marveled at all that had changed within the Republican conference—nothing. The leadership was pretty much composed of the same old crowd. There was the hardworking good guy, Jon Kyl. There was Trent Lott, who managed to get enough of the conference to forget his Strom Thurmond disaster to maneuver his way back into the leadership. And there was KBH with her cold, black eyes. What did I ever see in her? The only thing that was different, of course, was that Republicans had become identified with overspending, a couple of sex scandals, and a miasma of general incompetence.

One of the first things I had to do in my new job was to go office to office to convince Republican press secretaries to let us help them co-ordinate a message and book their bosses on TV and radio. Some of-fices welcomed our assistance. Their press secretaries were new and didn't seem to have a clue what to do. There were a few, like two highly capable young guys in Senator Jim DeMint's office, who worked hard to reach out to the media. Unfortunately, DeMint's principled conser-vatism and seventy-five cents would get you a copy of USA Today, which would never cover either DeMint or his principles unless, of course, he seemed to be violating them. Other press secretaries humored us. Sen-ator Olympia Snowe's press person palmed us off on lower-level staff while she was on the phone with NBC. (Snowe was a student of the McCain school of media attention—that is, she adhered to the creed that one's appearance on national news pages occurred in direct pro-portion to one's willingness to turn on the party.)

I also was asked by Senator McConnell to put together a Power-Point presentation for the entire Republican conference touting all the new communications services we'd offer. McConnell's chief of staff said I needed to keep the presentation fast-moving and colorful if I was to have any hope with that crowd. I was supposed to show senators things such as how we could use YouTube and blogs to spread our message. It was a frightening thought. Explaining new media to the Republican

Senate was sort of like explaining the Internet to your grandpa. A few, like John Cornyn, were very tech-savvy. Others, not so much. One senator called a computer monitor "that TV." Some didn't know how to use a computer at all. When I told them we could take a Senate floor statement, turn it into a computer file, and load it onto a website, many looked at me as if I'd invented a cure for arthritis.

We all knew what the most important Internet site was. When the *Drudge Report* first appeared in the 1990s, all the media elites poohpoohed it. Now Matt Drudge, according to most reporters I talked to, had become in effect their assignment editor. Their bosses would order them to cover whatever story that Matt Drudge was highlighting. Everyone on Capitol Hill and the White House routinely checked Drudge first thing in the morning. We all lived in awe, or fear, of what he might post. Ironically, then, the most powerful man in Washington lived in Florida. (Drudge is now getting competition from another rising power on the Internet, Politico.)

After my presentation to the conference, Pete Domenici, one of the longest-surviving members of the Senate, came up to me. "I know you," he said, smiling. "I saw your demonstration today." That made me feel good. I thought that if I could make an impact on at least one of the old-school senators and show them the importance of finding new ways to engage the media, my job might be successful after all.

"Thank you so much, Senator," I replied as he shook my hand.

I wondered what about my presentation had impressed him. I soon found out. "Yeah, you were that guy with the red face," he exclaimed. "But it's a lot less red right now." Then he walked off. This was going to be even harder than I'd thought.

I sighed. Here I was back in the Senate again, trying to teach men in their sixties and seventies how a digital camera worked and that it was Google, not "the Google." I was pretty much resigned to my fate.

Then in early 2007 I was in the lobby of my doctor's office in Alexandria, Virginia, for a routine checkup when my cell phone rang and I received the call that would change my life.

The doctor's office forbade us to use cell phones in the waiting room. So I had to go outside by the elevators while the phone kept ringing. The caller ID said "restricted." It was Bill McGurn, the chief speechwriter at the White House.

Bill had good news. The personnel office had actually come through. I was cleared for a position as a speechwriter. Could I come on board as soon as possible?

Wow. It was happening. It was finally happening!

At first I thought I must have been paranoid about the personnel problems, since I'd been convinced they would never let me through. But as it turned out, my move to the Senate had made all the difference. Since I was no longer at the Pentagon, Jim O'Beirne had no idea I was being considered for a White House position and was given no opportunity to object.

Bill offered me a presidential commission as special assistant to the president. He also managed to get me an acceptable salary, though $30,000 less than what I was making for Senator McConnell. Then came the pièce de résistance: an office in the West Wing! I felt as if I had just won both showcases on The Price Is Right.

As the elevator doors opened and closed and people pushed past me to get into the doctor's office, I was finally realizing the dream of a lifetime.

I walked back into the waiting room. Patients with rashes, acne, and sunburn were still sitting there as if the entire world had not changed. They didn't seem to realize that a few moments ago I'd walked out of that office a mere mortal. Now I'd returned as a full-fledged member of the White House staff.

I was so excited that it must have shown all over my face, because the nurse at the front desk stared at me as soon as I came in. I smiled at her. She smiled back. She looked like she wanted to tell me something. How could she possibly know? She motioned me over to her desk. I went there very proudly. Then she said, in a soft but authoritative voice, "Sir, I think you still have the key to the bathroom."

The nurse may not have cared about my news, but I knew my parents would. Two decades earlier, I'd been a shy, overweight kid from the middle of Michigan. Now I was going to sit in the Oval Office with our commander in chief and help him try to explain his policies to a doubting country in a time of war. At the White House, I'd finally get the answers to questions I'd always wondered about: How do you write a speech for a president? What was it like to work in the West Wing or ride on Air Force One? How did it feel to hear the words you'd crafted repeated on radio or television, mocked on Jon Stewart's show, or echo into history? For years, I used to take the Metro to McPherson Square and walk two blocks to the White House. I'd peer through the iron gates and wonder if I'd ever make my way inside. Yes, it looked like I finally would. I called my parents. Mom was happily stunned. Dad was proud. "You said you were going to do it when you left for Washington," he said. "And sure enough, you did it." My nephews, Michael and Eric, must have told every kid in school that their uncle was going to work for the president.

There was just one thing left before it was official. A minor formality, really, or so I was told. I was to have an interview with the president's chief of staff. I was advised that even though the meeting was a formality, it would be best not to do anything that might cause him any concern.

Josh Bolten had been with the Bush administration from the beginning. Before he became chief of staff, he'd served as director of the Office of Management and Budget. He was said to be a pragmatic, no-nonsense, nonideological type who was coming in to turn the floundering Bush presidency around. Everyone raved about his management style. He was going to clean up the mess all the other guys had made. Yes, Josh Bolten was a cleaner too.

The chief was the first person I met when I came on board at the White House. His assistant arranged for me to meet him in his West Wing office at seven o'clock in the evening. There was a freezing rainstorm in Washington that day. And as in most southern cities during an ice storm, the townspeople raided the grocery stores, hid in their homes, and waited for the number 666 to appear on their front lawns. I was from Michigan, so a little ice didn't bother me one bit. Still, since most offices in Washington had closed, I called Josh's assistant to confirm that the chief would in fact be in that evening for our meeting.

"Oh, he'll be here," he said firmly.

I walked to the front entrance of the White House, gave the guards my ID, and got my visitor's pass. Then I went through the metal detectors and walked to the lobby of the West Wing. The White House seemed pretty empty, which wasn't so strange considering the weather. I waited on the leather couch under the famous painting of Washington crossing the Delaware until I was called in to meet with the White House chief of staff.

The atmosphere was already intimidating. As I cooled my heels, I was sitting a few feet from the Roosevelt Room and maybe twenty-five feet from the Oval Office itself. Josh's aide, a rather humorless young man with dark hair and glasses, came into the lobby and greeted me.

"The chief is ready for you now," he said.

"Okay," I replied, taking a breath.

Josh's office was one of the larger ones in the West Wing. This was the same office that had been occupied by H. R. Haldeman in the Nixon years, by Don Rumsfeld during the Ford presidency, and by the ultimate of cleaners, Jim Baker, who served as chief of staff for Reagan and then secretary of state to the first President Bush. The chief had a spacious corner office with yellow walls, a marble fireplace, a modest-sized conference table, and two large sofas with a coffee table in between them. His office had large windows that overlooked the driveway where all the senior staff parked and the Eisenhower Executive Office Building, where most of the staff worked. I had the feeling that Josh would stand at the window late at night to see who was still working and who wasn't, whose car was gone and whose was still there.

Bolten was a relatively compact man with round glasses, a steady demeanor, and a consistently deadpan expression. He was a man of exacting precision—the kind of guy who would have subordinates write and rewrite even the most basic remarks or letters before he'd put his name on them. Even Christmas messages might go through several drafts.

He looked at the resume on his desk. It was clear he'd already seen it.

"So you just started working for Mitch McConnell," he observed. "Are we going to have a problem there?"

I said I didn't think so. In fact, the Republican leader had been very understanding and gracious when I told him about the job. And I'd been so over the top with my apologies to every person in the office for leaving so quickly that by the end they were pretty much begging me to get out of there and shut up already. That seemed to satisfy Bolten.

"Where are you from in Michigan?" he asked.

"Flint," I replied.

"Nice town," he said. He was the chief of staff, so I didn't argue with him.

"Thanks," I replied.

He told me a story about going to a Bikers for Bush rally in Flint with the actress Bo Derek. The idea of this soft-spoken, rather cold middle-aged man doing anything with Bo Derek was hard to believe. The idea of him with Bo on twin Harleys was impossible. "Here I was in this bar with a whole bunch of rather interesting-looking characters," he said. "And I was supposed to speak to them. So instead, I did the smart thing. I let Bo do all the talking."

I laughed. He didn't.

"The speechwriting office is very difficult," he began. "The president is very particular about his speeches."

I nodded.

"What portfolio are you going to have?" he asked. I assumed he meant, did I have any particular area of expertise?

"I don't know if I have any particular portfolio," I replied. "But since I come from the Pentagon, one thing I'd probably write a lot on would be defense issues, and the war."

"That's the Thiessen one," he said, referring to Marc. I didn't know if that was a statement or a question. So I just said, "Yes."

"Are you a fast learner?" he asked.

I said I was.

He said it was difficult to master the president's speechwriting style. He'd joined the Bush administration at the same time as Mike Gerson had. Even though Gerson was now revered as a master speechwriter for the president, apparently he'd had a hard time adjusting to the president's style at first. Gerson's style, Bolten said, was too lyrical and elegant.

That seemed like an odd, and troubling, criticism.

It must have been tough working for Rumsfeld, Bolten observed. He said that almost as if it were a compliment to Rumsfeld. I could tell he was curious to know what the defense secretary was like. I wasn't sure what to say, since Bolten had had a hand in removing him. "He was a good person to work for," I answered. "I learned a lot."

Bolten said the most important thing he wanted in employees was integrity and honesty. He said he was proud of the record of the administration on ethics. He called the administration "the most ethical administration in history."

"Looks like even Scooter Libby might get off," he added hopefully. (Oops.)

He asked about my attendance at the University of Michigan in Ann Arbor. I nervously mentioned that President Ford had gone to UM. "Well, that's pretty much common knowledge," he said.

Then I made matters worse by mentioning that I admired the pollster Bob Teeter, a resident of Ann Arbor. "He's dead," he replied.

As our conversation continued toward a disastrous crash, he told me he encouraged candor among White House staffers; if ever I had a concern, I should bring it up with him. (I had no intention of ever doing so.) Then he advised me to "have fun."

"Remember, my door is always open," he said matter-of-factly. I detected not a trace of sincerity in the remark. And I figured that if I was ever in this office again, it would only mean trouble. Meeting Josh Bolten was not the most auspicious beginning to my start at the White House. It was like getting a proctology exam from a doctor with cold hands. There was one thing I knew about Bolten, however: if I ever needed a ruthless divorce lawyer, he'd be the first person I'd call.

I guess I hadn't screwed up my interview that much, because before long my paperwork was formally approved and I was cleared to start at the White House. As promised, I was given some choice real estate: an office on the second floor of the West Wing. The office immediately to my right had once belonged to Hillary Rodham Clinton; it was said that her only addition to it had been a full-length vanity mirror. I also sat immediately above offices that housed the vice president and Karl Rove. Rove even used the bathroom across from my office a time or two. I was a five-minute walk from the Oval Office itself. My new office couldn't even fit two chairs in it. But I didn't care. I was finally here.

I thought back to when I'd first set out for Washington in that old Dodge Dynasty (which I had by now abandoned as junk after the car's engine caught fire while I was driving it with my friend Kim). Now I was finally at the place I'd set out for all those years ago, having blossomed into a modern-day Matthew Tyler Moore after all.

CHAPTER SEVEN
THE REAL WEST WING

It takes time for a new White House staffer to adjust to the fact that he actually works there. The oldest public building in Washington, D.C., the White House has been called home by every president since John Adams and remains a living testament to our nation's history. I was shown the black smoke marks on the sandstone of the building from when the British burned the mansion during the War of 1812. I stood in the large East Room, where Lewis and Clark camped out before their famous expedition out west, where Lincoln and Kennedy lay in state after their murders, where Franklin Roosevelt entertained Winston Churchill, where Nixon said his maudlin farewell to the White House staff and his successor, Gerald Ford, promised America that "our long national nightmare is over."

I was introduced to the quirks and miscellanea of the place. I never saw a White House ghost, though many people said they existed. There was the gray tailless cat that apparently had lived on the grounds for at least a decade. Every once in a while, he'd appear out of nowhere and then disappear again. I began to wonder if he was a sign of something I was supposed to figure out, like the four-toed statue on the TV show Lost. I learned an oddity about the construction of the premises: there is simply no way for a president to go from his living quarters in the White House to his office in the West Wing without walking outside. It seemed like a strange design flaw. A cobblestone ramp was installed between the residence and the Oval Office so that the polio-stricken Franklin Roosevelt could wheel himself to work every morning. There were rumors about secret tunnels in the basement of the White House, ones Kennedy reportedly used to sneak out and meet Marilyn Monroe. I heard people say they did exist, but I never saw them either. I have no doubt many presidents wished they could use them to sneak into the world and become a normal person again.

On my first day in the West Wing, I thought the tone was set. Melissa Carson, the assistant to our chief speechwriter, offered to take me on a tour. Melissa was tall and attractive with a warm California tan. She was also extremely bright and friendly, the kind of person I hoped I'd meet at the White House. Melissa and I walked past the famous rooms of the West Wing—the Roosevelt Room, the Cabinet Room, and a closed door where a tough-looking man in a suit and an earpiece stood.

"Where does that door lead?" I asked.

"To the Oval Office," Melissa replied. Oh.

We walked outside along the cobblestone path that I'd seen presidents walk down on TV. We passed the Rose Garden, which was smaller than I'd thought, and into the White House residence itself. As we walked through the first-floor corridor toward the Family Theater, where the First Family watched movies, we came across a group of tourists. They noticed our White House badges and whispered about us as we approached. After some discussion, one of the men in the group came up to us.

"Excuse me," he said. "Do you work here?"

Yes, I said excitedly, I did. I finally did.

A woman who appeared to be his wife was listening. "What do you do here?" she asked.

"We both work in presidential speechwriting," Melissa answered. She motioned to me. "He's one of the president's speechwriters."

The dad's eyes widened. "Can I shake your hand?" he asked. I looked at him skeptically, thinking, *He must have me confused with someone else.* But he was completely sincere.

"Sure," I said, and felt my face turn red.

As he took my hand, he looked me in the eye and said, "Thank you for what you're doing for the country."

The most moving moment of my entire time in the White House happened on my first day. In that one brief second, I realized that I was working not just for a Republican or for a president, but on behalf of the country. I felt giddy and inspired at the same time. It was the way I was supposed to feel as an employee in the People's House. I couldn't imagine that sensation ever going away. And I felt that way even as I adjusted to the fact that the West Wing wasn't exactly the way I'd imagined it.

Many people envision life in the West Wing as something akin to the old Aaron Sorkin TV show: where attractive young people walk briskly through the halls and discuss matters of great importance with snappy dialogue and sexual tension. That was not what George W. Bush's West Wing was like. Most of the senior staff weren't attractive or particularly young. They were balding, middle-aged, overweight men, with pasty white skin untouched by the sun. A 7:30 A.M. senior staff meeting was like walking into the lounge of a high-end golf course in Westchester, New York. The women were almost a perfect division between pretty, young, usually southern sorority girls with strong religious backgrounds and old warhorses who'd fought in the trenches against the Democrats for decades and showed it. Sexual tension was at a minimum.

In the real West Wing few people moved with any sense of urgency. Our dialogue was rarely snappy or clever. If people worried about the president's basement-level approval ratings, they never showed it. If they considered themselves on an urgent mission for their country, you could hardly tell. I looked all over for our version of Mrs. Landingham, the wizened secretary who offered daily nuggets of heroic truths. I never found her. And not one of the speechwriters bore even a slight resemblance to Rob Lowe. We were more like Rob Lowe's cousins—the ones who didn't go out much.

The Bush White House itself was run like most agencies in the federal government: haphazardly and with inconsistent rules. Also, as was true of other federal agencies, status—where your office was located, what your title was, what your rank was, what the president said about you last week—meant everything.

The top of the heap in the staffing hierarchy were the assistants to the president, or APs. They always got the best seats at White House events, and other special privileges. They were each allowed, for example, to join the president in meeting privately with the pope when he came for a state visit. (I was told that Speaker Pelosi had tried to get into that same meeting and was blocked at the stairs by the Secret Service.)

One of the most surprising things I learned was that assistants to the president were entitled to make use of the president's physicians at Bethesda Naval Hospital for their health care needs. I also was told that APs received health care at a heavy discount—the ultimate discount, in fact. Marc Thiessen, at least, claimed that their health care was completely free. I couldn't believe that the people closest to the president dealing with issues like access to health care were completely oblivious to its costs, to hassles with HMOs, and to the other burdens regular Americans faced. Marc, who prided himself on being a small-government archconservative, proudly told me that while he was at the White House he was going to get "every medical test known to man." He wore the expression of a kid told he could have all the ice cream he could eat.

Marc was true to his word. Once he became an assistant, he made generous use of his health care privileges. He told me more than I cared to know about his colonoscopy. He made frequent visits to a podiatrist. There even were rumors he took part in a sleep study. I half expected to walk into his West Wing office one day and see one of the president's surgeons walking on Marc's back, like Mr. Bentley in The Jeffersons.

Just below assistants to the president in the staff hierarchy were the deputy assistants to the president, or DAPs. They were followed by the special assistants to the president. I was a SAP. At the White House, this made me a commissioned officer, and was apparently a big deal. Supposedly I was equivalent in rank to a one- or two-star general. In actuality, the only thing it meant was that I got a few nice perks as well. (But I still paid for my health care.)

One perk was a large certificate stating my commission that was personally signed by the president and the secretary of state. In fact, I saw the president and Secretary Rice sign a few of them myself with black Sharpies. They issued a new certificate every time there was the slightest change to your title. I eventually earned two: one when I was special assistant to the president and another when I was special assistant to the president and deputy director of speechwriting. Marc, for example, had four or five displayed on his wall: one when he was a special assistant and senior writer, another as deputy assistant, another as deputy assistant and deputy director of speechwriting, et cetera. It took forever to get those things printed up, signed, and framed—at least several weeks. I had a sneaking suspicion they were outsourced to Mexico.

Another perk all commissioned officers received was getting "the Honorable" placed before our names on White House invitations. I'd get invitations to all sorts of events within the White House addressed in calligraphy to "the Honorable Matthew Latimer." I was so impressed with myself that I saved all the envelopes. And every three months we got a bag of swag—George W. Bush golfballs, George W. Bush playing cards, George W. Bush pens, and other trinkets. The idea was that you were supposed to give these keepsakes away to friends, family, and acquaintances and thus spread the George W. love all around the country. It was sort of a White House version of Pay It Forward. I said nuts to that and stored most of my loot in bags in my closet. I may have been an SAP, but I sure wasn't a sucker.

Underneath the commissioned officers were the "little people"—the staff assistants, researchers, fact checkers, and all the other folks who did the grunt work. In the status-conscious White House, they were the modern-day version of serfs. They didn't get any certificates, swag, or special seating at White House events. They were also the subject of constant torment by White House management. When a woman named Gena Katz was promoted from researcher to junior speechwriter, she asked for an office. The White House management gave her a room with no windows, no phone, and a slanted ceiling that made the office look as if the roof were falling in. Plus, they told her she could not call the room an office, but had to refer to it as a "workspace." None of their rules made sense.

I joined the Bush administration in the final two years of a second term that had not gone the way the president had hoped. The nation seemed to be on the verge of losing a costly war in Iraq. The Republican Congress that had gained power with such promise a decade earlier when I first came to Washington had been run out of town on a rail by an angry electorate. The president himself had won outright hostility from the voters who'd put him in office twice. Widely respected figures from the first Bush term had become as popular as Jennifer Aniston at an Angelina Jolie adoption hearing.

The first speech I was assigned was for remarks to a nearby American Legion post about the war in Iraq. I was given a memorandum about the event that contained details such as how long the remarks should be, who would be present, and what the general theme should be. Each of those things could be changed at a moment's notice. I was assigned the speech because I'd recently worked at the Pentagon and was familiar with the issues. At the time, the president was at a standoff with congressional Democrats over funding for the troops in Iraq. The speech was supposed to include an offer to meet with the Democrats to discuss their concerns but to hold the line against any demand on their part for an "arbitrary" deadline for the withdrawal of troops. The White House, at the time, was obsessed by what they called the Clinton strategy—appearing to sound conciliatory to the opposition without caving an inch. Bill Clinton might have pulled that off, but I doubted we could.

The lead writer of any remarks for the president would put his name at the bottom of the speech, followed by his office and cell phone numbers. I'd been warned that the president would call speechwriters on occasion to comment on a speech. Generally, with President Bush the rule was: no news is good news. The president was not known for calling writers up just to say, "I really liked that speech." If he called us, usually it meant he didn't like something.

I was told to come in at six-thirty every morning that the president had my speech. On most days, Bush arrived in the Oval Office around six forty-five. We needed to be available and on call in case he had a question. It probably goes without saying that the very notion of receiving a phone call from the president made me extremely nervous. That went for my parents too. "He's going to call you?" Mom asked with surprise when I told her. Imagine—the president of the United States calling her son!

One morning after my first speech was given to the president, I dutifully came into the West Wing at six-thirty as instructed. My usual ritual was to walk to the window of the mess and get a soda pop with a cup of ice. (I wasn't really a coffee drinker.) The White House provided us with as many sodas as we wanted, free of charge, though over the years they started to skimp on the ice by putting the cubes in small paper cups, so the ice melted within minutes.

At six-thirty in the morning, there were more people already working than I'd expected. No matter how early I arrived, Raul Yanes, the president's staff secretary, was usually already there in his basement office of the West Wing. The job of staff secretary is not well understood outside the White House, but it can be one of the most important in the West Wing. The staff secretary handled all the paper that flowed into and out of the Oval Office. He or she was responsible, for example, for getting legislation to the president for a signature. If the president was out of the country when a bill passed Congress, a junior member of the staff secretary's office personally would take the actual bill and fly with it to wherever the president was anywhere in the world, have the president sign it, and fly back. (There is an autopen in the White House somewhere, but not for legislation.)

As the person who had regular, constant contact with the president, the staff secretary could play the role of Rasputin—putting poison about other people on the staff into the president's ear. Or the staff secretary could be a roadblock to access to the president in order to advance his own interests. We were extremely fortunate to have Raul in that job. An enormously talented attorney who knew more about any issue than nearly anyone else in the West Wing, Raul was funny, even-keeled, and honorable. He treated every member of the White House with respect, paying particular attention to the junior staff members. Without exception, every person who worked for him loved him. And many people who didn't work for him wished they did. Though he was often the primary victim of the presidential temper, Raul was one of the president's most dedicated defenders.

Raul, or his deputy Brent McIntosh, spoke to Bush first thing in the morning and often were the last to speak with him at night. They were often a secret conduit for information to the president, who valued their take on things. I guess because Raul was Cuban American, the president called him "Chi-Chi." And since Brent McIntosh worked as Chi-Chi's deputy, he was dubbed "Choo-Choo." (Again, I can't say either nickname was particularly sophisticated.) I doubt Raul ever tried to persuade the president to take a particular policy position—Raul was a staunch conservative—but I always felt better that he was around as a counterbalance to Josh "Cold Hands" Bolten.

I'd probably been in my office for about ten minutes that morning when the phone on my desk rang. The display said "Oval Office." It was one thing to have been warned the president might call me to give me his edits, but it was quite another to realize it was actually happening.

I'd been working there for about a week or two and had never met him or talked to him. Now he was calling me directly. I just knew this was going to be the start of a wonderful relationship.

I picked up the phone, and said hello.

On the other end of the receiver, it wasn't the president but his secretary, Karen Keller. "Is this Matt?" she asked.

Yes, I said.

"The president has edits on your speech. Can you come down to the office?"

I paused. Nobody had told me I'd be going anywhere. I thought the president was just supposed to call on the telephone. I must have misheard Karen.

"The Oval Office?" I asked.

Karen was used to such inane questions. "Yes," she said patiently. "Please come right now." Uh, okay.

A little stunned, I grabbed a notepad and a pen and walked downstairs to the Oval Office. I was outside the office within five minutes.

Karen sat about a foot or so from the entrance to the Oval Office, within earshot of the president. She was an attractive woman with blond hair and glasses. She was probably in her thirties. She always seemed pleasant and efficient.

One of her jobs was to constantly update the president on the stock market.

"What's the Dow at, Karen?" the president would holler from his desk.

She always knew immediately.

Also seated at a desk near Karen was another assistant, a younger woman named Ashley. And across from them in a small connecting office was the president's personal aide, Jared Weinstein. For those who watched The West Wing television show, Jared was the Charlie character—the guy who always had what the president needed (mints, gum, bottled water, pens, pencils, whatever). He also was the person we all asked for the best read on the president's mood. Jared was something like a much younger version of the president himself—southern, good-looking, friendly, into sports.

One thing I noticed the very first time I met them in the small room outside the Oval Office was how impossible it would be for the three not to know everything the president was doing—and who he was doing it with—at any given moment. All three would have noticed in an instant if, say, a young intern walked in for a private "meeting" with the boss. There was even a reverse peephole on the Oval Office door so that any of them could see what the president was doing.

When I hurried in, Karen smiled and welcomed me. I noticed the Oval Office door was open. "Go on in," she said. "He's waiting for you." In a matter of seconds, I was going to meet and actually talk to the president of the United States. I tried to seem nonchalant about it in front of Karen, as if this were any other day at the office. (I'm sure Karen wasn't fooled.)

I walked into the famous room I'd seen so many times in the movies and on TV. The Oval Office was smaller than I'd imagined. In fact, so was the entire West Wing. The president did have a small study and dining room where he could escape (in what had to be a self-conscious joke about his own familial pedigree, he had hung a portrait of John Quincy Adams on the wall) but neither room was large and they didn't look particularly comfortable. Mrs. Bush had the Oval Office decorated with so much bright yellow that coming into the room was like entering the sun. With everyone looking in on you and windows all around, it must have been easy for Bush to get distracted. I could understand why President Nixon left the Oval Office whenever he could. He'd walk down the hall, down the steps, and across the private driveway separating the White House from the Eisenhower Executive Office Building. Then he'd enter a private hideaway office on the EEOB's first floor. Nixon's hideaway office is no longer used by presidents, but there are pictures displayed showing Nixon meeting with Kissinger there, or sitting alone, brooding in his weirdness.

President Bush was sitting behind the Resolute desk, the desk Kennedy and Reagan had used, carved from the timbers of the HMS Resolute and a gift to Rutherford B. Hayes from Queen Victoria. Portraits of Presidents Washington and Lincoln were on the walls. Lincoln, Bush said, was his favorite president. There was no portrait of his father, however. The president said, "Number 16 [Lincoln] hangs on my wall, but number 41 [his dad] hangs in my heart."

Bush was wearing his half glasses across his nose. He was holding a black Sharpie and looking at some papers on his desk, which I realized were my speech. I'll always remember his first words to me. "Hey there, buddy," he said, without looking up. "I'm on page three."

He went through the speech, page after page, dictating changes as he went along. He seemed less interested in the individual alterations than in schooling me on how to write for him. Also, I think he was sizing me up. There was another speechwriter named Matt who was currently in disfavor, and at first, I think, the president had confused us.

The president's editing sessions went like this: he talked, you listened and scribbled furiously whatever he said. On occasion, he might ask a question. But usually he wasn't too interested in the answer. Sometimes in the middle of your explaining something, if he felt he wasn't getting what he wanted, he'd interrupt and say, "Okay, here's what we need to do." This wasn't a process that encouraged dialogue or pushback on an important point. This was George W. decisively telling you what he wanted to say, and you writing it down. Got it?

But that was okay by me. This was my first meeting with the president of the United States. He was the one who had been elected by the American people, not me. To paraphrase the line from *Jerry Maguire*, he had me at "Hey there, buddy."

By the time the president had finished going through every page of the American Legion speech—pointing out words he didn't like to use and suggesting ways of reorienting several paragraphs—Bill McGurn had made his way into the Oval Office as well. Understandably, the chief speechwriter always wanted to be present when the president was talking to any of the other writers. Bill, in fact, liked to bring both of his deputies, Marc Thiessen and Chris Michel, to every meeting with the president to ensure that he didn't miss anything the president said, and also to shoulder some of the responsibility for the remarks.

Shortly after all of us had gathered in the Oval Office, the president asked us to come back in an hour or so to go over the changes. We were dismissed.

I didn't know how to take the president's very hands-on approach to the speech. He seemed to have a lot of edits. I wondered if I'd let him down.

"Well, that could have been a lot worse," said Bill McGurn. "He seemed happy with it."

"He made a lot of edits," I observed.

"He always does on an Iraq speech," he said. "But he didn't seem very annoyed about it, which is good."

The other writers commented on how surprised they were that I'd uttered a single word at my first meeting. I had spoken up for parts of my speech, having no idea that doing so was unusual. "It took me months before I said anything," Marc confided.

"He seemed to listen to you," Chris said. "I thought you handled it well."

Rather than send me off to put the president's edits into the speech, Bill, Marc, Chris, and I did what seemed a remarkable waste of resources: all four of us went up to Bill's West Wing office and went through the president's changes together, typing them into a new draft. Not only did this take up the time of four people, when one or two surely could have done the job, it also was an approach that inevitably led to chitchat and loss of focus. It was speechwriting by committee, and it never seemed to make much sense to me.

One of the people who made that point to us—in, predictably, the most unsettling and slightly taunting way possible—was the chief of staff himself.

"Well, if it isn't the lightbulb crew," Bolten once announced when he walked into Bill's office and saw us sitting there. We all laughed awkwardly. He didn't.

"Do you know why I call you the lightbulb crew?" Mr. Uncomfortable asked.

We didn't.

He said that the earlier Bush administration speechwriters, Mike Gerson, John McConnell, and Matt Scully, also used to sit around a computer screen together and work on a draft—which had given Bill his operational template in the first place. "So when I saw all of them together," Bolten continued in his crisp, unhurried manner, "I said I finally knew how many speechwriters it took to change a lightbulb. Hence, I called them the lightbulb crew."

Again, we laughed nervously. This was the perfect Josh Bolten joke—not particularly funny, but uncomfortable and slightly insulting. Assuming he was joking, of course, which by all appearances he wasn't.

When we finished making the president's changes to the speech, we returned to the Oval Office.

As one might expect, any speech on Iraq got special attention from the president and the rest of the staff. When we came back for round two of our editing sessions, Steve Hadley, the national security advisor, was there along with Raul and Dan Bartlett. Dan was then the head of communications for the president. He was in his midthirties, with graying blond hair and glasses. To my knowledge he'd never had a serious job outside of working for George W. Bush. He'd started as one of the president's bag carriers—a Jared type—and was eventually elevated to the president's counselor, in charge of the president's communications and message. Dan was a nice guy who had a rare talent for getting the president to change his mind about things. He also put the president in a good mood—which was not a quality to be underestimated in any member of a presidential staff.

And indeed, with Bartlett present, the president did seem much happier.

As we sat on the two couches across from the famous *Resolute* desk, the president and Dan were in the midst of laughing about something. Seeing our perplexed faces, the president asked, "Were you guys in the meeting earlier this afternoon?"

We all looked at one another, not knowing what meeting he was referring to.

Dan was still laughing. He said to the president, "Did you see—"

"Yes," the president interrupted jovially. "I couldn't look at him."

Dan noticed we were all totally confused. "Cheney fell asleep in the meeting," he said.

The president was almost broken up with laughter. "I saw his head go down and he dropped his papers"—more laughter—"and I didn't want to say anything, and . . ."

He and Dan were now in red-faced hysterics. They snickered like students laughing mischievously at their teacher after class. So naturally we did the only thing we could do when two people are having uncontrollable laughing fits: we laughed too. Hard. Until tears streamed down my cheek.

It was an unusual moment. Here I was sitting in the Oval Office laughing hysterically with the president of the United States about the vice president of the United States while we were gathered to discuss a speech I'd written on one of the most important subjects in his administration.

The president finally composed himself and started to go through the changes we'd made. During a second editing session, the president usually was given a document that highlighted in red type all the changes we'd made from the last draft he'd seen to the one he was reading now. This was to make sure his edits had been put in. As he looked through the speech, he seemed generally happy, saying things like "This is good . . . good . . . okay . . . yep."

By about page five or so, the president started to get bored. You could see it in his face. So, naturally, that meant the speech was too long. By page six, without really reading the ending, he decided it needed to be cut down.

I liked the ending. It was about the blessings of freedom and how America's system of government valued the individual and offered hope to people who'd lived their whole lives in the chains of tyranny. I thought it was nice, saying what the president had said many times before but in a different, more thoughtful way. I was going to make a case for it when the least likely of all suspects spoke up. Steve Hadley had once been Condi Rice's deputy at the National Security Council before taking charge of the NSC himself. Because of their concerns about Condi, conservatives eyed Hadley with suspicion as well. Bill and Marc had Hadley near the top of their secret list of troublemakers that they kept on Bill's computer.

In manner and appearance, the national security advisor seemed to fit the archetype of the Ivy League stiff. He had the demeanor of an English majordomo without the accent. I figured that he went to bed every night in one of those old-fashioned nightgowns with matching nightcap. Hadley was always conservatively attired, never raised his voice, never seemed to push too hard for anything. At first blush, he seemed to lack any ideology or emotion whatsoever. In short, I expected him to be the perfect cleaner.

Hadley was a master at handling the president. Though he was a very bright man, he liked to depict himself to Bush as the dumbest person in the room. He'd say things like, "Oh, Mr. President. I'm sure I'm completely wrong about this, but . . ." or "I have to apologize, Mr.

President, and feel free to 'calibrate' me, but . . ." This was the perfect way to talk to George W. Bush. He was the president's straight man, and the president loved it.

The main knock Bill and the others had on Hadley was that he'd never put himself on the line for a speechwriter, even if the president objected to something that had been Hadley's idea. I didn't find that to be true, though. It was certainly not the case on this speech.

As we were verging on a consensus to cut my ending, Hadley cleared his throat. "Mr. President, I didn't write this," he said, "but may I speak up for it?" Everyone looked at him, startled. He apparently had never done this before.

I broke the silence.

"By all means, please do," I said. He laughed. More important, so did the president.

Hadley went on to praise the same lines in the speech I liked. "I just think this is lovely," he said.

The president listened to Hadley, usually. "Well, just try to cut it down," he said in a brief fashion, clearly ready to move on.

When we were finished, it was evident to Marc that the president and I hadn't yet been officially introduced despite our two editing sessions. "Mr. President," Marc said, "I don't think you've formally met Matt yet." It was a nice thing for Marc to do.

The president looked at me. "Well, Matt, have we formally met yet?" he asked.

"I guess not, Mr. President," I replied.

"Well, I'm sorry about giving you that grilling earlier today," he said kindly. He looked at everyone. "I gave him a tough go this morning." He recalled it somewhat proudly, although I didn't think he'd been that tough.

"Oh no, Mr. President," I said laughing. "That was nothing. I used to work for Secretary Rumsfeld."

Throughout the Oval Office, there was an uncomfortable silence. Was I insulting Rumsfeld? Why was this guy bringing up a man the president had just recently let go?

The president's eyes narrowed and he cocked his head. "Now what does that mean?" he asked.

Oh no.

"I just meant, uh, I just . . . well, he could be a demanding guy to work for, but . . ." Why couldn't I stop talking? "But I liked him a lot."

The president remained silent for a moment. "He's a good man," he said finally.

I nodded vigorously. "Absolutely," I replied. *Get me out of here.*

The president looked a little uncertain. Then he extended his hand. "Well, thanks for coming on board, and welcome," he said.

I shook his hand, relieved. "Thank you, Mr. President."

"I appreciate your service," he said. Then I got out while the getting was good.

After all the painstaking, time-consuming work we went through getting the speech just right, the president ended up ad-libbing most of it. As for the ending, he dropped it altogether and did a riff of his own. But I didn't care. I was finally in the White House. I was finally writing for a president. I was going to be part of history. It would only be a matter of time before I made a difference.

Over the next several months, the president had a knack for calling me with edits on speeches at the most inopportune moments. Once he called while I was in the bathroom. Another time he called while I was driving home and I pulled over to the side of the road and wrote his edits in with a crayon I found in the car. Once he called me when I was headed out of the building to lunch. He asked if I had the speech in front of me. I didn't want to lie to him, so I said I didn't. He paused. Then he asked politely, "Well, should I call you back later?"

What was I going to say—*Yes, please call me back at a more convenient time, Mr. President?* Instead, I did the only thing I could do: I lied to the president of the United States. "I just found it," I said.

"Oh, good," he replied. As he gave his edits, I ran back into the building, down the hall, and into my office as quickly as was humanly possible, trying to memorize everything he said along the way. People were a blur as I flew past them, out of breath and sweating, until I made it to my desk. If the president noticed all the commotion, he didn't say anything. And he was the type of person who *would* have said something. From then on, I carried a copy of any speech I'd written with me at all times—even keeping it next to my bed.

Meeting and working with the president for the first time had been thrilling, nerve-racking, surprising, and exciting, all rolled into one. But there was one other person in those early days whom I was still eager to meet. I knew what everyone said about Vice President Cheney. He was the administration's Jabba the Hutt—corrupt, larger than life, sinister. The man who rubbed his hands together and stood in the shadows dreaming of planting oil wells all across America.

But the two people I respected the most during my time in Washington, Jon Kyl and Donald Rumsfeld, held a totally different view. Rumsfeld and Cheney were longtime friends, and Cheney had even gone out of his way at Rumsfeld's farewell ceremony to stick it to the president by saying Rumsfeld had been the best boss he'd ever had. And Kyl and Cheney thought the same way—they both seemed like low-key, serious conservatives.

Not only did Kyl like him, but there was a time not many years earlier when most of America did as well. When Bush picked Cheney as his running mate, many commentators breathed a sigh of relief. Cheney was the steady, solid, no-nonsense conservative who knew how to manage things. He'd been Gerald Ford's chief of staff (and Ford was no right-wing nut job). Though it soon came to be forgotten, he'd also been considered the winner of every vice presidential debate he was ever in— he'd outthought John Edwards and even outniced Joe Lieberman.

Cheney's big problem was the same as Rumsfeld's: he blew off the mainstream press. Maybe he even took a macho pride in doing so. In Cheney's case he also was hamstrung by a White House press operation, led by Dan Bartlett, who constantly threw Cheney under the bus while urging his office to be silent in response to bad stories so as not to give them "legs." But Cheney also didn't care one whit about his image and perhaps enjoyed a little too much the impression that he was some hard-edged mastermind. His staff reflected his personality. Those I met were very bright and could be quite engaging when you broke through their shell. But that shell could be hard. They were insular, kept to themselves, and always seemed to be keeping a secret that they weren't willing to share with outsiders.

Knowing that I was dying to meet the vice president, a friend who worked for Cheney invited me to a staff function at the vice president's official residence, the Naval Observatory. This was a nice-sized New England–style home at the very top of a modest hill in the northwest section of Washington.

The vice president was dressed casually, or at least in what passed for casual for Washington men of a certain age: a button-down dress shirt and khaki slacks. I introduced myself to him as one of the president's speechwriters. I also told him that I'd held the same job with Rumsfeld. He smiled.

"Well, then, you managed to accomplish something I never could—write something for Don that he liked," he said. As we continued talking about Rumsfeld, he added proudly, "I wouldn't be where I am today without him."

We talked about writing speeches for the president. "He takes a great interest in his speeches," Cheney noted. "I've always been impressed by that. He knows they're an important tool for communication." Within a few minutes, he awkwardly ended our conversation. Then, as he began to walk away, he stopped, turned back to me, and sheepishly apologized for going off to see other guests. Overall, he struck me as somewhat shy. He clearly preferred to seek refuge in the big canvas bag filled with books that he took on long trips than in conversing with people.

Lynne Cheney was far more assertive and talkative than her husband. She displayed a lot of zest and had a reputation for being a hard charger. What was well known in the White House, but not as well known across the country, was that Mrs. Cheney and their two daughters had enormous sway over the vice president. They were his protectors, his advisors, and probably his closest friends. The image of the gruff Cheney being supported by a group of women is not one he'd probably want publicized. But in a charming way, he was putty in their hands.

Nearly all the young conservatives on the staff idolized Cheney. And I quickly got a report from one about an encounter he'd had with the vice president at the White House Mess. Most high-level officials in the White House rarely went to the carryout window of the mess. The big guns usually had an assistant go down and pick up orders for them. Being above the menial task of fetching your own grub was something of a status symbol. Cheney was an exception.

One morning, he came out of the Situation Room and walked to the carryout counter. There were a few people already in line, so he quietly took his place behind them.

"Mr. Vice President, please go in front of me," one person said.

Cheney shook his head slightly. "No, that's okay."

The staffers all insisted, and Cheney continued to demur, slightly embarrassed. Finally, after being pressed, the vice president thanked them and went to the front of the line. He had a half-empty cup of coffee his hand.

The Navy steward at the window greeted the vice president and asked him what he wanted. Cheney handed him his half-finished cup. "Uh, fill this up a bit and nuke it for me, will ya?" he asked in his gravelly Wyoming drawl.

"I could get you a brand-new cup, Mr. Vice President," the steward replied.

"Naw," said Cheney. "Just nuke this. Thanks a lot."

As his coffee was being warmed in the microwave, the vice president dutifully picked up a pad on the counter and filled out his form just like everyone else ordering something from the mess. He put "Cheney" at the top and checked the box next to "coffee."

Over time, those who liked Dick Cheney belonged to an increasingly exclusive club, but the fact is, I liked the guy from the outset. I truly did. And unlike many people in the administration, he never once did anything that caused me to change my mind.

I wasn't quite as settled on my view of the president, however. But as my first few months at the White House went by I was starting to get to know him a lot better. Some of my most interesting glimpses of the president that year occurred during cross-country trips I took with him aboard Air Force One.

Getting on board Air Force One was an exciting experience. I'd traveled on many nice government planes, and this was certainly the best. The plane was divided into compartments. As you'd guess, Air Force One was arranged in order of importance from the front of the plane, where the president was grandly situated, to the back, where the media was crammed.

The president was accorded an office and bedroom. This was where the president and First Lady spent most of their time on board. The office was tan and rather spartan, but large, and could hold a modest-sized meeting.

Farther down from the president's suite was a conference room.

The room was dominated by a long desk with eight chairs around it. At one end of the table was the president's chair. Before him was a secure phone with a list of direct-dial numbers for the vice president, Condi Rice, the chief of staff, and other key officials. There was also a wooden box that held two decks of cards. The president, I was told, would sometimes play gin on the plane. There was also a long couch along one side of the room closest to the entrance. In addition, the room had one or two large TV screens, which could also be used to conduct videoconferences. Senior staff often used the conference room to read papers, watch TV, or work on laptop computers.

The president seemed more relaxed aboard Air Force One. He'd come by to say hello or participate in conversations taking place. On my first trip, we both found ourselves crammed into a narrow corridor. He was in a T-shirt and suit pants and was trying to squeeze by. "What's the word, Matt?" he asked.

I responded as cleverly as possible: "Uh . . ."

"Hot!" the president interrupted. "The word is hot." He was always hot.

On Air Force One there was no one demanding that people buckle seat belts. There was no stern order to turn off BlackBerrys and electronic devices and place them under the seat in front of you. (I always suspect there was no real reason for airlines to insist on that, but maybe the president's plane had some special BlackBerry-safe technology.) The first chance I got, I did what all newbies on Air Force One do: I called my mom just to let her know where I was at that very moment.

Presidential trips usually consisted of a lot of rushing and waiting. We traveled in huge motorcades of dozens of police cars and staff vans that contained hundreds of people—advance teams, Secret Service, local police, and communications teams. On my first trip, I shared a van with one of the president's national security briefers. I asked him what Bush was like. "He grills us," the briefer replied, "just grills us with tons of questions." "He does?" I asked, sounding more surprised than I meant to. That running around on our trip made me thirsty. So while we were waiting for the president to speak at some private fund-raiser, I walked into a small room and saw a blue bucket with two Diet Cokes in it. I grabbed one, opened it, and took a sip. At that precise moment, someone shouted: "Hey, who drank the president's Diet Coke?" For a moment, I considered running off. Instead, I confessed, and waited nervously for someone to replace it before the president found out.

For security reasons, our motorcade always seemed to arrive at dirty back entrances where the president would have to ride up on freight elevators. When we stayed at the Venetian Hotel and Casino in Las Vegas, we entered through the grungy loading dock. Then we arrived in our suites and saw the height of opulence. The president was given a two-floor suite complete with a billiard room and player piano. My own suite had three enormous rooms, a bar, a sit-in shower/sauna, and a floor-to-ceiling view of the city—all for me. Though the accommodations were usually top-notch for presidental trips, some cities' notches went only so high. The hotel we occupied in Kansas City, for example, had been on the news that very night for violating public health codes. A hidden camera showed maids using the same rag to clean the toilet and then wipe out drinking glasses that they then returned to the sink. On the air, the local news anchor said: "I hope the president knows what kind of place he's staying in."

One of the first trips I took with him was a swing to California. To tout the president's tax package and its effect on manufacturers, we went on a tour of a helicopter factory. One of the people who tagged along was California's governor, Arnold Schwarzenegger. He was shorter than I expected, and his face was more orange than tan. His obviously dyed hair seemed to be bronzed. He moved stiffly, almost as if he were just getting used to his body. In fact, his movements in general were so robotic that at any moment I expected him to pull out a bazooka and search for John Connor. Ahnohld then accompanied us to a fund-raiser in a swank house in Beverly Hills. This house was so huge that its wine cellar was bigger than most people's bedrooms. It had a garage to store classic cars, and a fifties diner–like counter where people could sit and drink refreshments. Even the bathroom had a massive chandelier. It made me think that no one should have this much money.

Most of the staff traveling with the president to a fund-raiser waited in one of the holding rooms or chatted on their cell phones. But whenever I could I tried to listen to the president instead. So at one event I walked into the backyard under a tent and stood by the Secret Service while the president prepared to speak to the wealthy donors.

He was introduced by Governor Schwarzenegger. "I enjoy talking to President Bush," the governor said, transitioning into a joke that I bet he'd told many times. "He is a normal guy. The other day he asked me how I stay physically fit. I told him that I still lifted weights. I lifted two hundred eighty-five pounds the other day. I helped Teddy Kennedy get out of a chair." The Republican donors, predictably, found that hilarious. (I did too.)

At the event, the president took a microphone and started talking off the cuff. In these off-the-record settings, as you might expect, he was more candid than usual. That day, his conversation ran the gamut. He talked with love and appreciation about his daughters. He told a story about how Vladimir Putin thought Bush had fired Dan Rather—evidence that Russia has no understanding about how a free press works. The president said he'd warned Putin not to repeat that myth in public, because he'd look foolish. But Putin went out and did it anyway. Bush shook his head good-naturedly. *What are you going to do?*

He talked about his own failings with alcoholism as the reason he supported his faith-based initiative. "My philosophy is, find somebody who hurts and do something about it," he said. "Don't wait for government to tell you what to do." He bluntly talked about his own situation. "I was beginning to love alcohol over my wife and kids. It got to a point when Billy Graham came into my life. But I was hardheaded and didn't want to listen for a while. And then I stopped drinking overnight. I am a one-man faith-based initiative. Alcohol was competing for my affections. And it would have ruined me."

He said things that could ruffle feathers, such as how he'd recently gone to a faith-based program run by "former drunks." He said he went to see a prison ministry program, noting that "everyone was black, of course." All eyes turned in search of the sole African American in the audience of donors. They wanted to see if he was offended. He didn't appear to be, and the president clearly didn't mean it in a derogatory way. He just liked making blunt observations to shock his audience.

The president also talked about criticism he'd received. "I haven't watched the nightly news one night since I've been president," he said, somewhat unbelievably. "My mood is important—and I can't go around all day being angry at everyone. I don't read editorials either. I can tell you what they say: 'If Bush is for it, I am against it.' I have enough of my mother in me and enough of Texas in me to say that if the *New York Times* thinks it's lousy, it's probably great." Predictably, the crowd applauded. I did too. (But it was dangerous to think the media was *always* wrong. That's what leads people to fall prey to delusions.)

And he talked about his dog, Barney, with surprising affection. "I never had a son," he noted. "So I take Barney fishing. He doesn't like most people, and that's fine with me." Barney, in fact, was mean. He moved around the White House grounds with a regal bearing, as if he knew he could get away with anything. When he finally bit a reporter in 2008, I wondered how Barney had restrained himself so long.

Beyond the presidential trips, I had other rare opportunities to see the president in a more relaxed setting.

At the end of my first year at the White House, I received a calligraphied invitation to one of the White House staff Christmas parties. The president would hold more than a dozen of these parties for members of the staff every year. Day after day in December, he and Mrs. Bush would stand in place for an hour or longer taking pictures with every staff member and their guests. He'd have a smile or a quip for everyone. It couldn't possibly be enjoyable.

Originally, I had asked my mom if she wanted to come. But as another example of how uninterested she was in the Bush White House, she declined, saying she didn't want to miss a day of work. So I invited Dad, who was only too happy to come. Dad still seemed amazed that I worked at the White House. He walked through the gates of the mansion and looked around in wonder. The real treat of the whole experience for him was running into veteran White House reporter Helen Thomas. "Do you think I should say hello to her?" he asked.

"Sure," I said.

He walked over to her table and chatted for a few minutes until it was time for our picture with the president. I was a little nervous about this. Even though I'd met with the president many times by this point, I didn't know what I'd say to him. He never seemed to have the remotest personal interest in me, or most of the writers, for that matter. When he met with us, he'd give us instructions and maybe joke around a little, but he never asked questions about our backgrounds or personal lives. He didn't have to, of course. My only point is that even after all that time, and a number of phone calls and meetings with him, I still wasn't convinced he knew my name. As we stood in line for a picture, someone made each of us fill out a card with our name on it just in case.

When my dad and I had our turn, the president waved us over. "Come on over here, Matt!" he said. Whether he'd read the card or not, I'd never know.

Dad seemed startled. "You know my son?" he asked.

"Know him?" the president replied. "I just say whatever he tells me to say."

The president laughed. I laughed. Mrs. Bush stood there without either movement or sound. The president touched my dad on the shoulder. "You should be really proud of him," he said, gesturing toward me.

Dad smiled, but I didn't think he'd heard him. Shoot!

The president noticed too, and very nicely he tried again. "I say, you should be very proud of your son," he said.

Dad smiled and looked proud. "I am," he said. "Thank you very much."

Then we had our picture taken and walked off. Dad seemed charmed by the president, and with good reason: he'd been charming.

As we walked off, I heard the president call to the next person in line, with the same boisterous, jovial tone. "Come on over here!"

This was the kind and gentle side to George W. Bush that had attracted so many voters seven years earlier. I ended that year with a warm feeling about the president. It was not the adoration or rapture that many of the younger speechwriters in our office seemed to feel. They'd never worked for anyone else in their entire lives and, unlike me, had no memory of another Republican president to compare Bush to. I thought he was a good person who meant well. I believed he wanted to advance the conservative movement, even though he was clearly experiencing stumbles along the way.

Still, I wasn't satisfied with my overall experience in the White House. I'd hoped I'd come on board, impress everyone, and craft the great speeches I'd dreamed of since childhood. That wasn't happening. In fact, the speeches for the most part were disappointing. And the speechwriting process at the White House was nothing like I'd expected it to be.

CHAPTER EIGHT

THE SECRET SPEECHWRITERS SOCIETY

By the time I arrived, the speechwriters who'd been with Bush from the beginning of his administration had dispersed in a rather ugly fashion. One of the most well-known, David Frum, left the White House quite early, wrote a book, and made statements that offered a mixed portrait of the president. Years later, people still hadn't forgiven him, and dismissed him by saying he'd never had much of an impact there in the first place. Apparently, three other writers—Mike Gerson, John McConnell, and Matt Scully—were at the top of the speechwriting hierarchy at that time. They helped craft the president's many memorable speeches in the aftermath of the September 11 attacks, which rank as some of the most important in recent history.

Unfortunately, in the years that followed, the trio had a very public falling-out. Not long after I arrived at the White House, Matt Scully wrote a cutting article for the *Atlantic Monthly* about the White House speechwriting process, aiming his attacks in particular at Mike Gerson. A copy of the article soon spread around the West Wing. Officially, no one would have admitted to having read it. Scully had violated the cardinal rule of speechwriters: never acknowledge your existence. Worse, he also violated a cardinal rule of the Bush family: never tell tales out of school. Unofficially, *everyone* read the article, some of us twice. We debated over whose side to be on.

Scully accused Gerson of hogging all the credit for speeches and accepting accolades he didn't deserve. Gerson claimed innocence, saying he always shared the credit and never asked to be singled out for attention in the media. At the same time, he was about to publish his own book, modestly called *Heroic Conservatism*, which seemed to highlight his own role as the Fonz of the speechwriting office while casting McConnell and Scully as Potsie and Ralph Malph. Those at the top—people like Karl Rove—sided with Gerson. Those at the lower levels of the White House seemed to believe Scully (and no one was surprised that Karl got it wrong). Raul Yanes called the Scully article "a suicide bomb" because it destroyed Gerson and Scully at the same time.

Yet on this one, Raul had it wrong. Neither Gerson nor Scully was permanently damaged. Gerson got a column in the *Washington Post*. Scully wrote the highly praised convention speech that Sarah Palin delivered in 2008, the only good speech in the entire McCain campaign. He also wrote a provocative and well-received book on the protection of animals. (Scully was a hard-core vegetarian and animal rights activist.) This prompted Bill McGurn to lament, "If only Mike Gerson had been a golden retriever, all this could have been avoided."

As a presidential speechwriter, I thought I'd be joining a salon filled with some of the finest writers and conservative minds in the country. I expected lively interaction with all the senior officials in the building, because the president's speeches were such an important tool for communicating their policies to the outside world. And I assumed we'd have a carefully crafted communications plan for every single event.

As it turned out, though, there were few if any stimulating meetings about eventful speeches. Mostly, we were asked to write remarks with a minimum of guidance. There was no apparent vision for the president's communications strategy or, for that matter, even a strategy. Sometimes speeches came about because the president was holding a political event in a particular state and his advisors needed to schedule an official event somewhere nearby so trip costs could be split with the taxpayers. (Speeches, in effect, became the Muzak for whatever political event the administration thought important.) Every year, the president gave a speech commemorating Asian/Pacific American Heritage month largely because Secretary of Transportation Norman Mineta, an Asian American, insisted that he do it and had invited his friends. Other speeches were scheduled for no apparent reason at all. Karl Rove was of the belief that the president needed to be out speaking every day no matter what the subject. Sometimes Bush would be at the podium four separate times in twenty-four hours, talking about the war in Iraq, the Olympics, the economy, or the birth of Thomas Jefferson. And the next day there might be another speech on Iraq, one more on the economy, and maybe a salute to Irish Americans. This obviously made it hard to broadcast a coherent message.

Sending the president out again and again to speak on the same subjects also tended to make his language stale, which meant that many people started to tune out, including the speechwriters. Our office was not the salon of geniuses I'd envisioned but a no-frills assembly line where overworked writers cranked out speech after speech as quickly as possible. Sometimes I'd test myself to see how far I could get into one of our speeches before my attention wandered. I usually never made it past page two.

I quickly discovered the answer to a question I'd been asked by people since I'd arrived at the White House: why did the president's speeches always seem to be so bad? It turned out it was intentional. On my very first day, Bill McGurn and Marc Thiessen both told me that the president was "okay" with a flat speech. All he cared about was logic and organization, not eloquence. As a student at Yale, the president had learned that all speeches should have an introduction, three points, a peroration, and a conclusion. I didn't even know what a peroration was. The president wasn't as insanely rigid about this approach, though, as Bill and the other writers thought he was. I'd read many of his finer speeches in his first term, and they rarely followed this pattern. But pushing the president to like a speech that was written differently was too risky. The writers all lived in fear that he'd blow up at them, which on occasion he'd been known to do. So in the quest for rigid logic—point A to point B to point C to conclusion—language that satisfied the president in one speech would be cut and pasted into the next speech and then the next.

The speechwriting process had three principal stages: a speech was assigned, then drafted, then sent out for comment throughout the White House staffing system. Assigning the speeches fell to the chief speechwriter and his two deputies, who at the time I started were Marc Thiessen and Chris Michel. The rest of the writers, about four of us, got a few of the big speeches, but mostly table scraps: talking points, small ceremonial remarks, and videotapings for those events the president couldn't attend in person. The tapings were always weird. The president would go to a room in the White House and read a one- or two-minute address off a teleprompter. Then, days or weeks later, his disembodied head would be played to a convention hall or conference room without the president ever being able to see the audience's reaction. The president hated doing the tapings.

One of the running gags among McGurn and the rest of the writers was that whoever Bill liked the least at the moment would get the worst speechwriting assignment of all: drafting a standby eulogy for Jimmy Carter. For many Republicans, particularly those from the Reagan generation, Carter was the political equivalent of what the Detroit Lions had been throughout my childhood: a hopeless, embarrassing disaster. On Carter's watch America had experienced an unprecedented economic crisis, an energy crisis, and international turmoil. No president could ever match that horrid record, right?

Bill thought it would be sheer agony to praise Carter. I actually thought it would be an interesting challenge. I used to come up with ideas for what I'd write without actually lying:

"Some presidents are so distinctive that they only come around once in a lifetime."

"We may have had our differences, but there is one thing we'll always be able to say about President Carter: he was an American."

"Jimmy Carter had a special way of looking at the world."

"I say this from my heart: America didn't deserve a president like Jimmy Carter."

In truth, the worst writing assignment in the speechwriting office wasn't a fake eulogy for Carter but the president's weekly radio address. The radio addresses were almost always cut-and-paste jobs based on whatever major speech the president had given earlier in the week. Hence, we all knew that being assigned the radio address was the equivalent of having a scarlet letter sewn to your shirt. I used to suggest turning the radio address into a video and putting some news in it instead of repeating old speeches. Whenever I mentioned that idea, people in the speechwriting office looked at me as if I were crazy. Think of all the work that would be. Weren't we already doing enough? Of course, years later, that's exactly what President Obama would do—wisely adopting the radio addresses for the YouTube era.

When we did receive advance guidance for a speech, it usually came from the head of the White House communications effort, the counselor to the president. When I first arrived at the White House, that was Dan Bartlett. Dan knew he wasn't a writer himself, so he offered commentary on our remarks but didn't try to craft them. His successor, Ed Gillespie, was a different story. Ed had been the chairman of the Republican National Committee. He was supposed to be our savior—a political genius Josh Bolten had brought in to turn everything around (just like Josh was supposed to). Habitually, Ed would predict confidently that we'd be back at a 40 percent approval rating anytime now, as if that were an accomplishment in itself. Ed reminded me of the congressional superstaffers I used to meet when I worked for Nick Smith. (I could even hear Ed thinking, *George Bush is elected to a third term in office in 2008. Now let's work backward.*)

Ed was a speechwriter's worst kind of boss: a lackluster writer who thought he was a good one. I'd read Ed's memoir before he came to the White House. The book was filled with clichés, from the obvious ("define or be defined"; "if you're in a hole, stop digging") to the weird ("cutting corners can cause bleeding"; "English beats math") to my favorite absurdism ("the more you get, the more you get"). All that was missing in the book was "there's no I in *team*" and "you know what happens when you assume." Ed meant well, but his tinkering usually made speeches worse.

Every week the speechwriters would go to Ed's office with a list of the speeches coming up in the month ahead. Ed's office was one of the larger corner offices on the second floor of the West Wing. It was apparently the only office that the president could look into at night from the top of the White House residence. Our meetings usually began with a discussion of the hit show *American Idol* (which Ed, a devoted father, enjoyed watching with his kids). That was usually the most interesting part of the meeting.

Whenever we talked about an upcoming speech, Ed almost never said, "Let me think about it" or "What do you guys think?" He never said, "Let's figure out what the message of the week is going to be." He usually just offered an instant reaction. The whole White House was like that—infatuated with decisiveness, dismissive of deliberation. I started labeling Ed's random decisions OTOHs, for "off the top of his head." It was not at all unusual for Ed to change his mind two or three times. He could send us in a certain direction one day and then in another two days later. Sometimes he had a last-minute speech idea—an address to the nation on the economy turned into a speech on the economy at the Chamber of Commerce turned into talking points at an Arlington, Virginia, tire dealership turned into cards for brief remarks by the president before he boarded Marine One. We'd often have to write something for each eventuality.

Like President Bush, Ed knew speechwriters had some of the most powerful jobs in the White House. The nature of our job meant that we got to know everyone at the senior levels of the White House. We sat in on meetings with the president on every conceivable issue. We met with him weekly, and sometimes more frequently. More than anyone, we helped him communicate with the outside world. It was therefore always amazing to me that few reporters, or congressional investigators for that matter, spent time talking to presidential speechwriters and finding out what they knew.

It was President Bush's speechwriters who articulated the concepts most associated with his presidency, for better or worse: "You are with us or you are with the terrorists," "axis of evil," "the Freedom Agenda," "the war on terror." A presidential speechwriter also could have a major influence on policy. When he was chief speechwriter, for example, Mike Gerson was widely credited with birthing the Bush administration policy of providing hundreds of millions of dollars in assistance to Africans infected with HIV.

Even I once created a presidential policy. I had been assigned to write the president's remarks for the National Day of Prayer. There were a number of similar events on the calendar throughout the year, including the annual National Prayer Breakfast, the annual Catholic Prayer Breakfast, and the annual Muslim Iftar dinner. It seemed as if we were always praying for something. Anyway, no one at the White House seemed to have the slightest interest in the remarks for the National Day of Prayer. So I decided to experiment with them a little. I thought it might be a nice idea for the president to propose an international day of prayer. This was a source of mockery among members of the staff—another day of prayer? But I thought the idea would appeal to the evangelical president. I had a vision of Bush urging Jews,

Muslims, Christians, and others around the world to spend one moment united in their common belief in a higher power.

When the speech went out for staffing comments, Raul called me. "Matt, who came up with this international prayer idea?"

"I did," I told him. "It was just a thought."

"But nobody told you to do that?" Raul asked.

Was I in trouble? I wondered. "Nope. You can take it out if you want."

Raul didn't ask to take it out. He just said, "Okay, thanks." And he hung up.

The day the speech was to be delivered, I'd just come out of the bathroom in the West Wing when my cell phone rang. It was Karen. "Matt?" she said. "I have the president for you."

I raced into Bill McGurn's office across the hall to find paper and a pen. President Bush was on the phone within seconds.

"Good afternoon, Mr. President," I said.

The president was in full Texan mode. "Hey, Matt, did you write this prayer deal?" he asked loudly.

"Yes, sir," I replied.

"Well, who came up with this international day of prayer idea?" he asked. He said it with his customary skepticism, his initial reaction to almost everything.

"I did, Mr. President." I swallowed hard. "It was a musing."

"Amusing?" he asked, sounding baffled.

"No, sir," I replied, laughing slightly. "Not amusing. A musing. Two words."

He paused. "What?"

"A musing. An idea." The other writers in the room were listening to the conversation in complete bewilderment. I could see them thinking, What on earth are they talking about?

That brief conversation was symbolic of our relationship: we never quite connected. "Uh, okay," the president replied. Then he hung up.

I didn't know what was going to happen next. Would the people in charge of our policies on prayer, whoever they were, call and yell at me? Or was the president just going to skip the line? Later that day I watched as the president went to the East Room of the White House before a group of religious leaders and Day of Prayer organizers. When he got to the part of the speech where I called for an international day of prayer, he said it as written. The president called it "a chance for people of faith around the world to pause to praise an Almighty. It will be a time when we can pray together for a world that sees the promise of the Psalms made real: 'Your house is ever before me, and I walk continually in your truth.' "

As the president offered this musing, he was interrupted with applause—something he clearly hadn't expected. One of the wire services sent out a news story with the headline "Bush Calls for International Day of Prayer." Afterward, someone in the policy shop sent an e-mail around asking, "Who came up with that?"

Though I was supposed to follow the preferred pattern of the flat, boring logical speech, I looked for every opportunity not to conform.

One of the best pieces of advice I ever received as a speechwriter came from Tony Dolan, whom I still spoke to regularly even though he was still at the Pentagon. Tony used to tell writers a story about the famed trial attorney F. Lee Bailey. Bailey was once asked what the key was to a successful case. People expected him to say a spellbinding closing statement or a good jury selection process or an impressive cross-examination of a crucial witness. Instead his answer was "investigation"—knowing the facts of your case up and down, forward and backward. Tony argued that the same held true for a good speech. The key was research: knowing everything about your audience, about the place where the remarks will be delivered, about everything that has led up to the planning of the event, and then tailoring a speech to those facts.

Though we had a small staff that was supposed to help with research, I usually preferred to do my own. My usual pattern was to find previous speeches the president had given on a topic. Then I looked at speeches on the same topic delivered by other presidents or other public figures. I examined where the president was speaking and investigated whether there was anything special about the place that fit into the event. I also checked the date to see if there were any notable anniversaries that could be mentioned.

This was the method I used, for example, to prepare remarks for an East Room event commemorating National Adoption Day. If I had wanted to merely follow the usual "Build a George W. Bush Speech from Scratch" kit, I could have written the whole speech in about ten minutes. The usual pattern would have been to start with a short, simple joke (two at most) and a brief, perfunctory mention of the audience. That would be followed with three or four paragraphs, each beginning with a variation of the same sentence: "We celebrate National Adoption Day because of X." (The sentences normally were underlined so the president could easily follow along as he read it.) Finally, the speech would end with a formulaic, lifeless anecdote about adoption. Once you wrote "God bless you and God bless the United States," you were done. Usually the audience would clap politely for a speech they had already forgotten.

This apparently was the Yale approach to a good speech.

I didn't take that tack for the adoption remarks. To hell with Yale. I'd gone to the University of Michigan, where we learned that speeches should be fun. (In Ann Arbor, we also learned that speeches could be followed by buildings being set on fire and campus-wide protests, but I digress.) I almost never wrote a speech with underlined sentences. I'd usually insert not one joke but two or three—and when I was feeling really frisky, sometimes even four! And I'd never end the speech with a by-the-numbers inspirational story. My whole speech was meant to be a story, with a beginning, middle, and end. (That this was considered revolutionary was a sad commentary on the situation I had found.)

In writing the Adoption Day speech, for example, the first thing I considered was the audience. I pictured the president standing before a large group of adoptive parents and their kids. I thought about the portraits of presidents that people would see just outside the East Room, including a portrait of an adopted son named Gerald R. Ford and another of an adoptive father named Ronald Reagan. And then I thought of the large pictures of George Washington that would be just to the president's left as he spoke. George Washington had been an adoptive father too, raising two children who weren't his by birth. (They were the children of his wife, Martha.) Searching the Internet, I found a letter that Washington wrote to his stepson while he was in college, complaining about his lack of attention to his studies. (I had our researchers verify its existence.) This led to a perfect joke for President Bush. After reading the excerpt to the audience, the president said, "Come to think of it, my dad once said the same thing to me."

I noted that Thanksgiving was approaching and so many new adoptive parents and children, including those in that room, would have the blessing of celebrating it together as a family for the first time. That thought made people cry. The president teared up. Even Mrs. Bush, who usually stood motionless while the president delivered his speeches, took an interest. She leaned forward and stole glances at the president's note card, as if to see how this was happening.

After the speech was over, one of the president's top aides, Kevin Sullivan, came up to me. He was the White House communications director, a title that hopelessly confused me. The overall communications effort at the White House was directed not by Kevin but by the counselor to the president. And most of the interactions with the press were handled by the press secretary. Which left the communications director doing . . . well, I wasn't sure. I do know that Kevin was the only person in the Bush White House who never uttered an unkind word about anyone. He told me that the Adoption Day event was one of the best the president had ever done. It turned out that Sully had adopted children of his own. But the event never would have been special without good research. I wished we all had done that a lot more.

On at least one occasion the person providing key research for a speech turned out to be the president of the United States himself. Of course, if the president had to fill in some important fact relative to a speech, it meant you'd really failed to do your job. But that's exactly what happened when I wrote the president's address to the men and women of the legendary USO, the group that, among other things, sends entertainers abroad during wartime to support the troops.

A few hours before the USO speech was to be delivered, I was at my desk when the phone rang. The caller ID had a code on it that I recognized as coming from the president's private residence.

"Matt, this is a nice little speech," the president said, which was usually the most praise he'd give. "But Laura says that my grandfather, Prescott, was the original chairman of the USO. If that's true, we probably want to mention that."

"Oh, absolutely, Mr. President," I said. I felt embarrassed that I hadn't known that. "We'll check it out, sir."

"Wait just a minute," the president said. "I think we've got a piece of paper somewhere on the Internet that mentions it. Hold on a second."

The president either put the phone down or put his hand over it. Either way, I could hear him talking to someone in the background. I assumed it was the First Lady. "Honey, can you find that paper?" he asked.

It sounded like Mrs. Bush was searching the Internet for something.

"No, honey, that's not it," the president said. "No, that's not it either."

He came back to the phone. "Hold on a second, Matt," the president said. "We're trying to find it."

"Yes, sir," I said. I wondered if I should even be listening to this.

They continued searching. I'd hear the president say, "No, that's not it...no...no..." He got back on the phone and whispered good-naturedly, "She's having a little trouble over here." Then after a few more minutes, he said, "Okay, yeah. That's it. Thanks, honey."

The president read the name of someone who'd written an article mentioning the president's granddad and his relationship with the USO. "So do you think you can have somebody verify this and make sure it's true?" Bush asked.

"Yes, sir," I said.

"I hope it's true," the president added. "Because I've already told that to people." He laughed with his distinctive "heh heh heh."

Over time, I developed my own little speech signatures, certain Latimer touches. One was "the Barbara Bush joke." There was something about that relationship between the president and his mother that humanized him. And he loved to talk about her. So I'd try to insert a joke about the former First Lady into every speech I could. In a speech to the National Religious Broadcasters convention—an audience that clearly shared Bush's spiritual values, I had the president acknowledge, "I learned early on the importance of obedience to a higher power. Speaking of which, Mother says hello."

At the farewell ceremony for General Pete Pace: "Some of you may think mothers are required to say only admiring things about their sons. Well, take it from me. It's not always the case."

At the Conservative Political Action Conference: "I think Dick Cheney is the best vice president in history. Mother may have another opinion. Don't tell her I said this, but mine is the one that counts." Other people told me that the president loved the riffs on his mom, though he never mentioned it to me. Nor did he seem to notice my Barbara Bush fascination (which is probably for the best).

Another Latimer signature was the surprise. The way that worked, I'd tell some story about an unnamed person and then surprise the audience by having it turn out to be someone unexpected. It was sort of a takeoff on Paul Harvey's *The Rest of the Story*. I did this in the USO speech, for example. "Looking back on those war-torn days," I wrote, "a former servicemember once said, 'I'll never forget the USO's positive impact during those dark and perilous times.' That statement has a special meaning to me because the man who said it was a Navy pilot named George H. W. Bush."

I also started a joyous kick for a while. Once, when I went with him to a private fund-raiser, I heard Bush call his presidency a "joyous experience." I liked the way that sounded. So in a speech to the troops, I wrote, "These Americans give me endless optimism about our future. And they have made my presidency a joyous experience." The other speechwriters snickered at the phrase. Later, when the president made an offhand comment to some of the writers that he loved using the word joyous, I was suddenly a genius. This led to an endless stream of "joyous" moments for the president. "This is my last [insert event here]. You have made my presidency a joyous experience." Eventually, it started to get a little much and the bored White House press corps caught on.

In a *New York Times Magazine* piece, "The Final Days," the author pooh-poohed the whole joyous business. "Bush refers to his time in office as 'a joyous experience,' " the writer wrote, "a phrase that seems jarring. A satisfying experience, pursuing important goals, maybe, or a vital experience, to be at the center of so many historic moments. But joyous? With all the heartache, the wars, the political attacks?"

We stopped using joyous. For a while.

The one ceremonial speech I'd always wanted to write since arriving at the White House was the president's remarks at the annual pardoning of the Thanksgiving turkey. This had been a presidential tradition since the days of Truman. I loved the thought of seeing the most powerful man on earth share the stage with two large birds that had the nerve to flap their wings and gobble throughout the president's speech. Reagan hated the event, or so I was told. The former actor simply hated working with animal costars who wouldn't reliably hit their marks. Bonzo was one thing. A bunch of turkeys was quite another.

I thought the speech would be a simple assignment: a few jokes, a bit of history on the Pilgrims, and then we'd be done. Nobody really cared what the president said at this event. They mostly wanted to watch the turkeys. But, much to my surprise, I was pulled into a controversy whose dimensions I couldn't possibly have foreseen.

"You heard about the pig, right?" a reporter friend asked me when I told him I was writing the pardoning remarks.

No, I replied, I hadn't heard about any pig.

"Well, it's a big debate," he said with complete seriousness. "I can't believe you haven't heard of it."

As it turned out, there was a movement afoot, led by a group of native Virginians, to have the president pardon a pig instead of a turkey, or at the very least a pig with a turkey. This was because some Thanksgiving fanatics insisted that the Pilgrims and Native Americans never shared a turkey for their famous dinner but ate a pig instead. They were really jacked up about it. *The turkey pardon is a sham!*

The issue actually became a topic at a White House senior staff meeting. Yes, such things were taking up space on the agenda of the most powerful people on the planet. In the end, turkeys and turkeys alone remained the guests of honor at the Rose Garden event. (But there's always next year.) I was disappointed. I wanted to be the first presidential speechwriter in history to pardon a pig.

Every year for the pardoning ceremony, Americans across the country were given a chance to vote on the names for the two Thanksgiving turkeys. The winning names were kept more confidential than the nuclear launch codes. In fact, I wasn't even allowed to know the winning entries until the very last moment. Who knows what I would have done with that kind of power?

Without yet knowing what names America in its wisdom would pick for the turkeys, I had the president launch a humorous barb at one of his favorite straight men: Dick Cheney. The vice president had famously shot a friend in the face during a hunting accident, and President Bush got endless mileage out of poking fun at it. So after the president revealed the winning names for the turkeys, I had him quip, "These names are a lot better than the ones Vice President Cheney suggested—'Lunch' and 'Dinner.' "

Josh Bolten, the White House chief of staff, was apparently so taken with the joke that he read it out loud at a staff meeting. Then he personally read it to the vice president to make sure he wasn't offended. He wasn't. In fact, the vice president didn't even get it.

Given the White House speech-vetting process, it was a miracle that any speech from the president was funny, moving, interesting, or memorable. The Reagan speechwriter Peggy Noonan once compared the White House speech-vetting process to the Hanoi Hilton and Heartbreak Hill. It turns out that was understated. When I was chief speechwriter at the Pentagon, no more than two or three people were involved in vetting a speech, and often it was just me and Rumsfeld (though trust me, that could be a challenge all in itself). The White House was very different. Every presidential speech was vetted through as many as a dozen different offices—including that of the vice president, the National Security Council, the Council of Economic Advisors, the Office of Management and Budget, and many others. The process gave you a glimpse of who in the White House possessed the most power. No one wanted to ignore a comment from someone the president liked or, alternatively, someone who was likely to go running to the president and complain that his or her comment had been ignored. When I first started, the vetters of highest rank were, in order of importance, Karl Rove, Dan Bartlett, Steve Hadley or Condi Rice (on national security questions only), and Raul Yanes. Over time, after Bartlett and Rove had left, the order changed to Steve Hadley, Raul Yanes, Ed Gillespie, and everyone else. In the final year, it was Ed Gillespie, Raul Yanes, Steve Hadley, and then everyone else. Sometimes it was Ed Gillespie and then everyone else. Making cameo appearances were the First Lady, Press Secretary Dana Perino, and the chief of staff, whose suggestions were usually carefully heeded.

Some of the hardest-working people in our office were the fact checkers. They were young, a few fresh out of law school, who worked long hours and many weekends to make sure the president's remarks were accurate. I remember one fact checker who spent the night in his office trying to verify a statement that I casually put into a speech about the number of Americans who pray daily. Unfortunately, the fact checkers rarely won appreciation, inside the White House or out of it. When Brendon Merkley enrolled at Stanford Business School and was introduced as the president's head fact checker, the audience laughed in disbelief. *Bush has fact checkers?* Bill McGurn told me that he once lauded their work to the president when the entire speechwriting team met with Bush in the Oval Office. "What do you expect me to do," Bush asked in front of them. "Thank them?" It didn't seem like he was joking, but the fact checkers were too dazzled to be in the presence of the president to take much notice of what he said.

It was always amazing to me how many big battles erupted during the vetting process over presidential jokes. For a speechwriter, jokes are one of the most important parts of any speech. They show that the speaker has a sense of humor, and they put the audience at ease and make it more receptive to the message being delivered. Unfortunately, the White House vetting system seemed determined to kill anything that hinted at humor.

I once wrote remarks for a Congressional Gold Medal ceremony honoring Norman Borlaug, the scientist credited with leading a revolution in grain production that literally helped feed the world. Most people, unfortunately, had never heard of the man, so it was even more important to make the president's remarks interesting and funny, to keep people listening. So at one point in the speech, I wrote the following: "A friend recently said that Norman spends half of the year in Texas, half of the year in Mexico, and the other half of the year wherever else he's needed. That's some interesting math. Madam Speaker, I was going to say that I bet some folks here wish we could use that kind of arithmetic during budget season. Then I realized—sometimes we do." It was not the most hilarious joke in the world, but I thought it would get a laugh.

This joke led to a raging debate. The head of legislative affairs at the White House strongly objected to the line because it insulted Congress. The Democrats in Congress never, ever would have said anything to insult President Bush, after all. Valiantly, Raul, the staff secretary, tried to save the joke. In response to the concerns about attacking the Democratic Congress, Raul pointed out that the joke could be read to insult the president as well: "Sometimes we do." The objection then became that the joke implied that we weren't rigidly honest in making our budget assumptions. (I thought the cat was already out of the bag on that one.) For whatever reason, the joke managed to stay in. The president thought it was funny and said it. After the speech was over, no one seemed to think that the joke had irreparably damaged relations between the White House and Congress, at least not any more than they already were.

Then there was the Battle of Jessica Simpson. She was one of the few major celebrities who went on USO tours to Iraq to visit the troops. She'd previously said nice things about the president, so I thought it would be cool if he found a way to mention her in his remarks to the USO. It might even make the sixty-one-year-old Bush look hip. So I drafted the president's remarks to include a Simpson mention. "There's been a lot of talk about the success of the surge in Iraq," I wrote. "But I think we all know the moment things really began to turn around in Iraq. It was when the USO decided to deploy Jessica Simpson." I thought that line would get a good laugh. Then I fought against a day-long effort to take the line out. First, Ed Gillespie objected to any mention of the success of the surge in Iraq. (It might be bragging.) Then I got an e-mail from the staff secretary's office. They objected to the Jessica Simpson joke because she'd visited Iraq before the surge began. She couldn't possibly have had anything to do with the turnaround in Iraq. Therefore, the joke was illogical.

It was left for me to point out that the president wasn't actually claiming that Jessica Simpson had anything to do with improving conditions in Iraq—and no one in their right mind would think that he was. The staff secretary's office wasn't convinced, though, and they usually had the power to kill something if they tried hard enough. So when the president called me about the issue of his grandfather's involvement in the USO, I decided to use the opportunity to my advantage. "Did you like the Jessica Simpson joke?" I asked.

"Yeah, sure," he said. "It was funny."

I waited for another e-mail to go around questioning the joke. Once it did, I used my new leverage, trying to sound casual about it. "Oh, by the way," I wrote, "the president told me he liked the Jessica Simpson joke." The line stayed. It got big laughs from the USO audiences. It was also mentioned in the New York Post, USA Today, and several other papers. And it was the "Quote of the Week" in the Washington Post. Not a single news article took the president to task for trying to give Jessica Simpson credit for the surge. And, in fact, it was the only thing in the speech that received even the slightest positive attention.

The speech-vetting process could often be misleading in a White

House notorious for its buddy system, where everyone wanted to be friends with everyone else. From my earliest days there, I'd get comments or a note from someone telling me a speech I'd written was moving or excellent. I was so excited. Someone had noticed me. My work was standing out. Then I realized that people said that about everything. "Great" talking points on the economy. "Great" taping for the Texas state GOP convention. Sometimes it seemed as if a writer could get praise from someone just by jotting down a grocery list on a Post-it note. In this environment, it was hard to know what was really good or helpful to the president and what was just being praised out of politeness. A rare exception involved Condi Rice. She once reviewed a speech on Romania and wrote only one comment on top: "Boring." To my fellow speechwriters, and pretty much everyone else, this was considered the rudest thing in the world. But I didn't see it that way. Many of the speeches *were* boring, but no one said so. Secretary Rice had the position and stature to be brave.

I developed a rule that I passed on to a few of the other writers. If someone asked me what I thought of a speech, I'd automatically, under any circumstances, say "great." This meant absolutely nothing. But if I used any other adjective—"good" or "interesting" or "elegant," for example—then that meant I actually liked it.

Perhaps it goes without saying that the speech-vetting process was the worst way to produce a decent speech. Any of the offices involved in the process could gum up the works at any point, and many tried.

The vice president's office played the role of Don Quixote. They fought against any language in speeches that tended to seem too pro-government or liberal. As the administration wound down, these comments were increasingly overruled, and the feedback from the vice president's office got increasingly angry. At one point, they disputed the word *snuck* in the State of the Union address with a snide comment. "This is not a word," someone in their office wrote. "Let's use proper English around here." Well, it was a word, and we kept *snuck* in. I also snuck it into other remarks just to show them.

The most scatterbrained comments usually came, frighteningly enough, from the National Security Council—the mammoth agency within the White House that seemed to have a specialist for every subject, domestic and foreign. One problem with their edits was that they were almost never on time. Another was that the NSC people rarely co-ordinated with one another, so edits would often be contradictory. More troubling was that they obviously hadn't read the president's previous remarks on the subjects about which they were supposedly experts. Frequently an NSC staffer would issue a warning in the strongest terms—"the president should never say this publicly"—even though the president had used that exact language in previous speeches. In one case, the NSC objected to facts they'd already approved and that the president had already asserted in his State of the Union address the night before.

One of the big criticisms of the administration was that it had "dropped the ball" in Afghanistan by turning all of our attention to Iraq. If the vetting process was any indication, there was every reason to believe that was true. Whenever we needed facts or edits from NSC on an Iraq speech, we were given a flood of information from a crack team of people. Whenever we created a speech on Afghanistan, however, it was nearly impossible to get timely or reliable facts from the NSC desk. One statistic in particular stuck in my mind. The NSC people were claiming things were improving in Afghanistan, and to support their contention they provided a metric indicating that we'd sharply increased Afghans' access to quality health care. The president had used this statistic before. It turned out, though, that this was a very questionable metric. To the NSC, "access" to health care meant that a typical Afghan would only have to walk something like eight hours to the nearest clinic. This was an achievement? We took the line out. And from then on, we had little confidence in any information the NSC gave us.

By far, the absolute worst office to deal with on speeches was the Council on Environmental Quality. CEQ always pushed and pushed for long speeches on their initiatives, wanting the president to take positions to the left of his party. Director Jim Connaughton was known to be so unmanageable in the speechwriting process that he was given a special deadline for turning in his comments—a deadline he usually ignored. We would have felt more comfortable ignoring him—what does the Council on Environmental Quality mean to Republicans anyway?—except there was one problem. Jim wasn't just head of the CEQ; he was Josh Bolten's brother-in-law.

CEQ was directly involved in one of the more interesting speech debacles that I experienced at the White House. Connaughton, Bolten, and others wanted the president to give a climate change speech. They thought that it would make our allies in Europe happy, and they were constantly pushing the president to the left on the issue. The small but merry band of conservatives in the White House—who were suspicious of climate change and the movement behind it—were opposed to any shift in our policy. They were adamantly against any speech supporting a cap-and-trade policy—a mandate on business to curb their CO_2 emissions. At one point, the words *cap and trade* were put into the climate change speech, with the president expressing his support for the policy. Then somehow this leaked to the conservative press. Republicans on the outside of the White House sent furious objections, and the words were removed. But only those words. The rest of the speech endorsing that policy remained. After days and days of postponements and fights, the president finally gave the speech. Conservatives in the West Wing were deflated by their loss in the policy battle. And then something miraculous happened. Because the speech had been so parsed and litigated, no one could quite understand what the president was saying. The press therefore assumed nothing had really changed. So the next day, the media reported that the president had in fact come out *against* cap and trade. A White House spokesman even said that the words *cap and trade* had never been included in any drafts of the speech, which was flat-out false. The president marveled at his good fortune. He'd changed his policy to please one side, but since he seemed not to have changed a thing, he'd also pleased the other. Indecipherable speechwriting at its finest.

On rare occasions the speech-vetting process would lead to exciting moments. I was writing the president's remarks for a ceremony honoring the holy leader of Tibet, the Dalai Lama, when I received a call from actor Richard Gere. Gere, who was very close to the Dalai Lama, left a message on my answering machine offering to share his perspectives. I thought it could be helpful to talk to him. I also thought it would be cool. So did many people on the speechwriting staff. In fact, many of the fact checkers and researchers came into my office just to hear Richard Gere's message on my voice mail.

But I did something dumb. I got cautious and asked our not exactly crackerjack press operation if it was okay for me to talk to him. I supposed there was a remote possibility that it could be leaked to the papers that the president was consulting with an actor from Hollywood on an important speech, but that really didn't seem all that likely. And who cared if that story came out anyway? It turned out that the White House *was* concerned, though. Someone in the communications office instructed me that I should absolutely not talk to Gere under any circumstances. I should just blow him off. (This also could have been a problem since Gere was going to be at the event and would certainly talk to the press.) Anyway, I never returned the call, but I felt bad about it. If it's any consolation to Mr. Gere, I've watched *Pretty Woman* six times—and not just because they play it endlessly on TNT.

Sometimes edits from staffers were revealing. I once wrote a toast for an event honoring America's Promise, Colin Powell's public service group. In the remarks, I had the president salute his former secretary of state and his wife, Alma. During the vetting process I received the following comment from the organization: "In the next draft can you change 'Secretary Powell' to 'General Powell'? He prefers to go by 'General' instead of 'Secretary.'" It looked to me as if Powell was trying to distance himself from the administration. I'm happy to report that the president didn't accommodate him. "Secretary Powell" stayed in.

We'd also sometimes receive interesting suggestions for themes to emphasize in speeches. For the Fourth of July, it was decided that the president should go to Thomas Jefferson's home, Monticello, to give a speech on citizenship. At the same time there'd be a swearing-in ceremony for legal immigrants who'd met the requirements to become citizens. It looked to be a nice event on a hot July day. President Bush's only instruction for the speech was to keep it short.

One afternoon, the speechwriter who'd been assigned the remarks—my old friend Horny—sent an e-mail to some of the other writers telling us about a suggestion he'd received from Barry Jackson's office for the speech. Barry was the White House political director, the guy who oversaw the president's political strategy and helped raise money for House and Senate candidates.

According to Jonathan Horn, Barry wanted the president to go to Monticello and give a speech that pointed out the similarities between the president's legacy and Thomas Jefferson's. In effect, he wanted Bush to go to the home of one of the greatest presidents in history and proclaim himself Jefferson's second coming. When Jonathan told us that,

I shook my head in disbelief. That couldn't possibly be what Barry had said.

I quickly made my way to Jonathan's office. "I've got to see this," I said. "There has to be some mistake."

Jonathan shrugged. He showed me the e-mail. I had to read it twice. There was no mistake.

Barry's team noted that Jefferson was proudest of three accomplishments in his life. These were the only things he wanted etched on his tombstone: father of the University of Virginia, author of the Declaration of Independence, and author of the Virginia statute for religious freedom.

The e-mail then asserted that these three achievements matched the president's own accomplishments perfectly. *Come again?*

Jefferson had founded the University of Virginia. Well, they said, Bush had gotten the No Child Left Behind Act passed. Jefferson had authored the Declaration of Independence. Well, Bush had launched the Freedom Agenda in Afghanistan and Iraq. Jefferson had authored the Virginia statute for religious freedom. Well, that was just like the president's faith-based initiative. It all made perfect sense!

I said that if we actually wrote such a speech, we all should be fired. I'd fire myself. And if Bush actually went to Monticello to proclaim himself the Thomas Jefferson of our day, there'd be grounds to question his sanity. I consoled myself with the knowledge that he never would. To this day I don't know what was more remarkable about the e-mail: that the president's top political advisor, a senior White House official, would propose such a notion, or that his entire office supported it.

The speechwriters received nonsense like this all the time, but our chief speechwriter, Bill McGurn, was deft enough to blow a lot of it off. Then Bill decided to leave the White House early to go to work for Rupert Murdoch at Fox News, and I knew the speechwriting office was in trouble. At first glance, Bill was a tall, large, white-haired angel of a guy. He was friendly and soft-spoken. But he also had the skills of a world-class schemer. In fact, as far as old-fashioned skullduggery went, Bill was a stealth bomber—agile, unexpected, and usually undetectable. Unfortunately, he'd never use his considerable talents to persuade the president to try anything new in terms of speeches. His approach was to keep the president happy by giving him what he was used to—the same old, same old. But if predictable, Bill was reasonable and collegial, whereas his deputy, Marc, was, well . . . not that way.

Even so, Marc became the new chief speechwriter, and Chris and I became Marc's deputies. Marc was chosen after what seemed an inordinately long delay. When Josh Bolten finally offered Marc the job, he apparently told him that it was a two-minute decision, and the first minute was taken up by getting a cup of coffee. (Marc casually repeated this line at least four times that week.)

Marc had good qualities. He was devoted to his kids and to his church. Still, I don't know if I would have taken the job had Marc been in charge then. That's how difficult I knew he'd be. As a boss, Marc could forget his assistant's last name or worse, mispronounce it. He called another staff member, who had worked there for a year at that point, by the wrong name. Marc liked to encourage a broad range of opinions from others, so long as theirs agreed with his. When Ted Kennedy was diagnosed with a brain tumor, I suggested that the president might at least consider awarding Kennedy the Presidential Medal of Freedom. Marc objected with the genteel diplomacy he was known for. "That's crazy!" he thundered. Kennedy was a liberal, he noted (of which I was well aware). This was the same sort of narrow thinking that led people in the White House to actually object to giving the author J. K. Rowling a presidential medal because the Harry Potter books encouraged witchcraft.

When Marc was writing remarks on the war in Iraq, he tried to browbeat a CIA analyst who was unwilling to state unequivocally that America was winning in the war on terror. "The president wants to say we're winning!" Marc thundered. Just what we needed—another accusation that the Bush White House wanted to politicize intelligence.

Then there were the thoughtless gaffes that Marc kept making to Steve Hadley. One day I was standing outside the Oval Office when Hadley walked up to us. "Marc, I think we need to get together to discuss the upcoming speech to the Institute of Peace," Hadley said politely. "The president is going to want to see it early."

Marc shook his head. "Steve, we've got a lot of work coming up, so we probably can't do it," he said. "We've got to shoot the wolves closest to the sled." I couldn't believe what I was hearing. This was a man who was holding the same job once held by Henry Kissinger, and Marc was casually blowing him off. For a millisecond, an unusual look crossed the very circumspect Hadley's face. Marc didn't notice it, of course. It was a look that said, *I'll get you for that, my friend.* (He did.)

A few days later, Marc, Chris, and I were sitting in the Oval Office with the president and Steve Hadley, talking about that very speech. The president didn't want to go to the Institute of Peace, but Hadley kept pushing him to do it. So when the speech came up, the president said, "The Institute of Peace speech. I call it the Steve Hadley Lecture." We all laughed.

Hadley went along with the joke. "As long as it's not called the Hadley Memorial Lecture," he said. We all laughed again.

Without looking at Hadley, Marc blurted out, "Well, it *will* be a memorial lecture if your office keeps sending all those edits to speeches." He laughed loudly. No one else did. I looked at Chris, who looked at me. We didn't dare look at Hadley.

A few days later, Marc came into his West Wing office, where Chris and I had been waiting for him.

Marc had a puzzled look on his face. "I think I insulted Steve Hadley," he said. No kidding.

"What happened?" Chris asked.

Marc said he'd been sitting with Hadley on the way to the speech and they started talking about the 2000 terrorist attack on the USS Cole. Marc was obsessed with all things terror-related; he liked talking about terrorism and quoting terrorists and prophesying doom. I was concerned about terrorism too. We all were, but Marc's interest veered to the extreme.

Marc said he told Hadley that the Bush administration's failure to respond convincingly to the strike on the USS Cole had led directly to the 9/11 attack. Since Hadley had been the deputy national security advisor before 9/11, Marc in effect was blaming him. Regardless of the point he was trying to make, even Marc seemed to figure out that hadn't been the wisest move.

When Chris and I were back in our office, I began taking stock of recent events. "Do you realize," I said, "that in the space of a week, Marc blew off Steve Hadley for a meeting, then basically threatened him in the Oval Office, and then accused him of complicity in the worst terrorist attack in our history?"

Referring to Marc's passion for ice hockey, Chris observed, "That's quite a hat trick." I laughed.

Even the president wasn't shielded from Marc's bizarre gaffes.

When we were preparing to write the president's 2008 address to the Republican National Convention, he asked us to read the speeches other presidents had given. One day the president asked if we'd finished going through them. We said that we had.

"How about Reagan's in 1992?" the president inquired. "I thought that was pretty good." I knew why. It was a speech in which Reagan had gone to bat for the president's dad.

"I didn't think that was a very good speech," Marc opined, for no apparent reason.

"You didn't?" the president asked, with a look of surprise.

"No," Marc said. "I don't think he had his heart in it."

"So you don't think Reagan had his heart in that speech?" the president asked, trying to conceal a smirk. I knew what Bush was thinking. This dude couldn't possibly be saying what he seemed to be saying.

Marc didn't get it at all. "No, I don't," he said.

The president chuckled. "Okay . . ."

Marc was now my supervisor, the chief speechwriter to the president of the United States. And he was making my old boss Nick Smith look like a study in sober statesmanship.

As I was just coming to terms with a White House speechwriting process that seemed designed to undermine the president and any message he wanted to communicate, I was invited to a gathering that made me feel even worse.

In the bowels of the *Washington Post* building, the Judson Welliver Society held one of its irregularly scheduled dinner meetings. Named for a man who, as an assistant to President Warren G. Harding, became the first official presidential speechwriter, the Welliver Society offered membership to all living practitioners of that mysterious art. The society's founder was William Safire. Safire had graying hair, merry eyes, and an arsenal of ready quips. Even at seventy-seven, he possessed the mischievous spark of that clever kid from the Bronx who went to the White House with Richard Nixon—and got out just before the administration's famous fall.

After his escape from Nixon, a year or so before the beleaguered president resigned, Safire built an impressive career as an author and columnist. He was an idealistic conservative who wanted the Republican Party to be what it strived to be, and was disappointed during the many years when it fell short. In 1992, Safire had become so disillusioned with a feckless and compromised Republican Party that he committed the equivalent of a mortal sin: he voted for Bill Clinton. He figured that a president named Bush had made such a mess of things that it was time for the country to try something else. Safire and Clinton would later have a very public parting of the ways when the columnist labeled Clinton's wife, Hillary, a congenital liar. (Actually, the term he used, with typical precision, was "habitual prevaricator.") In response, President Clinton offered to punch Safire in the nose.

Safire was our master of ceremonies for the evening's festivities, which commenced with a typical Washington fixture, the cocktail hour. Speechwriters from previous administrations carefully milled about trying to figure out whom they wanted to avoid and who was currently feuding with whom. Many of the people there had names most Americans had never heard before, including mine. It is the blessed curse of a speechwriter to toil anonymously, watch others receive acclaim for the words one has written, or, just as frequently, reap criticism for speeches that flop. Only a precious few ever manage to pierce the curtain and become known to the world.

Ted Sorensen was one who did. It was Sorensen who helped President Kennedy craft the famous line in his 1961 inaugural "Ask not what your country can do for you, ask what you can do for your country." The voice of the Thousand Days, Camelot, "Ich bin ein Berliner," and many other speeches I'd memorized as a child was now standing before me. For those of us who are Star Wars fans, it was like getting to meet C-3PO in person for the very first time.

Not far from Sorensen was the writer Richard Goodwin. He had wild black hair, white eyebrows, and a face that had weathered many adventures. He too had worked for the Kennedys—Jack and Bobby—and even for their nemesis, LBJ. He was credited with naming Johnson's ambitious domestic agenda "the Great Society." He was also made famous by the film Quiz Show as the lawyer who exposed the game-show scandals of the 1950s.

Richard Goodwin was joined by his wife, the author and famed presidential historian Doris Kearns Goodwin. I had read two of her wonderful books on the presidency—Team of Rivals, about the Lincoln years, and No Ordinary Time, about Franklin and Eleanor Roosevelt.

Chatting with the Goodwins and looking fascinated by their every word was the It girl of presidential speechwriting, Peggy Noonan. I came of age as a huge Peggy Noonan fan. She'd written a marvelous book, What I Saw at the Revolution, about the Reagan era and her time as a White House speechwriter. In the years that followed, I read her other books and her weekly Wall Street Journal column. And I watched her whenever she appeared on TV. Peggy was usually a no-show for these dinners, but Bill Safire personally had asked her to attend.

Standing not far from Peggy, but not too close, was my friend and personal Obi-Wan Kenobi, Tony Dolan. Tony wore a nice suit and power tie along with cowboy boots. Though he'd worked for Reagan far longer than Peggy had, Tony had never won her kind of fame. Then again, he'd never sought it. Still, when Reagan left office, the Gipper gave Tony a letter that showed where Tony ranked in the speechwriter pantheon. At the bottom, in his neat, small handwriting, the president wrote, "Tony, you were the keeper of the flame."

Safire invited a few of the writers to come to the microphone and share some stories. When Tony came forward to talk about the Reagan years, giving a lively and entertaining speech, one couldn't help but notice a certain tension in the air. While everyone else looked at Tony as he spoke, Peggy looked away. When others laughed at something Tony said, she smiled only slightly, revealing a flash of teeth. (Peggy apparently was not a fan of some of the other writers she'd worked with. She'd once dismissed them in a Wall Street Journal column, calling one "a hack" and another "a diseased leprechaun.") The other Reagan writers I met didn't seem to bear much affection for her either. Many thought she'd grabbed the Reagan limelight for herself. The stakes were high in this decades-long battle. The Reagan writers were fighting over something that mattered: their rival claims on the Great Communicator's legacy. Not all presidential speechwriters felt that way about their president. For instance, nobody was running around trying to prove they were the true voice of Gerald Ford.

That night we also heard from the oldest Judson Welliver Society member present, Ken Hechler, a spry ninety-two. He'd written speeches sixty years earlier for Harry S. Truman. He took us to school about the Republican Congress of 1948. "Did any of you know," he asked devilishly, "that Truman used to call them the 'Do-Nothing Congress'?" (We did.) Every time Safire gently moved toward him, Ken waved him away. "I know you're trying to give me the hook," he said to a laughing Bill Safire. "I've got a few more things to say." "Give 'Em Hell" Hechler proceeded to filibuster for twenty minutes, taking temporary control of the dinner from the amused emcee.

When Ken was finally finished, one of Bill Clinton's speechwriters came forward. He wanted everyone to know that all the rumors about the chaotic Clinton White House were undeniably, indisputably...true. Clinton had been a terrible president to write for, always second-guessing his speechwriters and seeking last-minute input from random outsiders. Incredibly, he even called up people for advice about his inaugural address the morning it was to be delivered. His speechwriter told us about the time he'd had to wedge himself into a limousine with Bill, Hillary, and his laptop so they could finally finish Clinton's 1996 Democratic National Convention address—while he was on the way to the convention hall to deliver it. It was no wonder most of the lines Clinton is remembered for came from him, not from his speeches. And I'm sure they weren't lines he hoped would go down in history ("That depends on what the definition of is is" and "That is one good-looking mummy. If that mummy were around today, I'd ask her out").

As I listened to each of these presidential speechwriters, I was completely enthralled. They'd reached the top of their profession, contributing to history in ways large and small. Now here I was—a kid from Michigan—at the famed Judson Welliver Society dinner joining their ranks. I'd thought that if I ever reached this moment, I'd feel, well...I don't know...exhilarated, I guess, excited in some way. I thought it would be thrilling. But as wonderful as it was to behold these speechwriting legends, it wasn't as satisfying as I'd expected to be inducted into their guild.

Safire called me and the other Bush speechwriters to a small stage and introduced us to the group. He asked us to raise our right hands and repeat a makeshift oath. Two minutes later, that was that. We were in. No oral exam, no cutting off the heads off chickens, no blood oaths. It wasn't exactly admission into Skull and Bones.

As the evening wound down, a dark thought took hold. It occurred to me that I wasn't destined to be the author of a speech ushering in the twenty-first-century New Frontier. I wasn't going to tell another Mikhail Gorbachev to "tear down this wall." No, my friends and I in George W.'s White House weren't going to be remembered that way. We didn't have a boss like Kennedy or Reagan whose oratorical gifts might burn our words into history. Rather, we were kin of sorts to the writers who'd toiled in the administrations of Carter and Ford. Mediocrity was the highest level our words would likely reach. We were the RC Cola of speechwriters, the Hyundais, the socks you get as Christmas presents. That was the best I was going to do with the job of my dreams.

CHAPTER NINE

THE MAYOR OF CONTROL

We wouldn't even have had a Bush presidency without Karl Rove. At least, that's what everybody said. Critics called him Bush's brain—because, of course, it was assumed Bush himself was lacking one. They looked at Rove as a real-life version of Voldemort—because, of course, Americans wouldn't really vote Republican unless they'd been bewitched. Karl, so the conventional wisdom went, was a rare genius—to some an evil genius, to others a corrupt one, but a genius nonetheless.

In 1999 and 2000, I watched in awe as Karl Rove maneuvered one prominent Republican after another into making the solemn pilgrimage to Austin to plead with then Governor Bush to run for the White House, as if the presidency were the furthest thing from Bush's mind. All Bush had to do was welcome his many visitors. He didn't even have to leave his house.

I thought I saw Karl's hand again in the campaign's coining of the slogan "compassionate conservative." The phrase gave many of my friends in the conservative movement considerable discomfort: Is he saying we aren't compassionate? But I thought it was clever. It made conservatives in the party think that Bush was one of us—he was just trying to placate the moderates and liberals. And it made moderates and liberals think Bush might be one of them—he was just trying to placate the conservatives.

Most of all, I was impressed by Karl's single-minded determination on election night 2000, when things were at their bleakest for the Bush campaign. The networks had famously called Florida for Gore.

The news anchors were telling us the election was slipping away. The Clinton machine would win yet again. No Bush restoration. No Republican White House. No endorsement of the conservative revolution.

Then came Karl, a bespectacled messenger from the gods. Word spread on the cable networks that Rove was vigorously opposing the Florida call. He was telling anyone who'd listen that the count was wrong and Bush had actually won. Refusing to back down, he pressured the networks to do something rarely seen on television: reverse themselves. They did. From that point on, even as the Florida count was disputed during the weeks that followed, the momentum shifted decisively in Bush's favor. Anything Gore did made it look like he was trying to take something away from Bush, who'd already been declared the winner. This wouldn't have been possible had it not been for Karl's relentlessness that night. Oh, how the Clintons hated him! And so did the pundits and prognosticators in the media. They saw his sinister maneuverings behind every move Bush made. They gave him credit for things he didn't do and sometimes spared him blame for things he did.

During President Bush's first term, you could definitely put me down as a Karl Rove man. But back then, Karl was only what I heard or saw on TV. It wasn't until the second term that I first came into contact with Karl Rove the actual human being.

In a White House where everything was just so, everyone stayed carefully in their own lane, and it was so quiet and polite that you couldn't even hear people's footsteps on the soft carpet, Karl was a traveling circus, a cavalcade, a stampede kicking up a messy cloud of dust. Everyone had an opinion about Karl, or a story. "Did you hear what Karl just said?" became a daily question. He was the only senior White House official who could walk around the West Wing handing out brownies his wife made and turn it into high drama. He brought one to me early on. I didn't really want one, but you didn't say no to Karl. You took it, you liked it, and you were grateful for the princely token.

Karl's practical jokes were the talk of the West Wing. One of his targets was Al Hubbard, the president's old friend and chairman of the Council of Economic Advisors. Al routinely left his keys in his car, which was parked just outside the West Wing. So Karl would take Al's car keys and move the car somewhere else. Each time, old Al would come out and wonder whether his car had been towed. (You might think that perhaps Al should have stopped leaving his keys in the car. But then, you probably don't know Al.)

Bill McGurn told me a story about another of Karl's targets, Steve Hadley. Steve was late to a meeting, and the rest of the senior staff was already there eating dinner. Then one of the NSC aides brought in Hadley's meal. While the rest of the staff ate on standard cardboard mess trays, they carried Steve's dinner on a silver platter complete with a silver covering dish. It looked like a meal you'd serve the king of England.

Of course, Karl spotted this and lay in wait. And as soon as Hadley came in, Karl interrupted the meeting, stood up, and put his napkin over his arm like a waiter.

Bill laughed as he remembered this. "Then Karl pulls out Steve's chair and lifts the silver covering dish and says, 'Your dinner is served, sir,' and he goes on to announce every food item on Steve's plate with great flourish."

Everyone was chuckling, including Steve. But the rest of them were laughing as hard as they were because Karl was so on target. Steve came across to most of them as stiff and aristocratic. His own staff strictly referred to him as "Mr. Hadley." (Still, I don't think he was ever served a meal on a silver tray again.)

Karl was a voracious reader. Like everything else, he threw himself into his hobby with in-your-face audacity. It wasn't enough for Karl to enjoy reading. He turned it into a competition with the president. I used to check the card that was kept just outside of the Oval Office tracking which of the two men had read the most (the record continued to be kept long after Karl left the White House). In typical Karl style, the card measured not just the number of books read but the number of words, the number of pages per book, and the total surface area of the books as well. (Karl would use whatever metric he could find to put himself in the lead.) In the first six months of 2008, Karl had read ninety-three books to Bush's ninety-one. Everyone was duly impressed. That is, until we started to think about it.

"How can anyone read ninety-three books in six months?" I once asked Chris.

"Yeah," he said as he did the calculations in his head. "That's like a book every other day."

"And even if they do read that fast," I wondered, "how much of it do they really absorb?" But I found out that people didn't ask a lot of questions about Karl. It was more fun to just watch what he'd do next.

The speechwriters were always anxious over Karl's edits. He almost always wanted more—more facts, more figures, more adjectives, more sentences. More, more, and then more. I was oddly excited by this news when I first arrived at the White House. It meant I'd have an instant link to Karl. He'd read all my speeches. And I'd have a chance to make an impression on him and show him what I could do. I wasn't sure how closely I wanted to be tied to Karl. But if I wanted to advance in the White House or make any kind of difference, he was where the action was.

Melissa Carson, Bill McGurn's assistant, had become one of my closest friends in the speechwriting office. Melissa dealt with Karl on a regular basis. Unlike most other people in the White House, Karl didn't write out his edits. He'd put a check mark next to a paragraph or scribble one or two words. He preferred to have you come to him to figure out what he meant. Melissa's job therefore was to decipher it all so she could pass it on to the writers.

"Does Karl ever praise a speech?" I asked Melissa. "Does he ever write 'This is great' and just leave it at that?"

Melissa laughed. She'd worked with Karl for more than a year at this point. "Oh, no, never," she said. "He *always* has edits."

"But has he ever praised one?" I persisted.

She thought for a moment. "I can't remember him ever doing that, and certainly not without wanting changes."

I slapped my hand on my desk. Melissa's head shot up with a start. "Melissa, from here on out it's going to be my life's mission to get Karl to praise one of my speeches," I vowed. "And I guarantee that I will write a speech that Karl not only praises to the hilt, but which he has absolutely no edits on."

I rarely heard Melissa say the slightest unkind word about anyone. True to form, she listened to my audacious prediction and replied, "That's wonderful." I could tell from her tone that what she was really thinking was, In your dreams, buddy.

Every week I was assigned to write a speech—some of them long and some short, some policy-heavy and some ceremonial. I'd work hard on it, send it off, and wait for Karl's edits. Within a day or two, Karl would dictate them to Melissa. I looked forward to those edits, incorporated them as best I could, and tried to get a sense of what Karl was looking for. And every week I'd try again to win his praise.

I wanted him to call someone in speechwriting and say, "Hey, this new writer is pretty good." Or, better yet, to call me himself. "Where did you come from?" he'd ask. "Come on down to my office, and I'll share all my secrets with you."

I knew Karl appreciated literature and history, so I'd search online and in history books for interesting stories or unusual quotes. Early on, for example, I got the president to quote James Joyce in a Congressional Gold Medal ceremony.

Melissa, of course, would do her best to put the best possible spin on Karl's edits. When he left a paragraph untouched, she and I would take that as a sign that he liked it. Or she'd try to interpret a nod when he spoke to her or a check mark he'd written as some hidden note of satisfaction. But it was mutual self-deception. I still wasn't getting the home run I craved.

Then, about three months into the job, opportunity beckoned. I'd been assigned to write remarks for another Congressional Gold Medal ceremony, this one honoring the Tuskegee Airmen, the legendary black aviators of World War II who fought discrimination at home to become pilots and defend the country. The event and the men it honored motivated me to try to give the remarks a special impact. I had the researchers send me a pile of books on the Tuskegee Airmen. I read other presidential speeches on these great men. Most important, I talked to other writers, including former presidential speechwriters, to get a sense of the moment and what the president might say.

The president didn't like to go on long at ceremonial events, especially when he was the eighth or ninth speaker at an event where everyone talked about the same thing. My first imperative was to keep the remarks short, lest he start cutting them down himself. My second imperative was to make them stand out in some way from all the other speeches that would be heard before the president spoke. They had to be something that only the president could say.

I came upon an idea I thought was inspired. I had the president begin his remarks by talking about his dad, who'd also been an aviator in World War II. Except I didn't compare the Tuskegee Airmen to former President Bush. I contrasted them. I noted that while the elder Bush was heroic in war, he was never judged every day by the color of his skin. And when Bush performed daring feats in the skies over Japan, he was never referred to condescendingly as "a credit to his race."

I then had the president note all the years these brave airmen spent living amid the bigotry of their own country even as they fought to defend it. I mentioned the white enlisted men who declined to salute a black officer. And I ended the remarks with the president directly addressing these black men, now in their seventies and eighties, some in wheelchairs and some with walkers. "Yours is the story of the human spirit," he'd tell them, "and it ends like all great stories do—with wisdom and lessons and hope for tomorrow."

Then came what I was hoping would be the kicker. Nothing he could say today would fully correct the wrongs the airmen had suffered, the president would acknowledge, "but I would like to offer a gesture to help atone for all those unreturned salutes and unforgivable indignities. On behalf of the office I hold, and a country that honors you, I salute you for your service to the United States of America." The president then would put his hand to his forehead and salute them.

When the president spoke to the airmen and offered the salute, I thought it would be simply a nice moment. So I didn't expect what happened next. In a hushed chamber, with leaders of Congress looking on, each of these elderly black men struggled to their feet, many with tears in their eyes, and returned the salute to their commander in chief. The president cried. The audience cried. The Democratic leaders on the stage looked startled; Bush wasn't supposed to be dramatic, was he? It was . . . well, it was a Reagan moment.

After the president sat down, one of the Tuskegee Airmen rose. He went to the podium and talked about the debt many people felt the Tuskegee Airmen were owed. Then he replied, "All I have to say is: paid in full."

Bush was thrilled with the event. It captured headlines and editorials and made a good showing on the news. And it overshadowed everyone else who spoke that day, including Nancy Pelosi and Colin Powell. (I especially liked that part.)

Later that day, I ran into Dan Bartlett in the men's room on the second floor of the West Wing. Dan asked if it was I who'd written the Tuskegee speech. I said I had. "Well, the president said that whoever came up with the salute was a genius," Dan said as he washed his hands. "So I told him it was me," he added jokingly (or so I hoped). The worst thing about this was that I probably never would have known the president had said that if Dan and I hadn't had to go to the bathroom at the same time.

I appreciated the president's compliment, indirect though it was. But perhaps more important was the one I received from someone else. The one I'd been waiting for. The day after the Tuskegee Airmen speech went out to senior officials for comment, Melissa came to my desk.

"Karl has a comment on your speech," she said.

"Let me guess . . . flawless?" I joked.

"Yes!" she said excitedly. "He said it was great—and he had no edits." She lowered her voice. "That has *never* happened before."

My heart soared. I'd pulled it off. Melissa couldn't believe it. Neither could I. After that, I waited for Karl to take special notice of me. But nothing unusual ever seemed to happen. I'd run into him in different places, and even once reintroduced myself, but he never mentioned the Tuskegee speech. He never seemed to have the slightest clue who I was.

By then, however, I wasn't sure I wanted to be in his orbit after all. As I was trying, and failing, to become a friend of his, Karl's friends on the outside were starting to turn on him.

Karl was supposed to serve as the eyes and ears of the conservative movement. He constantly was massaging conservatives, giving them the impression he was in their corner.

But as the second term wound on, conservatives were growing more and more disenchanted. Karl had tried to push for personal accounts for Social Security—a favorite cause for conservatives—but soon abandoned it as a failure. And he seemed to badly misread the feelings of many people in the base on a key issue: immigration reform. Many conservatives welcome immigrants who come to this country, stand in line, and play by the rules. In the words of former senator Fred Thompson, we wanted "tall fences and wide gates."

Yet, to my surprise, Karl and the president seemed to be caught off guard by the feelings of their own party on this issue. This despite the fact that the warning signs were everywhere. John McCain's push for a "pathway to citizenship," for example, had nearly upended his 2008 presidential hopes. Perhaps Karl thought he could charm his opposition or pretend they didn't exist. This time, neither tactic worked.

An intraparty civil war heated up for months. Many of my conservative friends were furious at the president for pushing this issue. But the president and Karl seemed more determined to pass their bill, whatever the effect on their party. Karl was nothing if not relentless. Both he and the president seemed downright furious at Republicans who opposed them. As the odds against their bill grew longer and longer, the president's frustration led him to make a very unfortunate comment.

I was walking back toward the White House from lunch when I got a call from one of my conservative friends on the Hill. "Tell me you didn't write that," he said, nearly breathless.

I had no idea what he was talking about.

"Didn't you hear the president's speech?" he asked.

The president had delivered remarks that morning on immigration. It wasn't an actual speech; he talked mostly off the cuff. "No, I didn't," I said.

"Well, check it out. You guys need serious help." He hung up.

It turned out the president had gotten so heated on the subject that he claimed that people who opposed his position on immigration "don't care about our country." To conservatives, it looked an awful lot like Bush was saying they weren't patriotic. It was a major mistake. It infuriated the president's base. And he later had to apologize. For many people, it was too late. The immigration effort—championed by Karl and his team—produced a sharp and lasting break between the president and his conservative base. And by the time the White House finally figured out the damage their position had done, it was far too late. Millions of people called Congress demanding an end to amnesty, and the Rove/Bush/McCain immigration bill was doomed.

But what most surprised me about the episode wasn't the administration's departure from conservative orthodoxy. They'd made that kind of break before (on global warming and campaign finance reform, for example). What most astonished me was Karl's and the president's apparent misunderstanding of how deeply conservatives thought about such a fundamental issue. Karl had made a terrible miscalculation—and the clumsiness of the effort further diminished his legend in my mind. I expected Karl's operation to be cunning. But I never expected it to be incompetent.

In the middle of 2007 Dan Bartlett announced he was leaving the White House. At some point during Dan's stratospheric rise to the top of the Bush hierarchy, he'd once worked for Karl. By the time he was ready to leave, he'd become Karl's equal, to say the least.

Though I liked Dan, he was part of what I called the president's "team of buddies"—a play off the term *team of rivals*, made famous by Doris Kearns Goodwin. These were mostly well-meaning people who rose to the very top because they were likable, not supremely qualified. Dan was a decent man who did his best. But he was put in a terrible position by the president; with little, if any, practical media experience, Dan was responsible for all communications during two wars and one of the most hostile media environments in recent history. It was like making a gifted intern the chief of cardiac surgery simply because he was great at telling jokes. Dan once told a group of us that the worst moment of his tenure was when the president retracted from one of his State of the Union addresses the sixteen words referring to the British government's belief that Saddam Hussein had tried to acquire uranium in Africa that could be used to build a nuclear weapon. Bartlett agreed to have the White House announce that the words never should have been in there in the first place. The "sixteen words" controversy immediately became an international sensation, which led to the charge that Bush and his team had lied the country into war. The retraction of those sixteen words, which the British government still stood by, nearly destroyed Tony Blair's prime ministership. It also almost cost Steve Hadley his job (though Hadley was Condi Rice's deputy at the time, he nonetheless took full responsibility and offered to resign). Dan told us that he'd made the decision to admit that the words never should have been in the speech while he was on a trip to Africa with the president and they were all jet-lagged. Nobody had thought the issue through or seemed to have any plan in place to deal with the obvious media fallout. I was so startled by Dan's disclosure that I had to ask someone else present if I'd actually heard it right. Two world leaders had had their reputations damaged and administrations endangered because Dan and his team didn't know what time zone they were in?

Nonetheless, Bush counted on Dan and liked him. He was so close to the president that I was surprised he'd decided to leave. As my boss explained it to me, "I think he was just sick of dealing with him."

"Who?" I asked. "The president?"

"No. Karl."

I looked surprised. I hadn't had the slightest clue that Dan didn't like Karl.

"He fights with Karl every day," my boss explained. "It's exhausting. Karl is just relentless. And he never likes any ideas that aren't his own."

It turned out Dan wasn't the only one exhausted by Karl. More ominously, Josh Bolten didn't seem to like him either. Which made perfect sense. Bolten was all about order and tidiness, and he seemed to judge ideologues with suspicion. In contrast, Karl was procedurally manic, bureaucratically messy, and he advocated—usually—the conservative agenda. One of Bolten's early actions in his new job as chief of staff was to strip Karl of some of his duties. (Karl had managed to put himself in charge of political operations, personnel, and policy. Bolten took the policy arm away from him.) As Bolten further solidified his power, Karl's freewheeling, hand-in-every-cookie-jar style seemed an increasingly poor fit.

But for a long time Karl had two things going for him. First, the president counted on him. And second, he was believed to be a political genius.

Karl had come to power promising to lead a Republican realignment not seen in the country since the days of William McKinley. Yet during his tenure it was the Democrats, not the GOP, who seemed to grow stronger.

Even the 2000 elections, which propelled Karl to the stratosphere as a political genius, were arguably his biggest failure. One could argue, in fact, that Republicans actually lost that election—if you cared about little things like who got the most votes. Hindsight, as is famously said, is always 20/20. Yet Rove spent millions on a last-ditch effort to win California that turned out to be a total waste of money, while the Florida effort had needed shoring up. Karl apparently just didn't see the trouble the campaign was in. One of the people who worked on the campaign remembered Karl's predicting the night before the election that they'd win with a comfortable 320 electoral votes.

Instead, the campaign spent the next month in Florida quibbling over dimpled chads.

In 2004, with the power of the presidency behind him, Bush barely won again. This after once leading by a sizable margin against a Massachusetts liberal elitist. In the 1980s and '90s the GOP used to take a guy like John Kerry—complete with his superelite lifestyle and pompous pronunciations like "Jen-jiss Khan"—and treat him like the political equivalent of a crash dummy. In this election, though, during a time of war, when Bush was still relatively popular, the Republicans ended up surviving by a few thousand votes in places like Cincinnati and Columbus, Ohio. (I speak as a Michiganian when I say that you know you're really desperate if you have to count on Ohio for anything.)

But regardless of the margin, those elections were both considered wins, and Karl was given all the credit for them.

The 2006 election was quite different. Not only was Karl wrong about the result of the election, confidently predicting Republicans would hold the House and Senate, he was spectacularly wrong. And he never recovered from it.

After the election, we started hearing rumors of Karl's imminent departure. They were followed by words of assurance from the White House that Rove had the president's confidence and had every intention of staying till the end of the administration. Of course, when the White House had to assure people you were staying, you might as well head to Kinko's with your resume. That's almost exactly what they said about Rummy just before they dropped the ax.

So with his reputation for political acumen damaged, a growing list of enemies, increasing disenchantment from conservatives who'd once cheered him, and his position at the White House more uncertain by the day, Karl did a curious thing: He started feuding with everybody even more—members of Congress, the media, Dan Bartlett, Karen Hughes, and others. My guess was, when he was in grade school he never scored well in the category "plays well with others."

I saw a glimpse of this firsthand. That June, the president was to give a speech at the rededication of the Islamic Center in Washington, D.C. I was assigned to draft the remarks. The "news" of the event was to be the president's announcement that he was going to appoint a special envoy to the organization of the Islamic Conference—the first such envoy ever appointed by a president. It was part of our effort to show that America was interested in greater dialogue and understanding with the Muslim world. Since Karen Hughes and Condi Rice, both backers of the envoy idea, were also both close to the president, Karl couldn't kill the idea outright. So he proceeded to try to sabotage it. That meant trying to sabotage the speech.

Karl became obsessed with moving one paragraph—the one talking about the appointment of the special envoy—to the end of the speech. I didn't agree with that suggestion because it ruined the ending. No one else seemed to agree with Karl's suggestion either, so we ignored it. Besides, how important could the placement of a paragraph be, anyway? As it turns out, pretty important—at least to Karl.

First, he came into the head writer's office in a fury, insisting that the paragraph be moved. Bill explained politely why we didn't think that was necessary. Karl ignored this and left without retreating. Having no success with Bill, Karl went to another writer on the staff, demanding his change. Since that writer had nothing to do with the speech, nothing happened. Then Karl went to the staff secretary's office, where Raul referred him back to the writers. Hours later, and well into the evening, Karl called our twenty-four-year-old head fact checker, Brendon Merkley. For Brendon, receiving a call directly from Karl Rove was like one of the White House groundskeepers' being invited by Dick Cheney to share a bourbon and brandy.

Yet Karl was on the phone with him, in a tizzy, insisting to this young man that he find a way to make the changes Karl insisted on. Brendon scribbled notes furiously and tried to figure out what to do.

"Karl Rove just called me," Brendon told me just after it happened, sounding almost like he thought this might all be merely a vivid dream. "He's pretty upset."

"What did he want?" I asked.

"He wants some paragraph moved. I didn't know what he was talking about. But he was yelling."

(This was such a bizarre experience that Brendon was still talking about the call a year later.)

I asked a speechwriter who'd worked there for years if he'd ever seen anyone carry on like this over the movement of a paragraph.

He shook his head. "Karl's never done this before," he replied. "I think he's coming unhinged."

Karl next went to Steve Hadley. Hadley had about one million more important things to do than discuss paragraph placements, but apparently he heard out Karl patiently. Then Karl came back to the staff secretary's office. He claimed that Hadley insisted on the change as well. And then Karl pulled out what he thought was his trump card: the president himself. He said Bush also wanted the change, and threatened to go to the president personally if it didn't happen.

It turned out, though, that Raul was wise to Karl. He'd seen this act once too often. Someone asked Hadley if, in fact, he'd agreed to Karl's suggested change. The ever diplomatic Hadley said that he'd listened to Karl and told him he didn't have a view either way. Then someone asked the president. The president didn't have any idea what Karl was talking about. He thought the speech was fine.

I couldn't believe it. On two occasions in one day, Karl had shown himself to be something less than a fanatic for the truth. And I must reiterate: *over a paragraph of a speech no one would even care about.*

"No wonder everyone is sick of him," I observed. This was probably how he'd gotten his way on everything.

The next morning, we were set for our weekly speechwriters' meeting in the Oval Office. Karl called our office to ask what time the meeting was, and sent word to us that he intended to be there.

My first thought: *Uh-oh. This is where it's all going to hit the fan.* Karl would never relent until he got his way, and now he was going to do it in full view of the president. The speechwriters would be painted as obstructionists, and we wouldn't be able to defend ourselves. And all over one stupid paragraph.

Then something curious happened. Our office received a call telling us the meeting with the president would be forty minutes earlier than scheduled.

"Did anyone tell Karl?" I wondered as we gathered outside the Oval Office. The answer, as it turned out, was no.

What followed was a surreal meeting with the president that had nothing to do with the speech. The closest we came was the president's passing comment: "So it looks like I'm talking to the Muslims."

Dan and the president exchanged a few playful glances. They

looked like two people who were in on a joke that no one else could share.

We stood around for a few more minutes, talked about football, and were dismissed.

As we left the Oval Office, the other speechwriters and I looked at one another quizzically. "What was that all about?" I asked.

No one knew. "That was the strangest meeting we've had yet," one of the writers observed.

To this day, I can't be sure. But it looked like the president and Bartlett had moved the time on purpose. They knew what Karl was up to, and they weren't up for the drama.

For six years, I had waited to see Karl Rove in action—and it was not at all what I expected—silly intimidation tactics. Boisterous claims that were easily disproved. Acting so insufferable that people avoided him. This wasn't the work of an evil genius. Karl was like the West Wing's version of Maude. And even more embarrassing for our own Beatrice Arthur was that his efforts ended in total failure. The speech went off as planned, and the paragraph was never moved. After all the crazed maneuverings, exactly nothing was accomplished. It made me wonder: Could Karl let nothing go? Could he compromise on anything? What did this say about his vaunted instincts on more important issues?

The Islamic Center event was unexceptional and got a minimum of coverage in the mainstream media. Except . . . in the weeks following the event, there was a small but noticeable number of op-eds and blog postings by conservatives who attacked the speech. I had the nagging feeling that Karl was behind them. Considering what I'd already observed, it wouldn't have surprised me at all if he still couldn't let the matter rest, even if his efforts embarrassed the president.

With this episode vivid in my mind, I took a cross-country trip with Karl and the president aboard Air Force One, which gave me a chance to see Karl in action once again. About an hour or so into the flight, I was sitting in the staff conference room with a few other aides when Karl walked in. He sat in a seat right next to mine and started typing away on a small laptop. He never said a single word to me (with the possible exception of "hello"). I hoped he wasn't still mad about that speech.

Sometime later, the president, dressed in his usual T-shirt and running pants, walked in as well. The president started joking about current events. He was particularly interested in a story about Senator Larry Craig of Idaho, who'd been accused of soliciting gay sex in an airport bathroom. Craig was just the latest Republican to become embroiled in a sex scandal. Former congressman Mark Foley had been caught up in a controversy involving male interns.

"What is up with all these Republicans?" the president asked incredulously. Referring to Senator Craig, he asked, "Is he married?"

"He has a wife," someone said.

The president shook his head.

While the president spoke to the rest of us, we stopped what we were doing to give him our attention. Karl kept typing who knows what on his laptop.

For his part, the president seemed to delight in provoking Karl. He started complaining about the campaign events Karl had arranged for the trip. The president kept asking about details that he clearly knew the answers to but Karl clearly didn't. When he caught Karl in an error, the president pounced.

"You don't even know what these events are!" the president declared. "Why am I even going to them?"

"These are very important events," Karl replied calmly.

"But you don't even know where they're being held and who's attending?" the president asked. "How important can they be?"

Karl kept typing away. "Very essential, sir."

Then the president asked why Karl wanted him to call one of the Democratic leaders. "I hate talking to this guy," the president said. (I forget who it was.)

Karl didn't back down.

After the president finished complaining and walked away, Karl kept staring at his computer screen, still typing. Then, several minutes later, looking at no one in particular, he said, "Never give an inch."

Was he talking to me? To the president? To the air? To himself? Who knew? But that sentence stuck with me. *Never give an inch.* That was Karl. Right or wrong, he never relented on anything. That was the source of his power, that was what brought him enemies, and ultimately that was the source of his downfall. The writing was on the West Wing wall.

Karl, of course, had long been linked to nearly every controversy or accusation or scandal in the White House, which, for a long time, I thought was a sign of his effectiveness in an odd way. Critics seemed desperate to pin something on him, because they wanted him out of the way. He was their "Great White Whale." Karl was accused of leaking an undercover operative's name in the Valerie Plame affair . . . accused of illegally subverting official records rules with non–White House e-mail . . . accused of pressuring investigators into indicting a Democratic governor . . . and on and on. Moreover, a curious number of Rove's current and former assistants were appearing in headlines like "Rove Aide Takes the Fifth" or "Rove Aide Subpoenaed" or "Rove Aide Resigns." The aides were becoming well-known and notorious figures. Susan Ralston resigned over ties to indicted lobbyist Jack Abramoff. Sara Taylor and Scott Jennings were called to testify in Congress over White House personnel practices at the Justice Department.

The most damaging allegations concerning Karl were that he'd improperly directed the hiring and firing of United States attorneys for political purposes. He was also accused of being involved in firing career employees at the Justice Department based on political motivations—a violation of federal law.

At the time, the Justice Department's White House liaison was a thirtysomething Republican named Monica Goodling. She was another member of the administration's "team of buddies"—young, in over her head, and given great authority over staffing a major cabinet agency. In light of my earlier battles with the liaison office at the Pentagon, the controversy rang many bells. Goodling was said to have fired a career attorney because she was a lesbian. Ding. According to a former Justice Department official, "She forced many very talented, career people out of main Justice so she could replace them with junior people that were either loyal to the administration or would score her some points." Ding again.

A report by the Justice Department's Office of the Inspector General found that under the White House Liaison Office at Justice, as the Washington Post put it, "connections and politics mattered more than competence and professionalism." Goodling, the Washington Post said, exercised what "amounted to veto power over a wide range of critical jobs, asking candidates for their views on abortion and same-sex marriage and maneuvering around senior officials who outranked her, including the department's second-in-command." Ding, ding, ding.

Under immunity from prosecution, Goodling admitted to Congress that she'd "crossed the line" in her hiring policies at the department. But she refused to acknowledge that Rove had played a role in any of it. Karl declined to appear before congressional committees to answer any of the charges himself. Through his attorneys, he denied any wrongdoing. As I started hearing about this, I became increasingly concerned. This was eerily similar to what had been going on at the Pentagon.

For a long time, I'd wanted to believe that the hiring troubles I observed when I worked at the Department of Defense were isolated incidents, or that Karl didn't know everything that the White House liaison people were doing. When they blocked the person I wanted to hire for a researcher job because of, I was convinced, her sexual orientation, I figured Rove couldn't possibly know. What would he care about the hiring of a low-level staffer for the secretary of defense? (Then again, why would he care about a paragraph in an unmemorable speech?)

But in light of the Justice Department scandal, I couldn't help wondering if Karl had been responsible for the whole thing. Might Rove have been deploying Monica Goodlings across the administration— young, unqualified people who were blocking qualified job applicants and forcing Bush loyalists into important positions where they were in way over their heads? This had happened time and again at the Pentagon, where, at one point, we even compiled a list of questionable hiring practices. When Rumsfeld tried to do something about them, it was Rove who personally stopped him. I recalled that Rove and his aides even called Tony Dolan once to discourage his helping me push for staff members that the White House liaison office wanted to block. The aides were pushy and threatening. It was only when I was at the White House, however, that it occurred to me that Tony and I had helped to thwart Rove. By exposing the activities of his minions at the Pentagon, writing memos and going to see Rumsfeld personally about what was going on, we created a situation where Rumsfeld fought these people and even removed one from her post. I wondered if Karl knew that. If he had, I would have been considered an apostate and heretic. It was not until later that I learned that O'Beirne had called the White House to protest my hiring and raise questions about my loyalty. (At the same time, another Rove ally, Dorance Smith, worked relentlessly to fire Tony from the Pentagon and failed.) While I was at the White House, reports also were surfacing of the same activities going on at NASA and the Department of Labor. But DoD was especially troubling, since it was a department responsible for the safety of the nation. Of course, in every administration some politicizing of hiring occurs. But these tactics, like everything else Rove was involved in, seemed over the top and ultimately harmful to the president, the administration, and the country.

I felt like someone who'd finally put together a very difficult puzzle, only to find the image wasn't at all what I expected. Karl was *not* the hero of the Bush White House, the brilliant behind-the-scenes strategist. He was what all the liberals said he was: the villain. And to make matters worse, a clumsy one at that. He employed ham-handed tactics, put forward obviously unqualified subordinates, and stubbornly defended them. He'd turned out to be less a Voldemort than a Boris Badenov chasing Rocky and Bullwinkle.

Under the weight of controversy and amid the active dislike of most of his senior colleagues, Karl didn't need a neon sign to figure out that he was overstaying his welcome. Still, it came as a shock to many of us when Karl announced his resignation. Once again, he did it his way—not delivering the news to most of his colleagues personally, but broadcasting it in an op-ed in the *Wall Street Journal*. This was sort of like going on the six o'clock news to announce you were quitting your job.

As soon as Karl's op-ed was published, the White House was filled with speculation over whether Karl's departure was really his idea. It shows you how far our view of Karl had deteriorated by then that most of us were reluctant to take anything he said at face value. Besides, there were reasons to believe he'd been pushed out. For one thing, nearly everyone who knew Karl believed he'd hold out until the bitter end. I certainly didn't think he'd voluntarily give his enemies the satisfaction of stepping aside. And he clearly loved his job and all the trappings that came with it. He was probably the most enthusiastic member of the West Wing staff I ever encountered. Plus, quitting anything simply wasn't in his genetic makeup.

There was something else that added to the curiousness of his departure. Karl told the newspapers that he'd decided to finally quit because Labor Day 2007 was the deadline imposed on everyone on the White House staff who planned to depart before the end of the president's term. If you were still in place through Labor Day, Karl maintained, you were expected to stay to the end. I'd never heard of this deadline before. Nor had anyone else I asked. Even if there had been such a rule, other senior officials on the White House staff didn't follow it. Many left after the supposed Labor Day deadline—sometimes long after. And Karl wasn't what you might call a stickler for the rules in any case.

Adding to the mystery was the fact that Karl had just hired a new assistant who was to start work only a week or so before Karl announced his departure. The young man would have been hired, presumably, when Karl already knew he was going to leave. Why would Karl hire a new assistant for a job he was imminently departing?

Karl, of course, denied all the rumors that he was forced out. (It would be just like Bolten to have planted them.) When asked if he was being "run out of town," Karl responded, "That sounds like the rooster claiming to have called up the sun." I still don't know what that means. Was Karl shown the door? It was certainly conceivable. To no one's surprise, Bolten was a happy executioner—the kind of guy who could smile at you in the morning, fire you at noon, and praise you to the papers at five.

When Bolten appeared on *The NewsHour with Jim Lehrer*, he was asked whether he'd convinced Bush that Attorney General Alberto Gonzales had to go. "I think Alberto came to the realization that, as unfair as the attacks on him over the last several months have been, at some point you need to let that unfairness, in a sense, stand, and step aside for the good of the department," Bolten replied. Answer: yes.

"And Rove?" Lehrer asked.

"That was completely up to Karl," Bolten said. "All of us at the White House would have loved to have had him stay and continue to contribute in the way he does, because he's a brilliant character, but everybody also accepted that this was the time in his life to move on."

Bolten, as I've noted, was a man who was very precise. If you looked closely, there really wasn't a word of praise in his answer. Karl could "continue to contribute in the way that he does" isn't the same as saying that his contributions were welcome. And sure, he called Rove "a brilliant character." Well, we had some brilliant characters in our family too, such as the guy who threatened our cat, but let's just say we didn't exactly trust them with the carving knife on Thanksgiving.

Whatever the true story of Karl's departure, Karl was really going. I happened to be with him when he took his final ride with the president aboard Air Force One as a member of the staff. Toward the flight's end, staff members were summoned to the conference room for an impromptu goodbye party.

As we entered the conference room, the president and Mrs. Bush were already seated at the long wooden conference table. The president nodded hello to us as we entered. Mrs. Bush glanced absently at a newspaper. As usual, she looked like a woman ready to go home. The president often mentioned that when he'd married Laura, he'd promised her she wouldn't have to give any speeches. But she'd given many, and my own impression was that she never liked it much—not speeches, not public life, and not politics. (She was secretly a Democrat for all intents and purposes, though it really wasn't much of a secret.)

Karl was sitting next to the First Lady, his face unreadable, except perhaps for a flicker of nervousness. The rest of us lined around the wall, until we almost circled the president, Mrs. Bush, and Karl. Though there was a couch immediately behind us, few if any felt comfortable enough to sit. Fox News—what else?—was displayed on the large television screen mounted on the wall directly opposite the president's seat. Someone had graciously put it on mute for Karl's farewell.

Once the president was satisfied that we all were there, he held court. He started with his familiar shtick—teasing the guest of honor and playing the room for laughs.

He looked at the cake on the table. Then he looked at Rove. "Karl, is it your birthday?" he asked.

"No, Mr. President," Karl replied.

"So what's the cake for?" the president asked, grinning.

"It's to mark my last trip, sir," Karl replied, gamely going along with the joke.

The president offered a look of mock surprise. "Last trip? Where are you going?" His audience started chuckling. We all were curious as to the answer.

"Well, I'm not sure yet," Karl replied.

The president turned his face to Laura. "Honey, did you hear? Karl is leaving."

Mrs. Bush smiled politely but said nothing. She wasn't going to have a part in this stand-up routine, thank you very much.

The cake was cut and slices passed around. After everyone started eating, the president turned to the guest of honor.

"Speech! Speech!" he called.

We all applauded, and Karl rose from his chair. He walked over to a spot just adjacent to the president. He looked around the room, mostly at people he barely knew. Then he took a breath.

Long ago, the president had nicknamed Karl "Turd Blossom." Apparently this was a reference to a kind of Texas flower that grew from cow excrement. In conferring that nickname, of course, Bush's message was double-edged. On one hand, it could be interpreted that Karl could even make cow dung look good. On the other hand, it was still dung.

Karl had the attention of the entire cabin. We knew, vaguely, that we were seeing a small moment of history unfold. This was a longtime aide to the president, a Bush loyalist, a man who'd twice helped the president get elected, and he was leaving.

Here was Karl's moment to tell the president what it meant to serve him. Here was a chance to tell the rest of us how much he appreciated working with us. Here was an opportunity to summarize the record the administration had assembled and to hint at what he'd do next. At the very least, this was a chance for him to make a few cracks about the liberals. He was good at that.

Karl didn't do any of these things. Instead he turned his eyes toward Kevin Sullivan, crouched in the corner at the far end of the room. Sully, who long had been overshadowed by Rove and didn't seem to like it, stopped chewing his piece of cake. I could see him wondering with a half-full mouth, Why is Karl looking at me?

Then the flower that grew from cow excrement finally spoke. "Sully, you are now the mayor of control!" he said.

With his mouth full, Kevin laughed politely and returned to his cake. The rest of us looked at one another in bafflement. The president, who was looking forward to some laughs, seemed confused.

Was this some secret code, indecipherable to us mere mortals? Or was Karl spending too much time at his vacation home on Jupiter? Sadly, the answer was far more boring than that. Karl was simply referring to one of the motorcade vehicles—called the control vehicle—which the senior staff usually rode in. Unsurprisingly, Rove had appointed himself the control vehicle's "mayor." Now he was offering that position to Sully. Actually, not offering it, but bequeathing it.

After Kevin said thanks, we all laughed nervously and waited for Karl to say more. He didn't.

Several delightfully awkward moments followed. Crickets chirped. Tumbleweeds blew by. Everyone glanced at one another uncomfortably. Had Mrs. Bush just looked at her watch? Finally, the president saved the moment.

"Good thing you weren't the speechwriter, Karl," he quipped. We all laughed. Then the president rose from his chair and turned to face him. "How 'bout a hug instead?" He warmly embraced a crying and red-faced Karl.

Karl then walked around and shook everyone's hand, including mine. And that pretty much was it. A private, emotional farewell aboard Air Force One that lasted about fifteen minutes and consisted of Karl saying about seven words. Still, in the history of famous farewells, surely the two most notable are "My only regret is that I have but one life to give for my country" and "Sully, you are the mayor of control."

That awkward Air Force One goodbye would be the first of many Rove farewells. There'd be a more formal one at Blair House. Then a senior staff meeting in which they showed old photos of Karl with the president. Once again, when given a chance to speak, Karl cried and said almost nothing. Was he that overcome with emotion—or did he just want to appear that way? I was never sure. Then there was a final goodbye when all of us were asked to stand on the steps of the EEOB and wave to his Jaguar as it left the White House grounds for the last time. Not coincidentally, this was in full view of the press corps, so that they could chronicle the love the White House staff supposedly had for him. All the interns went out—they were often used for rent-a-crowd purposes—but many senior officials didn't. Including me. For me, one Rove farewell was more than enough. And considering how much I'd looked forward to working with Karl when I first got to the White House, I still find it astonishing to realize how glad I was to see him go.

Yet even after Karl left the White House, he never really left. Months later, he was still giving orders to his former staff, still in regular contact with the president, and still showing up from time to time. Once he waved to me from his car, to say hello. I looked all around to make sure he was looking at me. (He was.) He was thick in the plotting of the Bush presidential library. Scheming to control the president's book project. And still in that deranged book-reading race.

In the 2008 election, Karl was writing op-eds pretending to advise both Obama and McCain and appearing on Fox News as an ostensibly unbiased analyst of the presidential election, but he wasn't fooling anyone. Everyone knew whom he wanted to win. At one point, Karl spread rumors through the White House that one of Obama's potential vice presidential running mates—and a United States senator—had beaten his first wife. "Karl says it's true," the president assured a small group of staffers. Then, knowing Karl, he quickly added, "Karl hopes that it's true."

In the end, Karl's relationship with the truth was as complicated as his relationship with most of the people who worked with him. He had promised a golden age of Republican domination, but the truth is that while Karl was running political affairs, the Republican president's approval rating had plummeted to an improbable low. The truth is that after Karl was promoted to run domestic policy in the second term, not a single major bill proposed by the White House passed through a Republican Congress. And the truth is that Karl oversaw an army of personnel directors who hired hacks, fired qualified public servants, blackballed others, and promoted incompetent partisans who disserved the reconstruction efforts in Iraq, federal prosecutors at the Department of Justice, and the president whom Karl was supposed to serve.

In hindsight, there were early warnings—scenes like the flashback that ends The Godfather, Part II, where you see a happy family, but you also see the tragic flaws that will kill two brothers and transform the third. On the one hundredth day of George W. Bush's presidency—back when a majority approved of Karl's boss, back when Bush was "a uniter, not a divider"—Tim Russert began Meet the Press innocently enough, by wishing his guest, Karl Rove, a "happy one hundred days." But Karl, being Karl, had to correct him. "Happy ninety-nine," he shot back. And while at the time it shouldn't have mattered whether it was the ninety-ninth day (it wasn't) or the one hundredth day (it was), the little comment was an early sign that no matter how unbelievably petty the point, Karl would never give an inch. That Karl had to have his say—and his way. And that Karl was often wrong.

CHAPTER TEN

GOING WOBBLY

By the beginning of 2008, only the most deluded White House staffers (and there was no shortage of them) remained unaware that President Bush was one of the world's most unpopular people. On any given day, anyone who walked out of the building could see people in hot pink shirts with bullhorns shouting, "You are a war criminal." (Maybe that's why most people didn't like to go outside for lunch.) To console ourselves, we made generous reference to Harry S. Truman. He was once deeply unpopular too, but everybody loved him now. So it would happen with Bush. Others weren't willing to wait fifty years. They sought any contemporary reference that might prove that Bush was secretly popular. Many senior officials believed they'd found it in the 2008 Batman movie *The Dark Knight.* For an uncomfortably long time, I heard people talk about how Batman's vigilantism was the equivalent of Bush's tough "war on terror" stance, how both W. and Bruce Wayne were unappreciated by the general public but were still desperately needed, and how the fact that the movie was a hit proved that people secretly agreed with Bush. I wasn't so sure about that, but my view was, hey, whatever floats your boat (or Batmobile).

I felt the sting of my Bush association at a very personal level—from a childhood friend. Working at the White House was so consuming that I rarely had much time to see anyone. We'd often work from seven in the morning till late at night. The strain of the job was so intense that I had to break up with a girl I really liked because she thought I just didn't have time for her. I hardly even had time for my old friend Kim.

During this time, Kim had left Debbie Stabenow's office to become a consultant. She also wanted to spend more time at home with her newborn son (whom she'd named after our hometown, Flint). One day, a mutual friend of ours from elementary school came to Washington with her family for a night. Kim knew how busy I was, but she browbeat me until I agreed to join her and our friend, Ruth, and catch up.

I pulled up to Kim's house in my new BMW, complete with my Bush-Cheney bumper sticker (taped to the window). In front of me was Ruth's family station wagon, adorned with a bumper sticker for every liberal lost cause known to man. I was happy to see Ruth. I said hello to her husband and we all ate dinner. But the conversation was awkward and uncomfortable. I later learned why. Ruth was afraid her ultraliberal vegan husband would have an angry confrontation with me if he found out I worked for Bush. So Ruth carefully maneuvered the conversation to keep me from innocently mentioning my job.

I saw this sort of thing many times over the years. It wasn't enough for some people to have voted against Bush. They had to portray him as the most evil person who ever lived, and anyone who worked for him as a tool of Satan. That's the way some Republicans view the Obama team, and it's why politics has become so empty.

If I'd been required to defend President Bush that day, I would have done so. But it would have been obligatory, not heartfelt. There were things about the president I liked, but I never felt the connection I was supposed to feel. For a long time I wasn't sure why it wasn't happening for me or why I'd come to work some days with a stomachache and sense of dread. As 2008 gathered steam, I finally found out.

The spring of that year began what the speechwriters fondly referred to as the "months of hell." Not all of us would survive them. It started innocently enough. The president was set to give two speeches in the Middle East. One was before the Israeli parliament, or Knesset, to celebrate the sixtieth anniversary of Israel's founding. The other was a speech in Egypt highlighting the need for political and economic reform. As we talked to the president in the Oval Office about the speeches, he told us to make sure we went to see Condi Rice to get her input.

I was thrilled. I had been an admirer of Condi Rice for years—her life story was inspirational, and I was proud she was a Republican. And I wasn't the only one.

With the possible exception of Laura Bush, no one in the White House seemed to have more influence on Bush than his secretary of state. She was close to being a member of the president's family. She'd go with the Bushes to Camp David for Thanksgiving. She was a frequent presence in the West Wing. She was around so often that I half expected her to walk down the hall one morning in a fuzzy bathrobe and slippers asking if anyone had put the coffee on yet.

The president used a markedly different tone around her. I was once sitting in the Oval Office when the president took a phone call from her. He offered gentle teasing. "Well, you're the secretary of state, right? . . . You are? . . . That's what I thought . . . Okay, will do. Goodbye." It seemed there was always idle speculation in the outside world about their relationship. One of the most widely read gossip columnists in the entertainment world, Ted Casablanca, published an item that suggested she and the president were closer than they should have been. Even members of my family believed this. It was talked about all the time in the tabloids. To me, the president's manner was more like he was talking to his kid sister. (This was confirmed for me when the president himself said, "She's like my sister.") Still, that was equally troubling. Maybe it was just me, but I didn't want the president's sister running America's foreign policy. What happens when she's wrong?

But as I thought about it, Condi Rice never seemed to be wrong. Through every misstep and blunder of the administration, somehow she always emerged unscathed. Even though she was intensely involved in the planning for the Iraq war, for example, no one held her responsible for its errors. It was all Rumsfeld's fault, or Cheney's, or Bush's. But never Condi's. During her eight years at the president's side, she managed to pull off more daring escapes than Harry Houdini.

This was not a happy accident.

Condi's team wisely understood that the key to getting good coverage in Washington was not to hope that reporters notice all your many fine qualities. Usually it helps to have someone point those qualities out to them. While Rumsfeld and Cheney blew off the big-shot D.C. reporters, Condi put in place at the State Department an aggressive and talented PR team headed by Jim Wilkinson. I'd known Jim a bit when he worked in the House of Representatives. He was one of the best communications operatives we had. (Unfortunately, not a large pool to cull from.) Condi was photographed well. Her speeches were leaked ahead of time to help shape the message she wanted to convey. This was a press team that knew what it was doing, as opposed to the house of horrors that was the press operation at DoD.

When Chris and I first attempted to meet with Secretary Rice, her office curtly declined our request. "The secretary does not meet with speechwriters," we were told. But when it was brought to her attention that the meeting was at the president's explicit instruction, they changed their tune.

So late one morning, Chris Michel and I were driven over to the State Department. As commissioned officers, we had a "carpet car" available to us at all times of the day, driven by a member of the U.S. military.

As we approached the State Department, it occurred to us that we were headed to the storied institution where brilliant minds had formed the Marshall Plan and NATO. And we were going as personal emissaries of the president to one of his closest confidantes.

As our car deposited us at a special dropoff point for VIPs, I felt like I was finally somebody. Chris and I walked into the building, our West Wing passes dangling from our necks, and were promptly met by . . . nobody.

We called our office assistant, Emily, who said she was sure somebody was planning to meet us. She said she'd look into it. Our egos deflated, Chris and I walked as mere mortals through the sunlit lobby, which was decorated with flags from every nation in the world.

We walked over to the visitors' desk. The employee behind the counter appeared to be asleep.

"There's no more fitting testament to the State Department," I told Chris.

We roused the employee and asked where the secretary's suite was. He said he didn't know.

"This is an even better testament," Chris quipped.

So we just stood around and waited. Finally, a man came over to us. "You guys from the White House?" he asked. "Come with me."

It turned out that we could access the secretary only via a special elevator. Her suite was totally isolated from the rest of the building— quite unlike the secretary of defense's office at the Pentagon.

When we arrived at the secretary's floor, the elevators opened to a long series of rooms, each decorated like we'd just entered the eighteenth century. They were filled with old-style chairs and narrow couches. Chandeliers hung from the ceiling. As we awaited the secretary, we looked like two gentlemen callers in a Jane Austen novel.

Chris and I were both excited and a bit intimidated to meet Secretary Rice. We'd never had any sort of lengthy conversation with her. We chatted nervously with each other while we awaited our summons. After a few minutes, we were escorted into the secretary's office suite.

The secretary's office appeared to be divided in two, with a large, ceremonial office that was elegantly appointed and a much smaller office in the corner that the secretary appeared to actually use. I was struck by how small the second office was—maybe a quarter the size of Rumsfeld's and even smaller than the speechwriting offices in the EEOB. The room had a regular-sized desk filled with papers and files, a small flat television screen, and a small fax machine. Football paraphernalia was strewn across the bookshelf behind her. I could only see one personal picture. It was not of her family—at least not her biological one. The picture was of her with Bush and Tony Blair, the British prime minister and close Bush ally. It was just the three of them casually dressed, perhaps at the Crawford ranch or Camp David. They looked like they were about to go on a hike or throw horseshoes. I found the picture strange, but maybe it's just me. Doesn't everyone in America decorate their offices with pictures of themselves hanging out with the boss?

Secretary Rice stood as we entered. She was dressed in an elegant black jacket and skirt. Her smile was broad and genuine. She said she was glad to meet us and urged us to make ourselves comfortable.

Chris and I sat in matching chairs while the secretary sat on the end of a small couch, about three feet away. I could see why people liked Condi Rice. She was very direct. She seemed to listen closely to us and to care about what we said. She shifted slightly in her seat as each of us spoke, giving us her full attention. I had come in determined not to be dazzled by her. Sure, she was the secretary of state, but she also was someone who seemed out to get Secretary Rumsfeld. That put her on the outs with me. And it was not as if I hadn't rubbed shoulders with celebrities. I'd gotten my picture taken with Marilyn Quayle, after all. And yet... I was dazzled. Sitting in that room, two or three feet from Condi Rice, I couldn't wait to tell my parents. They were sure to be impressed by this.

First, we talked about the speech before the Israeli Knesset. The secretary indicated that she liked the approach we'd outlined to her and just wanted to make sure we said something about the Palestinians. Then the discussion turned toward my Egypt speech. She said the president's most recent speech in the Middle East, which called for political and economic freedom, had been "wishy-washy" and "a dud." Chris and I exchanged knowing glances. We were both thinking the same thing: *I'm glad I didn't write that speech.* Of course she didn't know that.

"Let's make this a challenging, aspiring speech," she said.

I asked if there was anything we could highlight in terms of political progress in the Middle East. "Not really," she said bluntly. If anything, countries were backsliding. "I think we should give the speech some edge," she said. She spoke with authority, and I had no doubt that the president would agree with whatever she said.

After about forty minutes or so, the meeting was over. She was in no hurry to be rid of us. Our questions just ran their course. We shook her hand and left. I was excited that Secretary Rice wanted an edgy speech in Egypt. I thought it presented a perfect opportunity to advance the president's Freedom Agenda in the heart of the Middle East.

With Secretary Rice's blessing, Chris and I drafted our two speeches. Chris drafted a very nice Knesset speech with graceful touches to it, especially at the end. I made a few suggestions. Then as was our method, we trudged over to Marc's office on the second floor of the West Wing so all three of us could go through it together before we sent it to staffing.

With the Knesset speech, we were unusually lucky. Marc didn't have many changes. That is, until we got to a section where Chris warned of the dangers of negotiating with regimes such as Iran. It was nothing we hadn't said before, and it was a guaranteed crowd pleaser. The Israelis were understandably more worried than any other country about Iran.

"You know what we should do?" Marc asked. "There was a great line in a Rumsfeld speech once. Let me see if I can find it."

Whenever Marc took language out of an earlier speech, it was almost always one he'd written. This time was different. I was surprised to discover that the line he liked had come from a Rumsfeld speech he had nothing to do with. In fact, it was the American Legion speech, the one I'd helped write, that had led to one of Rumsfeld's biggest controversies only a year and a half earlier.

"Here's the line," Marc said as he scanned the speech. He proceeded to read aloud the quote from Senator William Borah that had caused all the controversy: "If only I could have talked to Hitler, all of this might be avoided."

"Isn't that line great?" Marc said, laughing. For a moment, I was speechless.

Chris was noncommittal. "Sure, but I don't know if that works here," he said.

"Don't you think?" Marc asked. "Let's try it." Then he added another line that called negotiating with people like the Iranians—which many Democrats wanted to do—"the false comfort of appeasement." Uh-oh.

Chris still appeared reluctant. So for a tie-breaker, Marc looked to me.

I opened my mouth, but words didn't come out at first. "Don't you remember what happened with the American Legion speech?" I finally asked. "This was the one that caused all the controversy last year when Rumsfeld was accused of calling all the Democrats appeasers."

Marc and Chris both looked at me as if it were the first time they'd ever heard of this. "You don't remember it?" I asked, dumbfounded. What had these people been doing back then? "It was a disaster," I added.

"Let's try anyway," Marc said again. We knew it was useless to argue with Marc—we'd done it many times before, to no avail. And he was our boss. Anyway, I figured someone would catch it during the vetting process. Surely someone would remember the whole controversy.

To his credit, Ed Gillespie flagged the "appeasement" line in the final editing of the speech, but not because of Rumsfeld's experience. He just wanted to be sure everyone was comfortable with it. The president, Hadley, and Condi didn't see any problem with it. They all said they liked the speech. In fact, the president assumed that if the appeasement line referred to anyone, it was Jimmy Carter. Bush was still peeved at Carter for trying to conduct his own makeshift diplomacy in the region, including a meeting with the militant terrorist group Hamas. "If I'm ever eighty-two years old and acting like that," the president once remarked, "have somone put me away."

When the speech was delivered, however, the media decided the target was not Carter—he was yesterday's news—but instead was Senator Barack Obama. At around that time, Obama was under fire by his primary opponent, Hillary Clinton, for wanting to sit down without preconditions with leaders from Iran. And wasn't Obama a senator, just like William Borah? Ergo, the media decided, Bush was attacking Obama! In Israel! On foreign soil! That was a hell of a lot more interesting than the headline we'd thought we would get: "Bush, in Speech, Wishes Israel a Happy Birthday."

The reaction to the speech was swift and predictable (but I wasn't one to say "I told you so"). "Bush Compares Obama to Nazi Appeasers," blared the Huffington Post. The White House may have forgotten the kerfuffle over appeasement when Rumsfeld had mentioned it, but the New York Times hadn't. "Thursday was not the first time the word 'appeasement' has cropped up in the Bush Administration lexicon," the paper noted. "In 2006, in advance of the midterm elections, then-Defense Secretary Donald H. Rumsfeld invoked the analogy as an attack against critics of the war in Iraq. Then, as now, it was controversial." It was perfectly reasonable for the Times to conclude that President Bush had mentioned it again deliberately. After all, how could anyone at the White House possibly have forgotten the controversy it caused the last time?

My friend Thayer, who was now chief speechwriter to Secretary Gates, called me from the Pentagon. Still in agony over his role in the American Legion speech, he got right to the point. "Uh, why the hell did you do this again?"

"I know, I know," I replied.

The Knesset speech, of course, was all good news for Barack Obama. He could not have hoped for a greater gift in his bitter primary fight against Clinton than for Bush to attack him. We might as well have dipped the pages of the speech in gold, wrapped a bow around it, and mailed it to Obama headquarters.

At the White House, Marc was thrilled with the reaction. He sent a mass e-mail to folks on the trip in Israel saying how great it was. At about the same time, an anonymous White House source falsely told a reporter that the speech was intended to be a direct hit on Obama, which fanned the flames even further. Meanwhile, in Israel, Ed Gillespie and Dana Perino were struggling to make the case that this was not an intentional attack on Obama. All I could think of was Chris. His wonderful tribute to Israel was now overshadowed forever by a quote he hadn't wanted in the first place.

As the media coverage turned increasingly sour, a reporter friend called me in my office. "Hey, do you know anything about this Israel speech?" he asked.

Oh, yeah, I sure did.

"Well, did Condi Rice object to the appeasement line? I have a source from her office saying that she tried to take it out."

Man, were they good. I told my friend, off the record, that I obviously wasn't on the trip but my experience was if Secretary Rice wanted something out of a speech, she usually got her way.

At first, the president tried to make the best of the reaction. Maybe this was a blessing in disguise? Maybe it put Obama on the defensive? Anyone? But he was clearly not happy. Now everyone on Air Force One started looking at every upcoming speech to avoid other controversies. At one point on that trip of doom, Condi Rice and Steve Hadley sent back edits to upcoming remarks on Cuba that so defanged the speech that it ended up praising the Castro regime for its reforms. If they had succeeded, the president's words, without any plan or warning, would have completely reversed our policy on Cuba.

It was in this foul and confusing mood that the president turned to the next speech—mine—for the World Economic Forum in Egypt. I knew right away it was going to be ugly.

The Egypt speech was another disaster, not because of what it said but because of what it didn't say. Any thought of a speech with "edge," as Secretary Rice had said she wanted, was out the window. Privately, the president was very critical of Egypt's human rights abuses. He said he'd always hoped Egypt would lead the way in the Middle East, but that nothing could happen as long as its aged dictator remained in power. Egypt was one of his biggest disappointments. But after Condi and the president rewrote the speech on the plane, it ended up saying just the opposite. "I applaud Egypt," the president said at one point in the speech. That's telling 'em!

There was one thing in the Egypt speech I really cared about. I'd included a call for the release of Ayman Nour. Ayman Nour was a cause célèbre of the global dissident movement. He'd been jailed because he chose to run for president against Mubarak. The Egyptians trumped up other charges, of course. But everyone knew the truth.

The president had called for Nour's release before, but only in passing and never in the Middle East. The president took great pride in having been called "the dissident president." To call for Nour's release in Egypt would show the president was willing to support the rights of dissidents, even when it wasn't easy.

The reference to Nour apparently was the subject of a fierce debate aboard Air Force One. Steve Hadley wanted the president to say it (another example of Hadley's ability to surprise). So did Ed Gillespie (and all of the speechwriters).

Secretary Rice, however, was adamantly opposed to the Ayman Nour mention. She said she'd called for Nour's release before. All she'd gotten was flak from the Egyptians, and Ayman Nour never even thanked her. The ingrate! He was still rotting in prison for following Bush's call to fight for democracy. Excuse him for not being thankful. Anyway, Condi Rice wasn't going to be bothered with this Ayman Nour business anymore.

There was something ugly about this episode for me, and it wasn't just Secretary Rice's political expediency. When Ayman Nour's name was still in the speech, someone at the State Department apparently saw fit to inform President Mubarak of that fact. (Didn't want the Egyptians to be caught by surprise, you know.) Mubarak apparently announced he was planning to attend the speech and to sit onstage while Bush spoke. I figured that the Egyptians were gambling that this might intimidate the president into not saying Ayman Nour's name and risk offending his host. It was an international game of chicken, and America blinked. For me, that was the worst part. Nobody outside a small circle of people ever knew George Bush had been going to mention the name of the famous dissident, but the Egyptians knew. And the fact that Bush backed down told them that this democracy business he'd made such a big deal about earlier in his administration simply didn't matter to him anymore.

As the Middle East speeches petered into disasters, the president looked for a target to blame. That was us. In a sense, I couldn't blame him. Presidents care about their speeches, and so many of the ones Bush was getting had been stale or unpersuasive. Bush had taken his chief speechwriters for granted—first Mike Gerson and to some extent Bill McGurn. He didn't know how to deal with a speechwriting department that wasn't working.

He seemed unhappy with everything, even criticizing well-crafted remarks that a skillful young writer named Troy Senik wrote for Memorial Day. Troy was told the remarks—for a ceremony honoring our war dead—were too "lofty." (Once again, Hadley, of all people, fought to have the president deliver the remarks as written.) Because there was so little time to revise, the president delivered Troy's version of the speech, to wide praise. But the president still seemed to have it in for us, and for Troy. Marc's solution was to banish Troy to the radio addresses and hope the president never saw his name again. Actually, Chris and I refused to go along with that—it would have demoralized a talented writer unfairly. Ultimately Troy rebounded in the president's esteem and he ended up writing many well-crafted speeches the president liked.

The president next hated remarks for the Furman University commencement address. First, the president objected to lines encouraging responsible home ownership, which meant urging graduates to only buy homes they could reasonably afford. (He indicated that was too harsh and judgmental.) Then Ed Gillespie wanted to insert some lines condemning gay marriage. This prompted the president to bridle. "I'm not going to tell some gay kid in the audience that he can't get married," he said. He claimed the whole address was too "condemnatory." (Which led Chris and me to walk around the West Wing for days saying to random people, "I condemn you.")

I managed to resuscitate the Furman remarks with some Barbara Bush jokes and a little bit of razzle-dazzle. The president accepted the later draft, grudgingly, but he was still on a tear.

Then came a speech innocently named "Remarks on Captive Nations Week." It should have been called "Remarks Commemorating the Beginning of the End." To this day I cannot contemplate that speech without shuddering.

Traditionally, Captive Nations Week was marked to remember

dissidents around the world still trapped in captivity. It gained special prominence during the Cold War when Ronald Reagan used the occasion to give speeches condemning the tyranny of the Soviet Union. Reagan publicly celebrated the anniversary over the strong objections of his State Department, which warned about offending the Soviets. I thought the speech would be right up President Bush's alley—another dusting off of his Freedom Agenda and a condemnation of dictatorships across the world.

But Ed Gillespie and Barry Jackson—the man who'd wanted to compare Bush to Thomas Jefferson—had another revelation. They'd looked at a series of polls and decided to "rebrand" the Freedom Agenda. They even held meetings in the EEOB about it, complete with PowerPoint presentations and colorful slides. To their apparent surprise, it turned out that all that stuff the president had been talking about—standing up to dictators and encouraging democracy around the world—was unpopular with the American people. The war in Iraq was even more unpopular. (Again, these are the conclusions that were being drawn in 2008.)

By contrast, fighting hunger and disease in places such as Africa and Latin America was viewed by Americans as a good thing. So it turned out that treating river blindness and elephantiasis and who knows what else was really what the president's Freedom Agenda had been about all along. (Wink.) As for the president's inaugural address, the one supporting democracy in Afghanistan and Iraq and calling for an end to global tyranny? Uh, never mind. Now assistance to Africa, our one popular initiative, was infiltrating our national security and foreign policies. The speechwriters were told to argue that battling HIV and malaria on a continent thousands of miles away was central, indeed essential, to America's national security. Rebranding the Freedom Agenda was our version of "New Coke."

So this was what Ed wanted the Captive Nations speech to be about. Steve Hadley and the NSC thought differently, though. Hadley was old school. He still wanted the Freedom Agenda to be what it used to be: a call to end tyranny and support the aspirations of dissidents around the world (like Ayman Nour). He also wanted the president to announce a new policy directive that would help guide future administrations in the effort.

I told Ed that Hadley wasn't supportive of his take on the Captive Nations speech, and I outlined what he wanted to do. "Fine with me," Ed responded over e-mail. "Elizabeth Dole rule." (Ed had once worked for Mrs. Dole. Apparently the rule was that if you learned to say, "Yes, Elizabeth, right away, Elizabeth," you save yourself a lot of trouble.) Ed was telling me to say, Yes, Mr. Hadley. Right away, sir.

At one of our weekly speechwriting meetings, I told the president the plan for the speech, based on Hadley's guidance.

"We thought it would be a good opportunity to counter the idea out there that the Freedom Agenda is dead." I looked at Hadley for affirmation. He nodded intently.

"The Freedom Agenda is not dead," the president said. His tone was oddly accusatory.

I nodded vigorously. "That's right," I said. "It isn't."

"So don't say it is," he said, shooting me an annoyed glare. "It's not."

"Yes, of course," I replied. Had he misunderstood me? "I meant to say that we are going to argue that the Freedom Agenda is not dead."

"That's right," the president said. "You are."

"Just to be clear, Mr. President," I tried again, "I was always intending to write the speech that way."

"Well, you are now," the president said with a note of triumph.

I looked at my fellow speechwriters for a life preserver. They were fresh out. "Yes, sir," I said. "I'll do that." What the heck was that about?

It was not a revelation to anyone that the president could be . . . well . . . a man with a generous supply of moods. And the president, of course, had every right to them—he was leader of the free world, after all. He could be quite short with people. The president himself knew that. When Ed Gillespie once asked Bush if he wanted cameras to follow him around to chronicle his last hundred days in office, the president shook his head. With a slight smile on his face, he said, "If I had a camera following me around all day, I'd look like a total asshole."

But this reaction was different from just being in a bad mood. I should have taken the Oval Office reaction to the speech as a bad omen.

I wrote a speech that talked about the Cold War and extended support to dissidents in places such as Syria, Iran, Saudi Arabia, and China. I also included a call for reorganizing the State Department to promote democracy abroad, just like Hadley wanted. It was a nice speech, but nothing too exciting. It went through editing without any particular controversy. Raul called me with two little nitpicky fact-checking issues, but a smaller number than usual.

"I'm sending it up to the president tonight," he said.

Raul was usually a spot-on barometer of the president's reaction. "Do you think he'll like the speech?" I asked.

"I think so," Raul replied. "It's good."

I came in early the next morning expecting to hear about the speech. I heard nothing. Hours passed. Since our policy with the president and speeches was no news is good news, I figured that was a positive sign. Then in the early afternoon I was called into the Oval Office to discuss the remarks. This was never a good sign. Marc Thiessen came with me as well. The third of our threesome, Chris Michel, was off on his honeymoon. With Chris out of town, we brought Horny along as a substitute.

As we were waiting outside the Oval Office, Kevin Sullivan came up to us. "Hey, guys, I asked the president if we could send out excerpts of this speech tomorrow afternoon," Kevin said.

"What did he say?" I asked anxiously.

Kevin shrugged. "He said wait until after the meeting this afternoon." This wasn't good.

There were more ominous portents. Raul, who always came to our speechwriting meetings, was nowhere to be found. Ed Gillespie also was not there. Even Hadley was missing.

We walked into the Oval Office. The president was sitting at his desk, looking grim. He had the speech in front of him. I knew we were in trouble when he asked, "What is Captive Nations week?" After I explained what it was, he asked, "Why are we doing this?" This was going to be ugly. I then received the most energetic critique I'd ever received for a speech from anyone. It was so "energetic" that I wanted to melt into the bright yellow sofa and disappear forever.

The president didn't like talking about the Cold War. He didn't like announcing new initiatives to promote democracy. He didn't like the reference to Captive Nations. "I would never use that term," he said.

The president turned the discussion to dissidents. He read this line aloud: "In my meetings with foreign leaders, I made human rights a high priority. When I last met [China's] President Hu Jintao, my message was this: as long as there are those who want to fight for their liberty, the United States will stand by their side."

The president glared at us, his half-glasses seemed to perch menacingly on his nose. "Where did you get this?" he asked me.

I explained that I'd taken that line, verbatim, from an off-the-cuff statement the president had made a few days earlier to a group of dissidents.

"You took that verbatim from me?" he asked skeptically.

"Yes, sir," I answered.

"Well, I never said that," he replied. Okay . . .

The president went through every paragraph, almost line by line, finding fault with one thing or another: "This doesn't make sense . . . Why is this in here? . . . See, this isn't a transition . . . Who told you to say this? . . . Reagan—no. Take that out." (Though Bush would cite Reagan on occasion, he never really seemed to like to do it.)

I'd seen the president annoyed with speeches before. But this reaction was so extreme it was almost unfathomable. I was convinced that he not only hated the speech but hated us and hated me personally. I was sitting in the Oval Office being yelled at by the president of the United States. And I wasn't sure why.

The NSC staff was equally baffled. They believed the only answer was that Condi had gotten to him. She was one of the few people who could set him off and turn him around on a speech that used a lot of language he'd used many times before. They speculated that Condi didn't like the speech because it bound the State Department to policies that the department actively opposed. Many employees didn't want to make the promotion of a democracy a fundamental aspect of their jobs, as we had outlined in the speech. (Naively, I'd assumed that the State Department always promoted democracy abroad.)

At the conclusion of this Oval Office skewering, the writers and I went back to Marc's office in the West Wing. Marc took over rewriting the speech. He decided the best approach would be to fold in large sections from speeches the president already had given that Marc had written (surprise, surprise). I happily let him take the wheel. I was so mortified and stunned by the president's reaction that I was not up for round two. In the new draft we still talked about the need to promote democracy. But we took out most of the things the president really didn't seem to like.

We went back to the Oval Office again. We stood in the small office just outside to wait for Karen to tell us it was okay to go in. The Oval Office door was open and the president was talking to Josh Bolten. I heard him say, "Those speechwriters just don't get it. I don't know what—" I think someone pointed out that we were standing just outside, because the president stopped speaking midsentence.

He asked us to come in. He hated the second draft of the speech as well but, perhaps feeling badly that we'd overheard him criticizing us, tried to be nicer about it. This time, he spoke very calmly and slowly, like we were pathetic dullards. "See . . . , this . . . is . . . not . . . a . . . good . . . transition." "No . . . this . . . is . . . not . . . what . . . I . . . would . . . say."

Ugh. This was even worse.

At the end of the remarks, I'd included a story about a time in the 1950s when the people of Hungary temporarily overthrew their Soviet occupiers and went on the radio begging the Western world to come to their aid. The West never answered, and their democratic revolution was crushed. As Soviet tanks closed in, a desperate Hungarian made a plea on the airwaves that I quoted in the speech. "The ship is sinking," he said. "Light is failing. The shadows grow darker every hour." As I was sitting in the Oval Office with the president, I felt the same way. Later, I sent an e-mail to Chris, who was sunning it up in the Carribean. "The ship is sinking," I wrote. "The shadows grow darker every hour." Chris had no idea what I was talking about, but he knew it wasn't good.

Now grossly dissatisfied with two drafts of the speech, the president finally told us what he wanted: a speech that recognized the Freedom Agenda as freedom from disease, freedom from poverty, freedom from despair. Oh, and freedom from tyranny too, if we could fit it in. It was true: the president really did want the Freedom Agenda to be about fighting river blindness in Botswana. I couldn't believe it. All the big talk about standing up for democracy around the world, well, that was clearly over.

We went back and changed the speech to what he wanted. It was something that I wish I could have removed my name from.

After two brutal, horrible editing sessions, I think the president decided he might have gone too far. To compensate, he poured praise all over us in the third go-round, slapping it on like honey-glazed goo.

"This is a pretty good little speech," he said. As we went through it, he nodded with approval at almost every paragraph. "This is good ... oh, this is good ... I like how you did this." He offered an unprecedented sixteen compliments for a speech that at best was mediocre. As he tossed us the compliments, Marc nodded eagerly. All was well again. My face remained expressionless.

Continuing to try to repair the damage, he came as close to an apology as he ever had.

"I know this speech wasn't your fault," he said. "You just got bad guidance from the NSC." Marc smiled and accepted the president's remorse.

He looked at me directly from his seat behind the Resolute desk. "But we finally made it through, didn't we, Matty?" he asked, eyeing me carefully.

There was a brief silence. Everyone turned to me. They looked terrified about what I'd say. "I suppose so," I replied, as quietly and coldly as I could possibly get away with in the Oval Office of the White House before the president of the United States.

The president smiled uncomfortably. Everyone did.

I should have been nicer, but I guess I was offended by the entire process. I used to shake my head at the people who took Rumsfeld's critiques so personally. Now here I was taking it personally from the president of the United States. But it was more than bruised feelings. I was genuinely confused about who this man was. The leader who'd said that pushing for freedom around the world was the hallmark of his presidency now seemed to be forgetting that calling. Worse, this reversal was only one of many the administration was now undertaking, without any explanation whatsoever. Suddenly, for example, we were willing to talk with Iran, after I'd been told for more than a year to write speeches saying that talking with Iran was like dealing with terrorists. We were supporting a time line for withdrawal from Iraq, though the president's rhetoric months earlier had been that a time line was the equivalent of surrender. We'd even made a deal with North Korea, though I'd always been told that a similar agreement had been the folly of the Clinton administration. The overture to North Korea came at Condi Rice's insistence. She wanted to remove the regime in Pyongyang from the list of terrorist-sponsoring nations in exchange for what some of the experts at the NSC considered very little in return. Vice President Cheney had been vigorously opposing this effort for years, but by 2008 he was no longer a power in the White House. Or, at least, that's how it seemed. Cheney seemed to have become the eccentric uncle of the administration, the "crazy conservative" nobody listened to.

"This is for the legacy," an NSC staffer explained to me when I had to draft the president's remarks announcing the North Korea deal.

"The president's legacy?" I asked.

"No, Condi's," came the reply. Rice apparently even objected to publicly holding North Korea to its promise to destroy a nuclear reactor on live television. (The reference to the reactor stayed in only at Steve Hadley's insistence.)

(As of this writing, the Obama administration is considering returning North Korea to the terrorist lists.)

The president loved being "the decider," but after observing all these turnabouts, I couldn't help feeling that he was more interested in making decisions that were bold than in making decisions that were consistent and right. Maybe, I wondered, this was how all second terms ended—with intellectual exhaustion.

The only core principle the president still seemed firmly committed to was cutting taxes—or so I thought. One day we were in the Oval Office discussing a speech that included a line mentioning that Bush, as president, had never supported a tax increase. Then Josh Bolten spoke up, which was never a good thing. He coolly pointed out that in fact the president had just signed energy legislation that included a tax hike, so we couldn't use that line anymore.

The president seemed to have forgotten that. He didn't seem particularly concerned that he'd changed his once-sacrosanct position. "Is that going to take effect before we give the speech?" was all he asked.

At this point, I didn't get what we were doing or why. In a quest to become more popular, the administration had thrown aside its more controversial figures—people who also tended to be a voice for conservatives, such as Cheney, Rumsfeld, and even Rove (though that was for the best). Filling the vacuum were cleaner types known more for their cold-bloodedness and managerial competency: Bolten, Gates, and increasingly Rice. Yet even as the administration became more soulless in this effort to ingratiate, it saw its approval ratings decline further. We were the political equivalent of PBS—at its most boring and unwatchable.

I saw how well the vaunted pragmatists were running the show just a few weeks later when Russia invaded the Republic of Georgia (a former Captive Nation that we didn't even mention in our doomed speech). Remarkably, Rice and Gates, who prided themselves on being foreign policy "realists," never saw the Russian tanks coming. (The ostracized Dick Cheney did, however. He'd been warning about Russia forever.) After Russia's invasion, Gates joked that it was ironic that both he and Condi Rice were considered Russian experts. Neither of them, he said, seemed to have done a good job managing the issue. No kidding.

As I tried to figure out why Bush had let the administration drift into ideological incoherence, my thoughts returned to a conversation I'd had with the president earlier that year.

I was always skeptical about how much the president truly believed in the conservative movement. Don't get me wrong. In his first term, Bush governed as one of the most conservative presidents in history, ushering in tax cuts, missile defense, and a discussion of Social Security reform. But I always felt that his conservative bent was more a tactic—a Karl Rove–inspired plan to get the base behind him and win with 50 percent of the vote—than a true philosophy. The president went through the motions, said all the right things to win, but I never thought he truly felt them in his heart. More than once, Bush bemoaned the treatment conservatives had given his father—and I didn't think he ever forgot it. The president also never quite made his peace with conservative opposition, led by the magazine National Review, to his choice for the U.S. Supreme Court in 2005, Harriet Miers. Conservatives were nervous about Miers's thin record on legal issues and not at all comforted by the president's "trust me" assurances that she would be a reliable vote on the court. I was nervous too, both as a conservative and as a lawyer. I don't know why the president backed down and withdrew her nomination, but he stewed about it for sometime afterward. When I arrived at the White House, I casually asked senior staff members about her. It was only then that I confirmed what I had suspected. Many who worked with Miers, including some who defended her publicly, confided that she was a very nice person who was fiercely loyal to

Bush. But few, if any, seemed to envision her as a qualified member of the Court.

One of the subterranean stories of the Bush years was his family's bonding with Bill Clinton, whom Barbara Bush referred to as their "adopted son." I was surprised by Bush's affinity for Bill Clinton. Apparently they talked somewhat regularly (Clinton kvetched about Obama during the primaries against Hillary). Bush appreciated his advice. Bill Clinton was many things, but a conservative he wasn't.

My theory about Bush seemed confirmed once I talked to the president about a speech to the Conservative Political Action Conference. CPAC had been established during the wilderness years of the conservative movement—the days when Ronald Reagan and William F. Buckley were trying to change the Republican Party from a bunch of moderates who graciously lost every election.

As the president edited the speech, he looked at me from across the *Resolute* desk with his usual look of skepticism matched with irritation.

"What is this movement you keep talking about in the speech?" he asked.

"Well, the conservative movement," I explained.

He looked at me skeptically.

"You know," I continued, "the one that started back in the sixties, when conservative groups first took root."

The president either had no concept of what I was talking about, didn't want any part of it, or both.

He leaned forward. "Let me tell you something," he said. "I whupped Gary Bauer's ass in 2000." Gary Bauer was a little-known social conservative who'd never mounted a serious campaign for president. But Bush seemed to think that beating him had been an important triumph.

"So take out all this movement stuff," he said. "There is no movement."

He couldn't possibly mean that. No conservative movement? He must not have understood what I was trying to say (which was a problem in itself).

Perhaps seeing my confusion, the president tried to explain what he meant. "Look, I know this probably sounds arrogant to say, but I redefined the Republican Party."

I wanted to say, but didn't, *Redefined it into what?*

It didn't really matter. After the disappointment of seeing what had happened to the Egypt speech and, during the Captive Nations debacle, having my eyes opened to the president's willingness to abandon core conservative principles, I realized, sadly, that I didn't care about the administration anymore. The president was not the evil person his enemies made him out to be nor was he a dummy, but he also wasn't the leader I'd thought he was. I have no doubt that he meant well, that he tried to do good, and he came to our country's defense after the horrors of 9/11, but he simply was not the president I wanted. He wasn't a conservative in the mold of Reagan or Thatcher. He certainly wasn't a liberal. If anything, he seemed to be adrift. All my life I'd dreamed of working for a president I adored, like those who had worked for Kennedy and Reagan (and, perhaps, Obama). But finally I realized it wasn't going to happen for me.

As this was going on, my friend Andrew came by for a visit. He was still working for Senator Kyl and was thrilled to have a chance to tour the White House.

As we walked through the West Wing, he seemed so happy for me. "This is such a wonderful opportunity for you," he said. "You must be in awe of this place every day."

I told him the truth: I really didn't feel in awe.

He thought I was being modest or trying to downplay things. "You're working for the president of the United States. This is what you always wanted to do, and you did it."

He was right. And yet my reaction was, oddly, "Eh."

Andrew still had faith in Bush, at least to some extent, but then he didn't know what I did. And I couldn't really tell him. I felt like I'd accidentally walked into a movie theater only to discover after the lights went down that I was watching the wrong film. And I was going to be stuck there until the movie ended and the lights came back on.

There was at least one welcome development during those several months of speechwriter hell—but even that occurred in typical Bush White House style: ineptly, somewhat deceptively, and in a way that didn't really satisfy anyone. After months and months of mismanaging the speechwriting office almost to the point of open revolt and his bizarre treatment of senior White House officials, Marc was removed as chief speechwriter to the president in all but name. Practically everyone in the West Wing was made aware of this—except for Marc. It was a desperately needed change that I strongly supported. Still, I felt badly about the situation, especially since Marc was the one who had helped me come to the White House. And most of the people in the West Wing who he naively thought were his allies actually weren't.

Instead of openly confronting Marc about the problems in his office, Ed Gillespie—in league with other senior officials—came up with the typical Washington solution: upward promotion. Ed told Marc that his skills were needed on a very important project. There was going to be a book written highlighting all of the president's major accomplishments, and Ed said he could think of no one better to write it than Marc. Of course, Ed explained somberly, this would mean that Marc couldn't be involved in the day-to-day speechwriting operations. The book would take up all of his time—every minute, in fact, until the last day of the administration. So Chris Michel would take over. That also meant that I'd be Chris's deputy.

Marc, as far as anyone could tell, never had a clue regarding what was happening to him. He thought he was getting a big promotion or something. The president even played along by holding meetings about the book, to fool him into thinking it was of major consequence. But nearly everyone else knew the truth. At one point, I literally was begged not to reveal it to him. The book ploy was the worst possible way to handle the situation. Chris had to run speechwriting while Marc still kept his West Wing office and title. Marc was given no opportunity to understand how badly he'd managed things. The taxpayers were paying a chief speechwriter's six-figure income for months while he wrote a book that was never utilized—at least not in the way he had billed it to us when he first took on the assignment. (I think it appeared briefly on the White House Web page, with as little fanfare as possible after being largely rewritten.)

I comforted myself with the knowledge that things couldn't get any worse. Wrong again.

CHAPTER ELEVEN

FINAL DELUSIONS

The global economy is more than strong. It's as strong as I've seen in my business lifetime.
> —Treasury Secretary Henry Paulson, March 6, 2007

We have not in our lifetime dealt with a financial crisis of this severity.
> —Treasury Secretary Henry Paulson, November 18, 2008

To this day, I don't really understand what happened. In the first several months I worked at the White House, I wrote any number of speeches praising America's economic prosperity. Over and over again, we'd write, "The fundamentals of our economy are strong." That was what we were told. We'd repeat the same refrain: there'd been month after month of uninterrupted job growth, after-tax income was increasing, exports were rising, inflation was down. At times, we even cited the stratospheric heights of the Dow.

As far as I could tell, the president was being told the same thing by his economic advisors, led by the secretary of the treasury, Hank Paulson. Paulson had been brought into the administration by Josh Bolten. They'd both worked at Goldman Sachs. Paulson had been one of the highest-paid CEOs on Wall Street, making at least $30 million a year, and had an MBA from Harvard (like President Bush). Paulson was supposed to be a nonideological, pragmatic, sensible type—another cleaner. He was bald with glasses and had a scratchy voice that sounded like he had a thousand-dollar bill caught in his throat.

While Secretary Paulson was telling the president that the economy was the strongest in sixty years, there were obvious signs that all was not well. Across America, the housing bubble had started to collapse, leading to a sharp increase in home foreclosures. At the White House, though, we were told that the housing bubble would correct itself. Even in the fall of 2007, Paulson was saying that the crisis was contained. Most of the big ideas we had for improving the housing situation required approval by Congress anyway, and Congress was doing squat. So to look like we were doing something, we announced various initiatives, such as assembling an alliance to encourage lenders to renegotiate loans. Another initiative was Project Lifeline. Housing Secretary Alphonso Jackson was about to announce this new program with great fanfare at a press conference, but then someone decided that, since the president needed to say something about housing, the announcement should be left to him. I kept trying to figure out what Project Lifeline was. Every time I asked, I got back gobbledygook. As far as I could tell, all the program did was send letters to people telling them to get help. They wanted the president to announce a letter-writing campaign? This was our response to the housing crisis? It was the lamest of the lame, the Jar Jar Binks of proposals.

For a while, the communications guys—Ed Gillespie and Kevin Sullivan—also wanted the president to give a toll-free number for Americans to call for assistance with their mortgages. I thought that was embarrassing, as if George W. Bush were Jerry Lewis. An additional problem was that the president kept botching the phone number. He thought, as I did, that it was an 800 number, but the number actually had an 888 prefix. So the president ended up telling Americans to call the wrong number. It seemed fitting somehow.

Unfortunately, I can't say that any of the president's top economic advisors struck me as having a firm handle on the economic mess ahead. The economic team the president put together at first included his friend Al Hubbard. He may have been a competent advisor; I really didn't know him. The only thing I knew about Al was that he went around putting whoopee cushions on people's chairs in the West Wing. There was Keith Hennessey, the head of the National Economic Council, his Mickey Mouse ears at the ready. And Eddie Lazear, the head of the Council of Economic Advisors. He and the president had gone to Harvard together. Eddie was in tip-top shape for a man in his sixties. He looked as if he ran around fifteen miles a day. He also frequently biked with the president. And, of course, Josh Bolten had been head of the Office of Management and Budget and, due to his Goldman Sachs background, was supposed to have a firm grasp on economic issues as well.

But even through the end of 2007, the president was told to say that the U.S. economy was "strong," "thriving," "flexible," and "resilient." We loved the word resilient. It implied whatever you wanted it to—it could mean that things are great or it could mean that things might not be great, but we'll bounce back and eventually the economy will be great again. Still, I had friends at the OMB who were telling me for months that things were in worse shape than we were letting on. One person relatively high up in the agency predicted a total collapse of the economy, but nobody was listening to him. He said that most of the senior economic officials at the White House were in way over their heads. I thought he was crazy, a natural pessimist. Things would turn around. We're resilient!

The president had a Harvard MBA, to be sure, but he wasn't expected to know all the intricacies of things most people had never heard of, such as mortgage-backed securities. Instead, he trusted his advisors. When they're all telling you that things will be okay, the fundamentals of the economy are strong, the economy will keep growing, what are you supposed to do? Still, I had a sense that the president felt uncomfortable going out and offering all these rosy economic scenarios. He always liked to convey the impression of confidence—he was a pretty confident guy—but he also was a natural skeptic. I had the sense pretty early on that when it came to the economy he figured something wasn't adding up.

By the beginning of 2008, the president was noticeably more concerned about the health of the economy. At one point, he told the public that it was "obvious our economy is in a slowdown, but fortunately we recognized the signs early." He proposed an expensive economic stimulus package, which he ultimately negotiated with Congress and passed, that would send Americans checks for a few hundred dollars. Everybody in the West Wing seemed to think that would solve the problem. For months the president believed it too. Even as the economy grew bumpier, he kept saying that we just needed to give the plan more time to work. It would take a while for these checks to get to people and for people to start spending. Once they did, the boost in consumer spending would energize the economy. Things would improve later in the year.

They didn't.

Major companies with household names like Bear Stearns found themselves in jeopardy. Then Fannie Mae and Freddie Mac seemed to be teetering, but Secretary Paulson assured Americans there were no plans for the government to inject any capital into them. (A short time later, the government did just that.) The situation with Freddie Mac was particularly interesting, since its top lobbyist was married to the First Lady's chief of staff. You would have thought we might have received some advance warning about its troubles. Following that, Lehman Brothers declared bankruptcy and Merrill Lynch was sold at a deep discount to Bank of America. It was the kind of chaos Wall Street hadn't experienced in seventy-five years.

By mid-September, it was clear to everyone that the nation faced a full-blown crisis. The president had been through so many shocking crises—9/11, Afghanistan, Iraq, Abu Ghraib, Katrina—that it was hard to see how he could rally himself for one more. People around him seemed to have adopted a woe-is-me attitude. None of the senior officials at the White House had expected to end the second Bush term this way, with what Warren Buffett called an "economic Pearl Harbor." In fact, Ed Gillespie, still in search of that elusive 40 percent appeal rating, was mapping out an ambitious schedule of "legacy speeches" for the fall and winter to trumpet all of the administration's achievements. We could strike "remarks on the robust economy" off the list.

As the economy nose-dived, pundits on TV started asking why the president wasn't saying more and what he was going to do. (The answers were: we had nothing to say and no one had any idea.) So our communications team, once again, did the usual: had the president go out and constantly talk about the economy to show we were doing something. The speechwriters were asked to insert remarks about the economy wherever we could, even putting an insert into the president's remarks during a state visit from the president of Ghana. We received very little guidance on what to say, so we threw in the old reliable— "flexible and resilient"—while saying that Secretary Paulson was on the case. Oddly, this didn't seem to calm the financial markets.

On September 16, 2008, the government bailed out the insurance giant AIG, which was on the brink of collapse. Everyone started to wonder which shoe was going to drop next and why the president wasn't just saying more but also doing more. Inside the White House, every-thing seemed even more uncertain. But after much debate and discus-sion, we speechwriters were asked to draft another short statement for the president expressing "concern" and reassuring the public that we were monitoring the situation. The statement lasted two minutes and was widely panned.

As the press started to froth, Dana Perino, the White House press secretary, asked Chris and me to write a speech for the president to ex-plain in understandable terms what was going on and get the press off our backs. Josh Bolten was not so sure the president needed to go out and speak. Bolten wouldn't reveal much, but it was clear that something more was going on. One of the president's top advisors started to tell Chris about further government action that was in the offing, but the topic was so sensitive that Bolten hushed him up.

After Chris, Horny, and I learned about the president's $700 billion bailout proposal and drafted the remarks announcing it to a stunned nation, Ed said the president wanted to see us in the Oval Office. The president looked relaxed and was sitting behind the Resolute desk. He felt he'd made the major decision that everyone had been asking for. That always seemed to relax him. He liked being decisive. Excuse me, boldly decisive.

The president seemed to be thinking of his memoirs. "This might go in as a big decision," he mused.

"Definitely, Mr. President," someone else observed with satisfac-tion. "This is huge."

The president asked his secretary, Karen, to bring him the Rose Garden remarks he'd just delivered announcing his action plan. He got slightly exasperated when she was delayed in printing them out. When he finally got them, he put his half-glasses on and looked at them. "See, this was fine today," he said. Then he seemed to channel Sammy Davis Jr. "We got to make this understandable for the average cat."

He proposed an outline for another economy speech that talked about the situation our economy was in, how we'd gotten here, and how the administration's plan was a solution.

"This is the last bullet we have," the president said at one point, re-ferring to the bailout. "If this doesn't work..." He shook his head and his voice trailed off. That wasn't good enough for me. If this doesn't work, *then what? We're done? America is over?* I looked around at everyone else. *What does that mean?*

As we started to craft a speech for the "average cat," the president was scheduled to give his final address to the United Nations. The address was conceived as calling for some tough reforms to encourage the spread of democracy. This was the president's last speech to that gathering, he reasoned, so why not make it tough and say some things he'd always wanted to say? But at the last minute, Condi Rice called the president and complained that we were being too hard on the UN. We needed to praise it more. So the speech was changed. It turned out fine but was oddly discordant. While every other world leader speaking to the UN General Assembly that day addressed the financial crisis, the president seemed slightly out of touch with his remarks on terrorism and the Freedom Agenda.

Since Chris went with the president to New York, I was tasked with leading the effort to write the "average cat" speech in the interim. The problem was no one knew when, if, how, or why he'd deliver it. The decision apparently was in Ed's hands, and it was another one of his "OTOH" moments. On Tuesday there were rumors this would be an address to the nation, then a speech to the National Restaurant Association, then an event in the Rose Garden, then some other forum, then no speech at all. Ed finally told us to write the speech as if it would be a prime-time address to the nation—the biggest of big deals in the speechwriting world—and assume that a deal had been reached with Congress. (He also wanted to make sure we put in that this was "a bold decision.")

As Ed and the president decided to give a prime-time address to the nation, Vice President Cheney was released from stasis and sent to the Hill to argue for our bill (a bill he may or may not have believed in) and was apparently hammered by House Republicans. There were reports that only four Republicans out of nearly two hundred supported the plan. From what I was starting to glean about the whole scatter-brained operation, four seemed like too many.

Hours before the president was to speak to the country, Senator John McCain's presidential campaign informed Josh Bolten that McCain was going to phone the president and urge him to call off the address and instead hold an emergency economic summit in Washington. If the president did speak that night, the McCain campaign said, they didn't want him to outline any specific proposal.

Of course, this threw the proverbial monkey wrench into our plans—and at the eleventh hour. I overheard the president call McCain's plan "a stunt." Dana Perino said the negotiations were nearly over, and suddenly he was going to swoop in and muck things up? The president's political advisor, Barry Jackson, was blunt, calling McCain a "stupid prick."

Now we were faced with a dilemma: should Bush still go out and address the nation, or should he cancel? And if he did go out (canceling didn't seem possible), what should he say? Ed, typically, told us to write two drafts for the address to the nation—one outlining the proposal as originally announced, and another that only discussed the "principles" the legislation needed to incorporate to win the administration's support. Chris and I looked at each other warily. *Two versions of a major prime-time address that may or may not be given hours from now? Sure, no problem.*

Ultimately, Ed decided to go with the second speech. But he clearly didn't share his plan with the president. When the president came into the Family Theater to rehearse the remarks in front of a teleprompter, he didn't like the idea of just talking about principles. It sounded like the administration was backing away from its own plan (which it was).

"We can't even defend our own proposal?" he asked. "Why did we propose it, then?" This was not bold decision making.

There were about a dozen people gathered in the theater to watch him rehearse, and all of us remained silent as the president looked at us for an answer.

The president walked over to sip some water from one of the bottles on the table near his lectern. "This speech is weak," he said. He looked at me and Chris. "Frankly, I'm surprised, to be honest with you."

Then he walked back to his podium. "I don't want to be melodramatic."

There was more silence. "Too late to cancel the speech?" the president asked into the air. He was joking . . . I think. Finally, Ed (who hadn't exactly rushed to jump into the line of fire) explained that we had to make this change to the address because the proposal the president liked might not end up being the one he had to agree to.

"Then why the hell did I support it if I didn't believe it would pass?" he snapped.

There was an uncomfortable silence.

Finally, the president directed us to try to put elements of his proposal back into the text. He wanted to explain what he was seeking and to defend it. He especially wanted Americans to know that his plan would likely see a return on the taxpayers' investment. Under his proposal, he said, the federal government would buy troubled mortgages on the cheap and then resell them at a higher price when the market for them stabilized. "We're buying low and selling high," he kept saying.

The problem was that his proposal didn't work like that.

One of the president's staff members anxiously pulled a few of us aside. "The president is misunderstanding this proposal," he warned. "He has the wrong idea in his head." Bush wasn't the only one; that's what I thought the plan was going to do too.

As it turned out, the plan wasn't to buy low and sell high. In some cases, in fact, the government wouldn't be buying these securities at the lowest prices. Secretary Paulson wanted to pay more than the securities were likely worth in order to put more money into the markets as soon as possible. This was not how the president's proposal had been advertised to the public or the Congress. The real problem wasn't that the president didn't understand what his administration wanted to do. It was that the treasury secretary didn't seem to know, changed his mind, had misled the president, or some combination of the three.

As Chris and I were in our office in the EEOB trying to put in the latest of the president's edits, there was a steady flow of people coming into the room. The economic team came in. Ed Gillespie came in. Tony Fratto, the deputy press secretary, was there. Marc Thiessen came by. Raul and Brent both were there. At one point there were twelve people crowded around our computer, trying to explain how the proposal worked. The economic advisors were disagreeing with one another. There was total confusion. It was 5:30 P.M. The speech was in three and a half hours.

After finally getting the speech draft turned around and sent back to the teleprompter technicians, we trudged back to the Family Theater, where the president rehearsed. In the theater, the president was clearly confused about how the government would buy these securities. He repeated his belief that the government was going to "buy low and sell high," and he still didn't understand why we hadn't put that into the speech as he'd asked us to.

When it was explained to him that his concept of the bailout proposal wasn't correct, the president was momentarily speechless. He threw up his hands in frustration. "Why did I sign on to this proposal if I don't understand what it does?" he asked. Now I was speechless.

The president was clearly frustrated with what was going on, but there was little he could do at this late hour. He went up to take a nap, saying he was beat. He looked it. I'd never seen him more exhausted. His hair was out of place and shaggy. His face looked drained and pale. Most alarming of all, he was wearing crocs. I thought, How many more crises can one guy take?

A few hours later, as the start of the prime-time speech approached, Chris and I went up to the East Room. The large room had been converted into a studio for the address. There was a big group of technicians present, and wires and equipment were everywhere. The president's lectern was set up so that we were to his left and out of his line of sight. His audience was a gold curtain next to a large portrait of George Washington. I worried that I'd do something goofy during the speech, like trip over a wire and unplug the president on live TV.

As Chris and I were standing together watching the speech get fed into the teleprompter, Josh Bolten walked over to us. There would be no sarcastic, off-putting comments to offer us tonight. Instead, he looked like he'd had a long day, and I felt a tinge of sympathy for him. He told us he'd gotten an earful from Speaker Pelosi and Senate Majority Leader Harry Reid. The Speaker had yelled at him for fifteen minutes and expressed her view that the president's speech was a mistake and would screw up their deal. "Talking to them is the hardest part of my job," he said quietly.

Then, with about thirty minutes until airtime, the president showed up, looking transformed from hours earlier. He was in a deep red tie and dark suit. The crocs, thankfully, were nowhere to be seen. His hair was neatly combed. His demeanor was completely businesslike. He made a few edits to the text and then read it through, flawlessly, from start to finish. He informed us that he'd called both the presidential candidates, Senators Obama and McCain, and asked them to come to the White House the next day for the summit McCain had wanted. Both candidates had agreed.

After the president finished his run-through, about ten of us walked over to him, forming a phalanx around him. We had little to say, of course. The speech was in ten minutes, so there wasn't time for any serious changes. We just wanted to be standing by him—it made us feel useful. And a few aides liked to be in the pictures that the White House photographers were taking of the president preparing for another historic speech.

Kevin Sullivan tried to be of use. "Mr. President, you were standing slightly to the left," he said.

We all looked at him, confused. So did the president. "What?" he asked.

"On the camera," Sully explained. "You were standing slightly to the left when you rehearsed. You might want to try to line your tie up in between the two mikes so you look straight into the camera."

The president looked at him sympathetically. "Uh, okay. Thanks."

Having accomplished little, we all trudged back to our places behind the bank of TV equipment and gave the president a moment to himself. Dana Perino showed up, mostly to stand around like the rest of us. Eddie Lazear, the chairman of the Council of Economic Advisors, ran in with seconds to airtime. He was sweating and out of breath. Nobody had told him he could watch the speech in the East Wing, he said. He'd been at home, so he'd changed back into a suit and hustled back over.

I watched the president seconds before he went live. His expression changed. He seemed to be trying to look more somber, but it came out as uncomfortable. The president had been relaxed only minutes earlier and seemed far more commanding. Now, live on the air, he was different. His delivery was stony and tense.

As the president was speaking, I stood next to Josh Bolten. Every so often, the chief and I would turn to watch the split television screen that showed all the major networks carrying the speech live. It was a surreal experience. I was standing in the White House watching the president give a speech I'd helped write, delivered live on every news channel in the country, on the worst economic crisis since FDR lived in this house.

The next day, when Senators McCain and Obama were set to visit the White House, a sizable group of White House staffers stood on the steps of the EEOB to see the motorcades arrive. I walked out to join them. When one of the black SUVs pulled up, there was a flurry of excitement. One of the presidential candidates was arriving! Young staffers craned their necks to see who it was. "Oh, it's just McCain," someone said. There was a collective sigh. Here I was, among the most loyal of the Republican Party loyalists, and nobody wanted to see our nominee. We were all hoping to see Obama. When the Illinois senator finally arrived, he walked through the West Wing, waving and saying a confident "Hello, folks" to stunned Bush staffers. He seemed right at home, and considering the terrible mess my party was in, I had no doubt he'd soon be back.

The proposal the president had announced to the nation would be soundly rejected by the House of Representatives. It turned out that Republicans in the House no longer listened to the president. Neither did they listen to McCain, who came out in favor of the bill. And the Republicans gave Paulson's warnings of dire economic collapse little heed. An eventual compromise was reached a week later. And I had to endure what I considered the biggest indignity of my entire White House tenure to help get it passed.

One of the things I'd believed since coming to Washington was that Jimmy Carter had been the worst president in recent history. This was carved in stone, so to speak, in a memorable episode of The Simpsons when the town of Springfield wanted to buy a presidential statue for the city square. The town couldn't afford one of the good presidents, so they had to settle for Carter. "Jimmy Carter?" a shocked townsperson shrieked. "He's history's greatest monster!" That epithet always stuck with me.

I mention this because one evening shortly after the address to the nation, I came into Chris's office. (Chris, as I've mentioned, had taken over the speechwriting office by now, in everything but name.)

"So we have an interesting assignment," he said. He had a sinister smile on his face.

"What is it?" I asked nervously. At this point, anything was possible.

"Well, we've been asked to write a statement on behalf of our financial rescue package for a VIP. If we write it, he'll release it."

"Who is it?" I asked, running a whole list of names by him. Bill

Gates? Warren Buffett? The guys who created Google? Ted Turner? No, we'd sunk much lower than that.

"One of your favorites," Chris replied, laughing. "James Earl Carter."

No. It couldn't be. History's monster himself? The guy Reagan beat? The symbol of all that was wrong and unholy in Democratic politics? Stepping up to bail out a bailout bill for a Republican president? It couldn't be true.

But it was. Chris took out a pen and scribbled the date on a Post-it note. He said he wanted us to remember when we'd "finally hit bottom."

We were now writing remarks for Jimmy Carter, of all people, because we'd been abandoned by nearly everyone else.

Carter delivered the statement our office provided nearly verbatim. Then, a week later, he launched a vicious attack on Bush's "atrocious" economic policies. It was just one more humiliation. First the administration had had to seek out Carter's help, and then the White House had been schooled on the economy by the president who'd brought you gas lines, an energy crisis, and high unemployment.

The worst of it was that the whole country was misled by the bailout plan. Paulson used scare tactics to get us all to act quickly—and then did exactly nothing with the money he'd said he urgently needed to save the economy. In the weeks that followed, he changed his spending priorities two or three times and seemed to rework the proposal on the fly into something different from what we'd thought it was. Incredibly, he'd been given the power to do with that money virtually anything he pleased. All thanks to a president who just wanted to act boldly and a Congress that didn't stop to think.

The economy was now *everything* to the speechwriting team. We were told to talk about the economy over and over and over. Forget about Iraq; that was so 2007. We were now writing speeches nearly every time the stock market flipped—never a smart thing to do. Meanwhile, the White House seemed to have ceded all of its authority regarding economic matters to the secretive secretary of the treasury. The president was clearly frustrated with this. I was told that at one Oval Office meeting he got very animated and exclaimed to Paulson, "You've got to tell me what you're doing!"

The president understood the danger of talking constantly about the economy, especially if he had nothing new to say. "It's hard to keep that kind of pace," he said, noting that people would start tuning him out. The real problem, which no one at the White House seemed willing to confront, was that the country already had tuned him out. The president didn't have credibility anymore.

At one point, during another of our marathon speechwriting sessions, Steve Hadley and Fred Fielding, the White House counsel, let us know that the president needed an FDR line—like "We have nothing to fear but fear itself." They regretted that they had no suggestion to offer, however. "Bush as FDR?" I asked. "Who do they think they're kidding?" The answer was obvious: they were kidding themselves.

The president had his own suggestion for such a line, however. "Fear feeds on fear." All Bush needed was a pair of Roosevelt-like glasses and a long cigarette.

So we produced a speech with no real information and our FDR knockoff line. Here were some of the kinder reviews: "lackluster"; "there is no news here"; "the president should go away for a while." The stock market dipped further.

As the Treasury started to use the bailout funds to invest directly in financial institutions, Ed wanted to come up with a name for the plan that made it sound better to the public, particularly conservatives who thought this was nothing more than warmed-over socialism. Yes, a catchphrase would solve everything. As we were working on this, Ed called a few of the writers on speakerphone with the idea he'd come up with: the Imperative Investment Intervention. (Try saying that three times.)

As Ed offered his suggestion, we all laughed in silence, not wanting him to hear us over the loudspeaker. "Oh, that sounds good," one of us lied.

We decided that if a catchphrase must be deployed, surely we could come up with something better than a tongue twister with the acronym III. Of course, we started out with dark humor: the "I Can't Believe It's Not Capitalism" Plan; the MARX Plan. I suggested that we also apologize to the former Soviet Union and retroactively concede the Cold War. Then one of the writers got serious and came up with the Temporary Emergency Market Protection Program, or TEMP. Not bad as gimmicks go. The writer who came up with that idea was Horny himself.

Ed liked it. But he decided that instead of dropping it into a speech, we'd leak it to the press that this was the phrase we were using internally. Ed's logic was that anything Bush said would be ignored. But if the press thought they'd got it from a leak, they'd find it more interesting and newsworthy. (TEMP never made it as a catchphrase regardless.)

In the meantime, the administration went back to talking day after day about the economy with no further news to offer. The White House was talking to itself—and not in a very compelling way. At one point, I conducted an experiment. I had one of the other writers read one of the speeches out loud to see how long he could go before I tuned out. I didn't make it past the third paragraph. I was bored with the statement I helped write. And I had every reason to believe that the country would feel similarly. When White House press secretary Dana Perino was told that 77 percent of the country thought we were on the wrong track, she said what I was thinking: "Who on earth is in the other twenty-three percent?"

I knew who they were—the same people supporting the John McCain campaign. As discouraged as I was by what the White House's handling of the financial crisis said about the administration's competency, the 2008 election race depressed me even more because of what it showed about the state of the Republican Party. The campaign had started with a weak field of candidates, at least as far as conservatives went. My candidate and the candidate of most young conservatives I knew had been former Tennessee senator Fred Thompson. But Fred's bid never really took off, so we were left with a bunch of prospects whom conservatives didn't really like.

There was Rudy Giuliani, a liberal on social issues whose only experience in governing was as dictator of New York City. (That's not an insult. I've lived in New York and it needed a dictator.) There was the former governor Mitt Romney, basically a nice-looking technocrat pretending to be a hard-edged ideologue. When he was running for governor of liberal Massachusetts, he'd bragged about not wanting to return to the Reagan years. Now, as a candidate for the Republican nomination, he had the nerve to attack everyone else for not being sufficiently Reagan-like. There was Mike Huckabee, a social conservative whom many feared was a liberal on everything else. (I actually voted for him in the Virginia presidential primary. He was my anybody but McCain candidate.) And of course there was John McCain, the temperamental media darling who'd spent most of the last eight years running against the Republican Party and the president. I figured there was no way in hell anyone would vote for that guy. I knew for a fact that Republicans on Capitol Hill and at the White House hated him. Choosing John McCain as the standard-bearer of the Republican Party would be the height of self-delusion. It would be like putting Camilla Parker Bowles in charge of the Princess Diana Foundation.

As it turned out, I was the one who was deluded. Most Republicans seemed to have no problem backing a guy who'd worked so hard to undermine them. By far the most surprising thing about the McCain campaign was the reaction of the people I worked with in the White House. These were the most loyal of the Bush loyalists. Many had been with the president from the beginning and had lived through all of his high-profile fights with McCain. Dana Perino was so sensitive to criticism of Bush that she once said she couldn't watch the Democratic convention because it would be "too mean" to the president. Naturally, I expected these longtime Bush loyalists to have some major qualms about our new party nominee. Instead, I watched them embrace McCain enthusiastically. It was a cynical bargain. They supported him because they thought he was the only Republican who could win that year. He was popular among the media. He was seen as an independent who'd stand up to the party.

Even people I admired were inexplicably on board. McCain had lambasted Rumsfeld practically every day, and even said he had no confidence in him as secretary of defense. I assumed Rumsfeld couldn't possibly stand McCain, yet he was for McCain as well. (Rumsfeld was always more forgiving than people thought.) Jon Kyl, a staunch conservative, was one of the chairmen of the McCain campaign. I knew they were both from Arizona, but still how could he?

The president, like me, didn't seem to be in love with any of the available options. He always believed Hillary Clinton would be the Democratic nominee. "Wait till her fat bottom is sitting at this desk," he once said (except he didn't say bottom). He didn't think much of Barack Obama either. After one of Obama's blistering speeches against the administration, the president had a very human reaction: he was ticked off. He came in one day to rehearse a speech, fuming. "This is a dangerous world," he said for no apparent reason. He was so upset, he summoned his inner Sammy Davis Jr. again. "This cat isn't remotely qualified to handle it. This guy has no clue, I promise you." He wound himself up even more. "You think I wasn't qualified?" he said to no one in particular. "I was qualified."

The president didn't think much of Senator Joe Biden either. "Dana, did you tell them my line?" the president once asked with a smile on his face.

"No, Mr. President," Dana replied. "I didn't."

He paused for a minute. I could see him thinking maybe he shouldn't say it, but as usual, he couldn't resist. "If bullshit was currency," he said straight-faced, "Joe Biden would be a billionaire." Everyone in the room burst out laughing. If I'd been drinking water, I would have spit it across the room.

Bush seemed to feel considerable unease with the choice of McCain as well. I think he liked Romney best. (The rumor was that so did Karl Rove.) My guess was the president hadn't so easily forgotten the endless slights he'd suffered at McCain's hand. But there was little he could do. To him McCain's defeat would be a repudiation of the Bush administration, so McCain had to win.

The president, who had quite a good political mind, was clearly not impressed with the McCain operation. I was once in the Oval Office when the president was told a campaign event he was to attend with McCain in Phoenix suddenly had to be closed to the press. The president didn't understand why when the whole purpose of holding the event had been to show Bush and McCain in a joint appearance so the press would stop asking why the two wouldn't be seen together. If the event was closed to the press, the whole thing didn't make sense.

"If he doesn't want me to go, fine," the president said. "I've got better things to do."

Eventually, someone informed the president that the reason the event was closed was that McCain was having trouble getting a crowd.

Bush was incredulous—and to the point. "He can't get five hundred people to show up for an event in his hometown?" he asked. No one said anything, and we went on to another topic. But the president couldn't let the matter drop.

"He couldn't get five hundred people? I could get that many people to turn out in Crawford." He shook his head. "This is a five-spiral crash, boys."

Again we tried to move on to something else. And again the president couldn't let it go. He was stuck on the Phoenix event. At one point, he looked off into space and said to no one in particular, "What is this—a cruel hoax?"

I laughed heartily at that. I was feeling exactly the same way.

Chris and I were tickled by that comment. For weeks, we would look for ways to use it. "They are out of Diet Pepsi's at the mess. What is this, a cruel hoax?"

I went to dinner with a friend. "They don't have cheeseburgers?" I said, looking at the menu. "What is this, a cruel hoax?" Then I laughed hysterically. My friend responded with a baffled stare.

If the president was cool to McCain, the feeling was certainly mutual. McCain treated Bush like a dim-witted nephew he had to hide from the public. So you can imagine the enthusiasm I mustered when I was asked to write the president's 2008 Republican National Convention speech. The next indignity the president would suffer from McCain came when the McCain campaign told us that Bush had to keep his remarks at the convention to ten minutes or less. This was an embarrassing gauge of just how unpopular Bush was and how little regard McCain held for him. I had my problems with the president, but this was just disrespectful. The McCain campaign also ordered us to write the speech with a light emphasis on the president's record and heavy praise of . . . take a wild guess.

This might—just might—have been worse than writing for Jimmy Carter. To me, praising McCain was basically slapping Ronald Reagan and William F. Buckley in the face. One thing I absolutely refused to do was to type the words "President John McCain" into any speech draft. I could type "president." I could type "John." I could type "McCain." But never would those words appear together.

Ed Gillespie, the former Republican Party chairman, wanted to help McCain as much as possible. He wanted the president to use his convention speech to praise McCain by attacking his own cabinet. Ed had crafted a line that credited McCain with having seen the wisdom of the surge in Iraq before members of the president's administration had. I'd supported the surge too and certainly thought that opponents, like Condi Rice, were wrong. Condi's opposition to the surge—a position the president called support for "managed failure"—was one of the few instances that I knew of where he overruled her. But to have the president attack people who were still on his staff and loyal to him, all to help a candidate who'd been disloyal to the president for years, was too much.

"The George W. Bush I know will never say this line," I told Chris. "He'll never throw his own people under the bus like that." By this point, I may not have liked the president that much, but I knew he was a loyal guy.

The next day, Bush read Ed's line out loud at a meeting in the Oval Office where we were going over the speech. Ed said he thought it was an important line. The president had an uncertain look on his face. "You *really* want me to say that?" he asked. Then he looked around the room to gauge our reaction. I was the only one who shook my head—and vigorously. Whether that made a difference or not, I don't know, but Bush took it out.

Nobody was really comfortable praising McCain regarding anything other than his support of the Iraq war or his undeniably heroic experience as a POW in Vietnam. After talking about McCain's POW experience, Ed wanted the president to say of McCain, "When he was released, his arms had been broken but not . . . his . . . honor." Ed thought long pauses between the words were dramatic. I thought they sounded ridiculous. And the president repeatedly flubbed it. Sometimes he'd say "but not . . . his honor" or "but not his . . . ." He never quite got it right. Ed kept insisting on it, though, and the president played along.

Finally, in the last rehearsal for the speech, Josh Bolten stood up and said, "Mr. President, I don't think that line sounds natural."

The president agreed. "It doesn't feel right," he said. He stopped doing it. But would he have done it if Josh hadn't said anything? Or had he persuaded Josh to say that? Who knows?

Later on, Chris and I said to one of the other writers, John McConnell, that we were glad they'd taken those weird pauses out.

John nodded. "Yeah, that never worked," he said matter-of-factly. All of us had apparently thought this, but none of us had spoken up.

That was true of a lot that occurred in those days. We were all just going along with whatever happened.

After we worked and worked on the convention speech, a massive hurricane struck the New Orleans region, putting the entire convention on hold and canceling all Monday night events, including the president's speech. At one point, the president said he'd have to stay at the White House and skip the convention altogether to monitor the storm. Katrina had so damaged Bush's image that he didn't dare do anything but appear to be in crisis mode whenever another serious storm posed even the most minor of threats.

Thankfully, the hurricane missed most of New Orleans and the damage, while extensive, wasn't as bad as feared. The convention resumed the next day, and the president decided he wanted to go after all. The McCain reply was swift: "Thanks but no thanks." They'd lucked out by canceling Monday's events and now told the president not to come. He was too unpopular.

This infuriated everyone at the White House, including me. I understood why Bush was unpopular. I wasn't his biggest fan. But he was a two-term Republican president who deserved a farewell, and I felt surprisingly protective of him. And since McCain was going to be tarnished by his relationship with Bush in any event, what was the harm of letting the president go and rev up the conservatives who still supported Bush (and hated McCain)? McCain had always made such a big deal about his principles and vaunted courage regardless of the polls, and then he turned around and stiffed the president because of the polls. The McCain campaign was, as the saying goes, like school in the summer: no class.

In the end the president was reduced to speaking to the convention via satellite. It was my understanding that the president's parents, who were at the convention, were extremely proud. The president himself didn't betray any anger over this, at least not overtly. But at the last minute, he took a line out of his remarks that praised McCain for "not chasing the public opinion polls." It wouldn't be honest to keep that line in, the president said. I thought: Honest? *If we were really being honest, we'd have to throw most of the speech in the trash.*

If my colleagues at the White House were even momentarily scared straight about McCain over the convention fracas, the clarity wore off just as quickly as it came when the very conservative governor of Alaska, Sarah Palin, was picked as McCain's running mate. McCain apparently had selected her after meeting her only a couple of times. He seemed to take more care in choosing his gardener than the vice president of the United States.

I had nothing against the governor—she was definitely a conservative, but I knew little about her. Besides, I was in a guilt-by-association mood when it came to McCain. So I wasn't initially wowed. Still, she energized thousands of conservatives in a way John McCain never could. The overall reaction to Palin at the White House, however, was almost frenzied. I think what was really going on was that everyone secretly hated themselves for supporting McCain, so they latched on to Palin with over-the-top enthusiasm. They acted like they'd been on a starvation diet and she was a coffee cake that had just popped out of the oven.

Even the normally levelheaded Raul was overtaken by Palin mania. He'd been slightly annoyed with me for not jumping on the McCain bandwagon and for saying aloud that I thought McCain was a certain loser. Now, of course, I had to be enthusiastic about the ticket. "You still think we're going to lose?" he asked me laughingly.

"Yep," I replied. The Palin choice had given McCain a bump in the polls, but I figured that wouldn't last. McCain, after all, was still McCain.

Raul looked incredulous. "Well, you obviously don't believe in facts!"

I didn't quite know how to respond to that, so I didn't. I started to tread carefully whenever Governor Palin was mentioned. And I nodded slightly, but said nothing, over the next few days as one White House staffer after another confidently, and desperately, predicted that the Palin choice had won us the election. Or didn't I believe in facts?

Some uncomfortably suggested that McCain, who was seventy-two, was likely not to survive his first term anyway. Marc Thiessen even printed a Palin-centric bumper sticker that he gave White House staffers that said "Vote for the Hockey Mom." (I half expected a Sarah Palin action figure.)

I was about to be engulfed by a tidal wave of Palin euphoria when someone—someone I didn't expect—planted my feet back on the ground. After Palin's selection was announced, the same people who demanded I acknowledge the brilliance of McCain's choice expected the president to join them in their high-fiving tizzy. It was clear, though, that the president, ever the skilled politician, had concerns about the choice of Palin, which he called "interesting." That was the equivalent of calling a fireworks display "satisfactory."

"I'm trying to remember if I've met her before. I'm sure I must have." His eyes twinkled, then he asked, "What is she, the governor of Guam?"

I laughed. Everyone else in the room seemed to look at him in horror, their mouths agape. She'd hardly done a single thing on the campaign yet. Still, how could the president not love her?

When Ed told him that conservatives were greeting the choice enthusiastically, he replied, "Look, I'm a team player, I'm on board." He thought about it for a minute. "She's interesting," he said again.

He went on to talk about something else, but eventually came back to the subject. "You know, just wait a few days until the bloom is off that rose," he said. Then he made a very smart assessment. "This woman is being put into a position she is not even remotely prepared for," he said. "She hasn't spent one day on the national level. Neither has her family. Let's wait and see how she looks five days out."

It was a rare dose of reality in a White House that liked to believe every decision was great, every Republican was a genius, and McCain was the hope of the world because, well, because he chose to be a member of our party.

Governor Palin, of course, ended up receiving disastrous reviews, at least from the mainstream media. In one interview during the campaign, she didn't seem to be able to name a single newspaper or magazine that she read. She was asked what the Bush Doctrine was—a reference, I presumed, to the president's belief in preemptive war that justified the invasion of Iraq. She clearly didn't know what the doctrine was, which led to laughter among the press corps and many Americans.

As it turned out, neither did those of us at the White House. The next day, Josh Bolten asked some of the speechwriters to help define the doctrine. By the time the writers were done, the doctrine had three or four parts. I found that funny. It was the fall of 2008, more than seven years into the administration. And we still couldn't define our most central policy.

The White House devotion to Palin seemed to go hand in hand with an almost visceral hatred of Barack Obama. Which, again, made me odd man out. I didn't dare say it, but I liked Obama. He inspired people. Even my seven-year-old niece, Olivia, was talking about him. I thought he was a smart and thoughtful guy. He seemed like he wanted to do things differently, and was far more authentic to me than, say, Hillary Clinton and every other retread in establishment Washington. And he seemed far more levelheaded and stable than McCain, the human bobblehead doll.

Yet some Republicans were calling Obama a terrorist lover. I had friends who said they'd never support any candidate whose middle name was Hussein. In desperation, some in the White House speculated about a terrorist attack that would change the election. One high-ranking White House official talked about the prospect of terrorist attacks so much that he terrified his own kids. Of course, endlessly warning about a terrorist attack on Obama's watch could easily be misinterpreted as rooting for one.

All we beleaguered Republicans had left, it seemed, were personal attacks. We had a candidate that most of us, in our heart of hearts, didn't really believe in and who certainly didn't believe in us. And it was becoming difficult to criticize Obama on policy grounds, since we'd abandoned our own principles. How, for example, could we credibly claim Obama would be a liberal big spender when we'd spent more than any administration since LBJ's?

Still, there were those who believed that the importance of McCain's winning the election trumped any reservations one might have about his flaws. Tony Dolan, for example, shared all of my concerns about McCain, but still liked him. As with nearly everyone else I knew in the party, he was fiercely on board the McCain bandwagon. Tony invited me to a small dinner at Café Milano in Georgetown. The guest of honor was the man I'd wanted to be president, Fred Thompson. Fred was eagerly backing McCain as well.

I sat with Fred, Tony, and a few others for two or three hours. During that time, Fred tried out his pitch on McCain. His argument was typical—he urged me to support McCain by attacking Obama. Obama was a threat to the country. Terrorists would bring us a mushroom cloud if he was elected. Fred tried everything he could think of to show how terrible Obama would be. Many things he said made sense logically, and I wasn't one to lightly cross the tough guy from *The Hunt for Red October*, an actor I'd been a fan of since I was a kid.

The trouble was, my response was emotional, not logical. "I just don't trust him," I said. McCain would abandon all the conservative positions he was now espousing just as easily as he'd abandoned them before.

Fred never backed down. At the end of the dinner, he smoked a cigar. It was like watching him in one of his movies. He was exactly the same on-screen and off. After coolly taking a puff, he looked at me. "Well, Matthew," he said in his deep southern drawl, "have I convinced you about John?"

"Senator," I replied politely, "if anyone could, it would be you."

He seemed to like that, and he smiled. "Well, then I'll quit while I'm ahead." He continued puffing on his cigar.

"I didn't say you were ahead," I corrected him. Others at the table squirmed uncomfortably.

Fred laughed jovially. "Well, then I'll quit while I'm behind!"

While I continued to grapple with why so many people I respected would get in line behind someone who was the ruin of our party, I poured out my disappointment to one of my best friends in Washington. He was a prominent newspaper columnist who came from a conservative family. "Your problem is simple," my friend said. "You're an idealist." Nobody really wanted McCain to win, he said. They just wanted Obama to lose even more.

At another point during the campaign, I was at a dinner party with four or five Republicans who'd been involved with every GOP election since 1976. Without exception, they hated McCain. "He's a lunatic," said one. Others attacked him from the right as a betrayer of the faith. Another attacked McCain from the left, saying he was too quick to go to war.

Yet I was the only one of the entire group who balked at voting for him. They'd all vote for someone whom they admitted was a "lunatic," a "liar," a "sellout," and a "traitor" because, as one of them put it, "getting elected is the name of the game, right?" To these people, politics was just a business. They might have hated McCain, but Republicans gave them contracts and consulting fees. They didn't care who led them or what they stood for as long as they stayed in power. I was reminded of what a philosopher said early in the twentieth century: "Every great cause begins as a movement, degenerates into a business, and becomes a racket."

It was the same, it appeared, with the once-principled conservative echo chamber in the media. The cynical, lame, unprincipled McCain campaign was embraced by the same people who used to disavow him. The conservative standard-bearer, *National Review*, which used to rail against conservatives of convenience, was now enthusiastically on their side. All those once in good standing with conservatives—Kathleen Parker, Chris Buckley, and others—were banished for criticizing McCain or Palin. This was not the sign of a mature or healthy movement. It was not how Ronald Reagan would have handled disagreement, but it was how Karl Rove would. ,

I was facing some hard truths about the party and movement I loved and the public officials I'd chased around for autographs only a dozen years earlier. Professional Republicans no longer cared, it seemed, about supporting candidates who believed in our ideals. They were more interested in keeping their cushy houses in Georgetown or Cleveland Park, and their contracts with the revolving door of Republican bigwigs. It was all about being close to power for the sake of power. The Republican Party I believed in—smaller, smarter government—was unidentifiable. We'd thrown it all away amid excessive spending, corruption, dishonesty, and petty partisanship. By abandoning our principles, we'd paid the price—the loss of Congress, the loss of our party's popularity, and the impending loss of the presidency. During the economic crisis, someone at the White House at one point wanted us to refer to the economic theory of "creative destruction," the idea that a capitalist economy has to let weak businesses fail for the overall system to survive. Well, that's what I thought we needed for the Republican Party—to disinfect ourselves and start over again.

Long before the election, most people at the White House knew the McCain campaign was over. But the morning of the election, Barry Jackson, the president's top political advisor, was heard to say in the senior staff meeting that McCain still had "a path to victory." He may have been the only one who saw it. Toward the end of October, I'd started working with Chris on drafts of the president's speech for the morning after the election. We'd written a version if the victor was Obama and another if the victor was McCain. But I think only the Obama one ever went for vetting.

Writing a speech acknowledging either candidate's triumph was somewhat disheartening. I wasn't sure which man I wanted to win, or if it even mattered. So to relieve some of the anxiety, Chris and I started to get silly. I insisted we consider what we might say in the event that third-party candidate Bob Barr, a libertarian, won the election.

We imagined the president's remarks. "Yesterday evening I had an interesting conversation with a stunned President-elect Robert Barr," the statement began. "I expressed my congratulations to him on a startling come-from-behind victory. I also placed calls to Senators Barack Obama and John McCain. They were, frankly, as baffled as I was. I am sure they will continue to serve in the United States Senate, but I don't see how. Anyway, I guess we'll be all right. But who knows what's going to happen next? My best wishes to Bob and his wife, name unknown, and their family, names unknown. God bless."

Barr was notoriously skeptical of law enforcement. There was a story going around that he refused to carry a BlackBerry because he thought the government might be tracking him. So Chris suggested a change. "I tried to call the President-elect," Chris wrote, "but we couldn't find his phone number and he refuses to carry a BlackBerry. So if you're listening, Bob, congrats."

Chris thought it would be fun to also assume what the president would say if he offered condolences to Bob Barr after Barr lost. I suggested, "I know Bob Barr supporters are very disappointed today. They believed. They hoped. They dreamed. Today they woke up."

Chris suggested, "He brought important issues before the American people, from his well-intentioned queries about our law enforcement practices to his vow to abolish the Federal Reserve."

"Today the voters may have broken Bob Barr's spirit," I went on, "but not . . . his . . . honor."

I quit the White House before the election results even came in. People thought I was crazy to leave before the administration ended, maybe even disloyal. But I wasn't into blind loyalty anymore. I didn't believe in what we were doing—didn't believe in the administration or its "team of buddies" or, in its present incarnation, the Republican Party. And I didn't want to be there when the election woke everyone up and it all came crashing down. I drafted a resignation letter to the president and had to redraft it because some of the writers thought that I, you know, might want to say something in it that praised him. I *was* grateful for the opportunity he'd given me and I said so. Then, sadly but without a moment's regret, I gave up the job I'd wanted all my life.

On election day, I was contacted by a friend in the White House. "You really should see what these people are doing now," she said. Apparently, a group of senior White House staffers assembled what could only be described as scarecrows in the Cross Hall of the residence, for the president to see when he walked by. The scarecrows were cut-out faces of former and current administration officials attached to sticks. Some of the sticks were wearing Bush or McCain T-shirts and had inspirational messages attached, like "We love you, Mr. President" or "You're the best." I guess the reason for it was to buck up Bush on what was probably going to be a disappointing election night. But scarecrows—harkening to the *Wizard of Oz*—might not have been the best of ideas. I wasn't at all surprised to hear of them. The White House had become something of a cult of personality by then—a domain for the last holdouts when the country wanted something else. Eventually, these scarecrows were displayed outside the cafeteria in the EEOB. One of my friends told me of watching David Addington, Vice President Cheney's dour chief of staff, walk by the display, chuckle, and shake his head. Another surreal moment in a surreal year.

The morning of the election, I stood in line for an hour to vote. The line was ten or twenty times longer than I'd ever seen in my liberal-leaning precinct in Alexandria, Virginia—a sign of people's excitement over Obama.

During the long wait, two people immediately behind me in line started talking. One, a man, spoke about the enthusiasm he felt about Obama's campaign. "Finally, we're going to get a handle on health care," he said.

The other, a woman, was more restrained. "I hope so," she said. "It's a complicated issue."

"It's only complicated because Bush and the Republicans are beholden to the insurance industry," he said.

"Well . . . ," she said. Then the conversation petered out. He figured out she was a Republican. I looked back at her for a moment. We exchanged sympathetic glances and an unspoken message: *Yes, today is going to be bad.*

As I stood in that line, I realized that for the first time in my life I had no idea how I was going to vote. I'd voted happily and proudly for every Republican who ever ran for anything. I'd even voted without hesitation for Bob Dole, and he was a sure loser. Now I'd lost so much faith in my party that I wasn't even sure I was a Republican anymore. I'd come to town idealistic and excited, and now I was cynical and disillusioned.

I walked to the voting booth and stood there staring at the screen longer than I ever had before. I hadn't a clue what to do. In Alexandria, we turned a dial over various names and then pressed a button to select the ticket of our choice. I first turned the dial to Obama and Biden. Then I switched to McCain and Palin. Then I switched to Bob Barr and whoever he was running with. I even lingered on Ralph Nader. I used to make fun of the "kooks" who supported a third party. Now I easily could have been one of them. I could have gone any which way. That was shocking enough.

I switched my dial back to McCain again and thought about it for a moment. I knew he really didn't share my principles. He'd run an erratic campaign. But he was the president's choice. He was my party's choice. I'd voted Republican all my life. I'd made it all the way to being a senior official at the White House. I'd vowed I'd never support McCain, but could I really turn my back on the party?

Then I thought more about Obama. Had I been so disappointed by the Republicans that I could vote for a liberal Democrat? Obama had run a brilliant campaign. He inspired people. I thought of my thirteen-year-old nephew, Michael, who, just like Obama, was a mixed-race child being raised by white grandparents—my mom and dad. He too was growing up in an era when the temptation of drugs was all around him. Every day I prayed that Michael would stay away from them. And every night I worried that he couldn't. With a president like Barack Obama, I could offer the child I treasured more than a plea. I could offer a hopeful example. That alone might have been almost enough for me to cast my ballot for the Democrat.

Michael and I, in fact, had talked on the phone a few days before

the election. He and his nine-year-old brother, Eric, considered themselves Republicans because they knew I was. But Michael now wanted
to support Obama. He seemed to want my okay.

I remembered what my mom had said all those years ago when I
was casting my first vote for president and begged her to vote for the
Republicans. "Just this once," she'd told me.

Now, as a little boy I loved so much asked if it was okay to support
Obama and the Democrats, I smiled. "It's all right," I told him. "But just
this once."

At the age of thirteen, Michael was interested in politics for the
very first time. He believed in his chosen candidate, just like I did when
I was his age. But now, for the first time, I didn't know if I believed in
anyone in politics anymore. I took one more long look at the voting dial
and then, seized by an impulse, made the only choice I felt I could live
with. Indeed, it was a choice that would satisfy only myself.

As I walked out of the polling place and climbed into my car, I realized that a presidency was ending. So too was my career in politics.
Months later, I watched on television as President Bush delivered his
farewell address to the nation. My friends and colleagues from the
White House sat in the East Room audience to help ensure applause.
"Regular Americans" were lined up in front of the president, to serve, in
effect, as human shields. I didn't miss the place one bit.

A few days later, I watched a very different scene as President
Obama took the oath of office. He was welcomed to Washington by
millions of true believers who engulfed the capital city. They had the
same look in their eyes that I'd had twelve years earlier when I'd met
Bob Dole, of all people, for the very first time. Even after all I'd been
through in Washington, I saw that day of Obama's inaugural the magic
that still lingered in politics, the faith that change could come. As I left
politics, I knew more than ever what I believed. And though I didn't
know where I'd land next, I was going to keep searching for that place
in America where people meant what they said and where principles
still mattered.

Maybe I'd try Hollywood.

W hen I first left Michigan for Washington, D.C., it had not been my intention to write a book about my experiences. Who was I to think my life story was so important? But recently I remembered something. I'd actually become interested in pursuing a public service career after reading the terrific memoirs of presidential speechwriters from the past. Two in particular stood out, those authored by William Safire and Peggy Noonan. Their books captured an era and made it accessible to people across the country. They certainly inspired a shy kid from Michigan to try to come to our nation's capital and achieve his dream. For that I'll always be grateful.

On that journey I was blessed with the unquestioned love of my parents. There was never a moment that I felt without it, and I hope this book shows them how much it's meant to me. I also express my appreciation to other members of my family: Marlan and Barbara Latimer, Tim and Annette Latimer, Jennifer Latimer, Jackie Kozlowicz, and their children. My thanks as well for the encouragement I've received from a group of lifelong friends, including Todd and Nicole Wade, John Galaviz, Kimberly Love, Maiselle Shortley, Alec Rogers, Kurt Schmautz, Dena Battle, and a few others who, because of their jobs in the media or Republican politics, asked not to be named in my book. You know who you are. More important, so do I. Thank you all for your support. (This is starting to feel like the Academy Awards.)

Then there are those who are entitled to a special place in these acknowledgments not only because of their impact on my life but because my mother politely insisted they be listed. Mom and I happily thank my godparents, Lue and Larry Venyah, the Avery family, Paula Jones, Pearl Morrow, Maggie Cooper, Pat Banner, and Joanne Wood. While I'm at it, let me also thank in advance the dean of admissions at Harvard University, who will be receiving my nephew Michael's admissions application in three years.

Everybody has that special teacher who inspired them to achieve, and I was no exception. In fact, I had two. One was my elementary school teacher, Maureen Hearn. The other was my professor at Columbia Journalism School, Judith Crist, who taught me essential rules such as "shorter is better" and "murder your darlings." In fact, I thank all of the faculty and staff at my alma mater, Columbia Journalism School, particularly those involved with awarding the Pulitzer Prizes (hint, hint).

When you write a book like this, you have to be careful whom you thank, lest they look like accessories to some of the stories you tell. Many people I worked with over the years spoke to me privately as I worked on this book. A sizable number called or e-mailed, urging me to put in this story or that under the condition that I not mention their involvement or their names. I've happily obliged. I do want to send my best wishes and appreciation to everyone I worked with in the Bush administration. We endured historic times together, even if we didn't all end up looking at things the same way. Of special mention are the members of the president's speechwriting team I worked with most closely: Chris Michel, Meghan Clyne, Troy Senik, Jonathan Horn, Mark Busse, Gena Katz, Jim Hickey, Emily Soeder, Melissa Carson, Niklas Warren, Brendon Merkley, Staci Wheeler, Matt Larkin, Aaron Cummings, Mike Robins, Anneke Green, and Matt Robinson. I also want to mention my friends and colleagues at the Department of Defense, including Bryan Whitman, Kevin Kellems, Charley Cooper, Thayer Scott, Alston Ramsay, Justin Walker, Keith Urbahn, Bonnie Sciarretto, Bonita Ruff, Tara Jones, Matt Kenney, Randy Lee, James Dillon, Terri Lukach, Matt Konkler, Bill Turenne, Nicole Schofer, Lauren Weiner, and Dave Romley. On Capitol Hill, there were a few people I felt especially close to: Andrew and Rebecca Wilder, Elizabeth Maier, Don Dempsey, Kimberly Wold, and Noah Silverman. Thank you all.

I will always be deeply appreciative of my former employers—

Spence Abraham, Nick Smith, Jon Kyl, Donald Rumsfeld, Mitch McConnell, and George W. Bush. I learned something important from each and I'm grateful for the opportunities they gave me to see Washington up close.

As I started writing this book, I learned how many creative and talented people are involved in making a book a succes. It's a shame that they only get a brief mention, while the author gets all the attention. I do want to single out a few people, beginning with my terrific agent, Howard Yoon, of the Gail Ross Agency in Washington, D.C. I also thank the legendary Gail Ross herself and their associate Anna Sproul, who helped me polish the manuscript. My thanks to the wonderful people at Crown, including its publisher, Tina Constable; my editor, Rick Horgan, who routinely went beyond the call of duty to help make my book a success; and the intrepid Nathan Roberson. I thank Annsley Rosner at Crown and my friend Carol Blymire for answering the phone (most of the time) even though she knew I'd be calling with some crazy question. And I thank one of the finest young writers I know, Justin Walker, for his friendship, patient input, and advice. I also thank his mother, Deborah, for taking the time to read my drafts and give me the perspective of a real person outside of Washington, D.C. (proving once again that moms usually give the best advice).

Most of all, I thank all those people in Washington—conservative and liberal—who stand on their principles and believe that their government should be about something more, something better, than egotism and self-interest. This book was really meant for you.

Index

Index